T0318463

Dance and Organisation

"This is a must-have book for anyone applying the arts to management, human resource management, or training. It has excellent ways of doing feminist studies in the social sciences."
—David M. Boje, New Mexico State University, USA

Dance and Organisation is the first comprehensive work to integrate dance theory and methods into the study of management, which has developed an interest in the arts and the humanities. Dance represents dynamics and change and puts the moving body at the centre of research, which has been ignored and oppressed by traditional management theory. 'Being' a leader, however, also means moving like one, and critical lessons can be learned from ballerinas and modern dancers. Leadership is a dialogue, as in the work of musicians, conductors and DJs who manage groups without words. Movement in organisational space, in a museum or a techno club can be understood as a choreography and site-specific performance. Movement also is practically used in leadership, and employee development workshops and can be deployed as an organisational research method.

By taking a firm interdisciplinary stance in dance studies and organisational research to explore management topics, the book reflects on practitioner accounts and research projects, and seeks to make an innovative contribution to our understanding of the moving body. It generates new insights on teamwork, leadership, gender in management, organisational space, training and research methods. It comprises an important contribution to the organisational behaviour and critical management studies disciplines, and pushes the boundaries of the academic literature.

Brigitte Biehl (Biehl-Missal) is a Professor at SRH Hochschule der Populären Künste hpdk, Berlin, Germany, and a Visiting Fellow of Essex Business School, the University of Essex, UK.

Routledge Studies in Management, Organizations and Society

For a full list of titles in this series, please visit www.routledge.com

This series presents innovative work grounded in new realities, addressing issues crucial to an understanding of the contemporary world. This is the world of organised societies, where boundaries between formal and informal, public and private, local and global organizations have been displaced or have vanished, along with other nineteenth-century dichotomies and oppositions. Management, apart from becoming a specialised profession for a growing number of people, is an everyday activity for most members of modern societies.

Similarly, at the level of enquiry, culture and technology, and literature and economics, can no longer be conceived as isolated intellectual fields; conventional canons and established mainstreams are contested. **Management, Organizations and Society** addresses these contemporary dynamics of transformation in a manner that transcends disciplinary boundaries, with books that will appeal to researchers, student and practitioners alike.

Recent titles in this series include:

Dance and Organisation

Integrating Dance Theory
and Methods into the Study
of Management

Brigitte Biehl

Routledge
Taylor & Francis Group
New York London

First published 2017 by Routledge

711 Third Avenue, New York, NY 10017
2 Park Square, Milton Park, Abingdon, Oxfordshire OX14 4RN

Routledge is an imprint of the Taylor & Francis Group, an informa business

First issued in paperback 2018

Copyright © 2017 Taylor & Francis

The right of Brigitte Biehl to be identified as author of this work has
been asserted by her in accordance with sections 77 and 78 of the
Copyright, Designs and Patents Act 1988.

All rights reserved. No part of this book may be reprinted or reproduced or
utilised in any form or by any electronic, mechanical, or other means, now
known or hereafter invented, including photocopying and recording, or in
any information storage or retrieval system, without permission in writing
from the publishers.

Notice:
Product or corporate names may be trademarks or
registered trademarks, and are used only for identification and explanation
without intent to infringe.

Library of Congress Cataloging-in-Publication Data
A catalog record for this book has been requested.

ISBN: 978-1-138-93551-8 (hbk)
ISBN: 978-0-367-02653-0 (pbk)

Typeset in Sabon
by Apex CoVantage, LLC

To Norman Nodge

Contents

Acknowledgements

This book has been in the making for a year and is looking back on the rather young history of dance theory and practice in organisation studies. Dance stands for constant dynamics and change and during the process of writing, many things in my life have changed as well. I am happy that the book is now finished and grateful for the support of those who sent over positive vibes. For a period for about almost four years I have collaborated with different people in the area of organisation studies, dance studies and practice and benefited from their intellectual input and their creative inspiration. I would like to thank Claus Springborg who has been involved right up front in the academic endeavour with the co-ordination of two academic conference streams and the first special issue on dance, leadership and organisation. Steven S. Taylor has from the start supported our interest in dance that is linked to research on the aesthetic side of organisations. Dirk vom Lehn has discussed with me sociological perspectives on movement and we have published on movement in consumption spaces and museums. I am deeply grateful that I have met Christina Volkmann, who started working with me on social choreographies with dance workshops and a research project, which also benefited from Kelly Vadukar's support. I would like to thank Sam Warren who has supported our research endeavour and a funding application at our time at Essex Business School, and has inspired peers with the first academic DJ set at a management conference. Naneci Yurdagül, a techno music lover and inspirational artist for the past 17 years has been challenging myself and my views and I am particularly grateful for his presence this year.

Related material on the topic has appeared in journal articles and I benefited greatly from feedback from editors and reviewers and co-authors and would like to thank Jo Brewis, and Donna Ladkin. My thanks go to Anke Strauß and Mai Kawabata for their participation in field research, including visits to Berghain. Paulina Kleingarn has done a great job when helping to gather data, interviewing DJs on their leadership practice. I would like to thank Daniel Ludevig for his enthusiasm and the insights he allowed me into his practical work as a leadership consultant. Nina Bozic-Yams has exchanged critical and innovative ideas on the topic. Other dear colleagues

x *Acknowledgements*

that have discussed dance and organisation and have encouraged me are Anneli Hujala, Wendlin Küpers, Katrin Kolo, Fides Matzdorf and Ramen Sen. I am also grateful to many former colleagues at Essex Business School for their interdisciplinary drive and interest, including Phil Hancock and Christian De Cock. I also have in mind Heather Höpfl and her work on gender and organisation and theatre that has inspired me much more than I could tell her. My thanks also go to Herbert Fitzek and the interdisciplinary exchange on dance and gestalt psychology at BSP Business School Berlin.

Introduction

"Life is dance" because the world is full of movement. Organisations in particular are full of embodied interaction that has largely been ignored in a management tradition that focuses on the rational mind and overlooks many elements that are in the moment and in motion. This book on "Dance and Organisation" is intended as the initial interdisciplinary work to integrate dance theory and methods into the study of management, for researchers and practitioners in two worlds that may seem very different and distanced at first sight. By doing so, it adds to and develops an increasing interest of organisational scholars in the world of arts and the humanities and in explorations of the body in organisations.

The link between organisations and dance is the moving body that has always been at the centre of dance studies. Organisation studies has long ignored and continuously oppressed the body and only over the past decades has developed an interest in the human body and its aesthetic perceptions. In organisations the felt, sensory and emotional aspects have become increasingly relevant with regard to how we situate ourselves in the world and how we interact with others. Leadership has been considered an 'art' and organisations have been likened to theatres, jazz bands and orchestras to emphasise creative, visionary and social approaches that are required in a dynamic environment. Practically, workshops with painters, actors and poets have been deployed in organisations to bring in new perspectives and to generate innovation. What we see now is an emergence of 'dance' in both theory and practice.

The book situates itself at a nexus of two disciplines coming together: Dance studies always centred around the body in motion. Rather than merely decoding dance as an 'art work', an increasing emphasis was put on kinaesthetic experience, on processes of co-creation in choreography, on the politics and social power of movement, and on the potential of dance to work with people and as a research method. Broad interdisciplinary attention has been given to the dance discipline and sociology, gender studies, psychology, robotics engineering and many other perspectives use theories and concepts from dance studies to explore human movement and social interaction. It does not come as a surprise that organisation studies now also draws on dance studies. Dance as an abstract, non-verbal and transitory art form has met more reservations in organisation studies that in other fields, given the tradition of positivist management thinking and seemingly rigorous method—that can however hardly capture the aesthetic, subjective and dynamic nature of organisational life. Dance as a collaborative practice and embodied form of interaction demonstrates how people cooperate socially and empathically and how they coordinate their actions without words, connecting to spaces and contexts and each other, 'leading' and 'following' and making sense of the spaces in-between. Dance studies has a broad theoretical potential when considering issues of perception and knowledge, gender, space, leadership and research methods.

More broadly, dance as an ephemeral art has become a model for a society that emphasises acceleration, transience and global movement, constant social, technological and economic change. Dance is a paradigm for modern and postmodern times, exemplifying that people and structures are in motion and change constantly. Sociologically there are obvious links between the world of dance and performance art and today's business world. Performers and dancers have been the pioneers of the creative economy, doing exhausting and personalised work, cooperating in projects, often in precarious conditions. The performing arts are social arts par excellence. Different from visual and plastic arts that can be seen as 'immobile' arts, in dance human bodies are 'in motion', interact in dynamic ways, constantly cooperating and creating temporary networks. Going beyond a sociological analysis or the use of dance as an analogy, this book looks into a range of topics in organisational life and in leadership situations that are 'in motion'. After all, when it comes to thinking, cooperating and interacting, despite and because of intellectual and virtual work, we remain in our moving bodies as 'embodied minds' and need them to understand what 'moves' us and others, to make sense of ever more abstract and changing environments.

Before proceeding to an overview of the individual chapters of the book, I shall say a few words on the perspective taken. I am passionate about the argument that is made to broaden organisation studies and to include dance as another arts perspective that has much more to offer than a metaphor on organisational life. An interdisciplinary and aesthetic approach to organisations has for the last decades worked against the positivist view in management and organisation studies that has so many shortcomings, oppressing the body, women's bodies, and critical perspectives, and has failed to provide sufficient methods to access what people feel and what drives their interaction. An orientation at the arts world has been associated with supporting precarious working conditions and exploiting work, but a perspective bringing arts into organisations has also been heralded as a view that is more human centred and sustainable and helps 21st-century organisations to engage in more innovative ways of managing and thinking.

Keeping this in mind, I am not proclaiming a universal view on 'dance and organisation', but I speak from a certain set of perspectives that is rooted in my knowledge and background and my academic activity in the field, and my experiences from the world of performing arts. Having done research on theatre and management, I observed and also supported an emerging interest in dance and organisation. With Claus Springborg from Copenhagen, I hosted the first stream and also the subsequent stream on dance and organisation at the AoMO Art of Management and Organization Conference in 2014 and 2016 and published the first special issue on the topic in 2016 in the journal "Organizational Aesthetics". The many scholars that are involved approach the field from different angles, for example draw on their passion and experience as ballroom or tango dancers or modern dance choreographers that they then link to leadership and organisation research or practical consultancy in the field. Others come from business schools and benefit from their interdisciplinary experiences and also were among the first to work with dance-based methods. Scholars from around the globe have simultaneously approached organisation theory and leadership with dance, drawing on a slightly different but still related theory.

Personally, I am looking back on more than a decade of publishing on theatre and management, drawing on my background with a PhD in theatre studies that explored the world of management, developing studies on postdramatic theatre (Hans-Thies Lehmann) that considers the actual performative, aesthetic side of organisational life. On the practical side, I have done some artistic performance work but my dance experience remains mostly in the field of clubbing, social and leisure dance, including an early, not very talented, introduction to ballet in the 1980s, more enthusiast jazz dance in the 1990s and beginner ballroom courses. Dance practice and theory is in my scholarly context however very close to and overlapping with performance studies (Richard Schechner), and I have also devoured American cultural studies scholarship that has included dance (Jane Desmond), also from a feminist view and with an emphasis on critical theorizing (Susan Leigh Foster), as well as international contemporary choreography (Jo Butterworth). The perspective adopted here also draws on research originating in a German development of dance studies, with a sociological and interdisciplinary focus that considers movement in social life in sports, play and leisure (Thomas Alkemeyer) and seems well suited to be extended into the organisational world, accounting for questions of theorising dancing (Gabriele Brandstetter; Gabriele Klein; André Lepecki). Literature on site-specific dance that brings to life space and context also has attracted my interest having experienced their magic when studying in Wales (Mike Pearson and Heike Roms) and looking back on my research interest in space, atmospheres and aesthetic approaches to social life (Gernot Böhme). Being based in business schools during my academic professional life, I have brought together topics of performance with management, leadership and marketing. The theoretical trajectories adopted in this book to summarise extant research on dance and organisation and to build a theoretical basis for further inquiry have been chosen with the past interdisciplinary experience in mind.

All knowledge that we have from the arts is locally embedded and contextual and the book would be different if my existence and education had happened in some other place in the world. I have been fortunate to spend my education and life in a European context, particularly Germany, France and the UK, as the first two in particular, despite unfortunate cuts, consider culture a valuable asset that is supported and funded more than in many other countries. I have seen many theatre and dance performances by international acclaimed and also avant-garde artists that were invited and able to perform at festivals and in culture institutions nearby. Being based in Berlin, I have also observed a growing international scene and the hype of the creative industries that affects and develops traditional contexts of management and work. When talking about dance and leisure in particular, I have developed an interest in DJ culture and have experienced the vivid techno scene centring around clubs such as Berghain and other places that in some ways relate to the former underground scene and to a particular pedigree of Berlin that attracts so many international ravers who want to experience this and be part of it.

What is presented in this book is a summary of work on dance and organisation and an interdisciplinary application of dance studies literature to develop topics that are of interest to the broader field of organisation research, including gender, leadership, space and research methods. The book follows a broad programme from applying dance as a metaphor for organisational life to the actual practical application of dance for training and as a research method. In Chapter 1, "Dance and Organisation Studies," I discuss how studies on organisations can be linked to dance studies, using as a bridge aesthetic approaches and studies on the body. Chapter 2, "Dance as a Metaphor," shows the beginning of research in this field by discussing how dance was used as a metaphor for organisations, along with other arts metaphors such as theatre and jazz for example. Both chapters develop an argument for a focus on the kinaesthetic practice of bodily movement, which is the basis for the other chapters.

Chapter 3, "Kinaesthetic Politics (Gender)," discusses movements that have not attracted much scholarly attention in management studies as movement was long taken for granted or considered 'natural'. Movement however is not natural, rather gendered and depending on age, gender and physical ability and also on the ways in which people adapt to situations and to others. Movements, like outer appearances, are a central media of interaction and self-presentation and the notion of 'kinaesthetic politics' is used in this book to explain how personality, gender and social role are related to movement and its perception. To be a leader means to move like one. As 'kinaesthetic politics', movement is a political practice when it confirms, and particularly when it challenges, negotiates and changes social interaction. This section draws on sociological studies of movement ('Throwing like a girl') and includes dance studies on ballet and modern contemporary dance, which are linked to research on the body and on gender in management, showing limitations and also opportunities in the performance of movement.

Chapter 4, "Kinaesthetic Empathy (Leadership)," uses the notion of kinaesthetic empathy to approach the embodied perception of others and forms of coordination and collaboration, also applicable to organisational leadership. The notion of kinaesthetic empathy that refers to processes of taking-in, or tuning-in to others' movements and bodily expressions is used to develop studies on leadership that emphasise embodiment and aesthetic, sensual communication. Leadership is not a merely rational practice but an embodied form of interaction. While many studies over the past decades have considered this embodied nature of leadership, the kinaesthetic, movement-related dimension remains under-researched. In this chapter, the role of movement in leadership practices is discussed, also with reference to how DJs in dance contexts use their kinaesthetic empathy to make people move.

Chapter 5, "Choreography (Collaboration and Space)," uses the notion of choreography that is central to the dance discipline and has different definitions that revolve around movement, embodied practice and collaborative work. In organisation studies it is particularly promising to apply choreography not as a metaphor, but as an analytical term to capture how people coordinate and cooperate, creating social orders and constellations that are in motion. Such an approach is able to explore that movements may be connected in ways that cannot be accessed with extant organisational theory, and are dynamic and permanently negotiated as social choreographies. The notion of site-specific dance is used to link dance studies to scholarship on organisational space, showing how space is experienced, sensed and brought to life. Research on movement in museums and consumption spaces in integrated, and I look at Berghain in Berlin, one of the world's most famous techno clubs.

Chapter 6, "Kinaesthetic Training (Arts-Based Interventions)," considers the growing use of dance as an arts-based intervention along other methods such as organisational theatre, painting and crafts work, to develop certain capacities and skills in leaders and organisational members. With increasing scholarly attention there has been a proliferation of consultancy activity in this area. Dance and movement interventions help participants to tap into feelings and hidden understandings that guide their decisions and actions— a competence that is said to be of particular importance in contemporary situations of uncertainty and ambiguity. The experience can also be critical in the sense that is tests new forms of body politics and social practices of collaboration. Drawing on the previous discussion in the book, a framework is used that integrates metaphorical versus kinaesthetic approaches on the individual level (kinaesthetic politics) and group level (choreography). Barriers and factors that speak for the use of dance are presented and different applications of dance are presented and critically discussed.

Chapter 7, "Dance as a Method (Research)," explains dance as a research method, inspired by research in the area of performance studies and social studies, which look back on a longer tradition of using movement for research. Applying dance links to embodiment research and phenomenological approaches that promote the body as a central source of data and that have led to a general increase in dance as a methodological tool in other disciplines. Examples are presented of how organisational scholars have used dance, along with frameworks such as Laban Movement Analysis and performance analysis. The final chapters on practical applications of dance are rounding up the argument that started from a theoretical perspective and the mere use of dance as a metaphor, showing that dance studies has much to offer to understand the dynamic, fleeting and invisible structures of interaction in organisations and how they are constantly negotiated and, possibly, changed.

1 Dance and Organisation Studies

Organisation, Art and Aesthetics

Dance stands for constant change, temporary structures and dynamics. It appears to be an intriguing model for today's organisational world and a promising field of study and practice. In a post-Fordist and digital era, capabilities linked to the arts world such as innovation, creativity and collaboration are required and skills such as learning, reflection and co-operation are thought after (Adler, 2006). The world of dance exemplifies many of these issues, particularly with latest developments in contemporary dance and choreography that emphasise co-creation and new ways of working. Organisation studies has broadened over the past decades and came to include a diversity of cultural studies approaches and interdisciplinary theory to account for social, technological and economic developments. Dance studies as a young academic discipline reaches out into the humanities and even into natural sciences research, and, eventually, has made its way into organisational research. Research on dance and organisation is much more than yet another art metaphor for organisational life that emphasises the creative, innovative and human centred approach of many 21st-century organisations. Efforts to integrate studies of dance into organisational research can be seen as interdisciplinary advances that put the (moving) human body and its capacity to generate meaning into the centre of attention. These advances come from research areas such as leadership, gender in management, organisational behaviour and others, but in many cases find their origin in the larger field concerned with the 'art' of management, most commonly referred to as 'organisational aesthetics'.

I will sketch developments in organisation studies that parallel and, in most cases, follow crucial developments in dance and performance studies: We witness an increasing interest in aesthetic perception in both fields, along with a growing attention not only on the body, but its movement. In this section I link some of the central developments of the two different fields of organisation and dance studies to build a basis for a dance perspective on organisations. An inclusion of dance studies and the movement-related, kinaesthetic dimension is a promising extension of not only the organisational aesthetics research field, but organisation studies and management in general. To show this, I will also address issues such as embodied and tacit knowing and briefly review studies on the body in organisation, which have not yet considered the moving body to an appropriate extent. The moving body stands for constant dynamics and also points to many opportunities of change in today's times, which makes dance a theory and practice of critique that adds to organisation studies.

Historically, organisation and management studies have for a long time almost exclusively focused on the 'rational' sphere of work and organisation with notions of scientific management. Shortcomings soon became apparent, as outlined in Weick's (1967) "Social Psychology of Organizing" that introduced into conventional management theory the consideration of subjective aspects of organisational life. These aspects often were largely disregarded in the organisational discipline. Exceptions come for example from Gestalt psychology that has conducted early organisation studies with the works of Kurt Lewin on socially inter-related processes, which only three decades later re-emerged in research on organisational culture, firstly in the USA, soon thereafter in Germany (Biehl-Missal and Fitzek, 2014). Such early approaches also made mention of atmospheres and aesthetic perception in organisations, which over the decades was further developed in many popular and academic works.

Following long periods of research that focused on questions of efficiency and effectiveness, from the 1990s we witness an increasing interest in the aesthetic sphere of our existence in organisations. Aesthetic studies in organisations that were enabled by new works in the emerging field (Carr and Hancock, 2003; Linstead and Höpfl, 2000; Strati, 1999) used the notion of aesthetics in the sense of Baumgarten as concerned with knowledge that is created from our sensory experiences (aiesthesis). A range of publications have formed the basis of an ever growing field of organisational aesthetics research (Taylor and Hansen, 2005), as did conference series (The Art of Management and Organization conference AoMO; The Standing Conference on Organisational Symbolism SCOS), and special issues on 'aesthetics' in management journals. Meanwhile, we have seen the emergence of specialised journals such as the "Organizational Aesthetics" journal. The aesthetic approach assembles works that draw on philosophy, cultural studies, theatre, film and media studies, architecture, aesthetics, psychology and many more, and also includes a range of different traditions within the social sciences, including critical theory, poststructuralism and postmodernism. The inclusion of dance studies adds to and develops the field's interdisciplinary scope.

The aesthetic approach achieved recognition in management handbooks as well, for example the "Sage Handbook of New Approaches in Management and Organization" (Barry and Hansen, 2008). In Germany for example, research in this area is quite young and driven by artists cooperating with businesses in areas such as organisational theatre, and cultural studies researchers drawing on international research (Biehl-Missal, 2011). This approach situates itself in a positivist mainstream business studies tradition that is less open to interdisciplinary research than, for example, international business schools. Research in the US and the UK in particular benefits from the diversity of business school lecturers educated in sociology, the humanities, the arts and psychology (Rowlinson and Hassard, 2011).

A focus on the aesthetic, sensual perception of organisations parallels developments in philosophy and art history. This is reflected in the 'new aesthetics' by the contemporary philosopher and aesthetician Gernot Böhme (2003), which has been received in organisational scholarship as well as in dance and performance studies. The 'new aesthetics' is concerned with 'aisthesis', i.e. the sensual perception of the reality—and links with organisational research that emphasises the importance of the body and sensual perception. The 'new aesthetics' differs from traditional aesthetics, which was developed in the 18th century as a theory of art or of the work of art, typically concerned with aesthetic judgements and categories such as the beauty or the sublime. The task of the new aestheticians today is not to deal with only the fine arts but to make the broad range of aesthetic reality transparent and open to critical analysis. Böhme (2003: 72) uses the term of "aesthetic work" to not only refer to art, but to "the totality of activities which aim to give an appearance to things and people [. . .] to endow them with an aura, to lend them an atmosphere, or to generate an atmosphere in ensembles", i.e. the work of painters and artists, as well as music producers and designers, and marketers and organisational communications professionals. Aesthetic work applies to all those who use their aesthetic capabilities to interact and cooperate in organisations, including leaders. This book discusses how movement-related issues such as kinaesthetic empathy and co-operations or choreographies also are part of 'aesthetic work' in organisations and beyond. Explicitly critical is this view when problematizing manifold attempts of contemporary power and control in organisations that go beyond the surfaces and operate on the bodily level by sensual and implicit manipulation (Böhme, 2003) via atmospheres, spaces and movement politics. A cultural studies perspective on dance explores the body as something that is influenced and formed socially, the aim and result of power that is fugitive and difficult to capture but reproduced and negotiated through movement.

The philosopher Wolfgang Welsch has further argued that aesthetics is not only a phenomenon on the surface of things and processes (and organisations) in the sense of a sugar-coat and beautification, but goes much deeper to affect their inner constitution. The epistemological aestheticisation (Welsch, 1997: 47) refers to a fundamental shift in people's perception of what reality and truth are, when everyday modes of reasoning involve an awareness of the aesthetic and constructed character of 'reality'. Aestheticisation in this sense occurs not only within the world of organisations, marketing and consumption that sugar-coat products and services, but take place in underlying processes. With regard to the perspective of dance taken in this book, this means that organisational processes, including leadership inter-action and service processes, are not only 'like dance' on the surface, but are co-created, negotiated and performed. Leader–follower interaction for example is not created by a representational surface, but through shared and mutual practices involving kinaesthetic empathy and collaboration.

Aesthetic approaches have made their way into organisation studies as attempts to build knowledge differently, acknowledging a 'crisis of repre-sentation' within organisational research that emerged with the shift from positivist and functionalist to interpretive and critical perspectives in organ-isation studies and their associated problems of representation and form (Taylor and Hansen, 2005). It includes analyses of how people sensually perceive spaces, relations, imagery, atmospheres and interactions and how they use their five classic senses of vision (sight), audition (hearing), tactile stimulation (touch), olfaction (smell), and gustation (taste) in their bodily response to situations. Aesthetic inquiries have studied many different forms of aesthetic perception and how different influences affect the body, includ-ing smell (Riach and Warren, 2015), tactile phenomena (Rippin, 2013) and bodily existence in architectures and spaces (Chapter 5). These studies on the aesthetic dimension of organisational life however have only rarely explicitly considered the kinaesthetic dimension, which is central to dance studies.

A kinaesthetic perspective is concerned with movement, more specifically with the act of setting in motion: kīn(eîn) and the sensual perception of it (aesthesia). Movement is difficult to grasp, to analyse and to describe with words. Responding to developments in organisation studies that ques-tion the status of objective knowledge, dance studies is a useful addition as it considers movement as an embodied practice of knowledge that is cre-ated and transmitted through movement between actors, a dynamic and culturally resistant form of knowledge (Huschka, 2009). Movement in organisations is worth exploring as movement is a pervasive phenomenon that relates to many issues of identity and social (organisational) practices. Kinaesthetic exchanges enable different relationships between people (kin-aesthetic politics), mediate interaction and coordination (kinaesthetic empa-thy), facilitate different forms of collaboration and perform and produce social orders ('choreographies') that are transitory, difficult to pin down and not fully visible.

Organisational aesthetics research combines different perspectives and forms of academic inquiry that are concerned with aesthetics not only in the content of inquiry, but also as a mode of inquiry. Following a two by two matrix developed by Taylor and Hansen (2005: 1217), aesthetic stud-ies in organisations can be structured as 'intellectual' methods with an 'instrumental' or 'aesthetic' content. The instrumental approach includes the application of art metaphors such as the organisation 'as theatre' and efforts to learn theoretical lessons for management from the arts (e.g. by reading Shakespeare or poetry), while the aesthetic content revolves around the sensory experience of the day-to-day reality in organisations, including aesthetic services, products and spaces. The second approach are 'artistic' methods with intellectual or aesthetic content, which include artistic forms used to work with individual issues (e.g. art therapy), artistic forms used to work with organisational issues (arts-based interventions), as well as aesthetic forms used to illustrate and present intellectual arguments and the direct sensory day-to-day experience in organisations.

Expanding the organisational aesthetics field to include dance entails both additions to the intellectual and to the artistic methods. I shall develop a more detailed argument about what dance as a metaphor has to offer for organisation studies, whereby the value of the intellectual approach lies in a consideration of organisational life in terms of the 'aesthetic', of movement, kinaesthetic empathy and choreography that links to dance studies. Dance can provide a strong methodological contribution, developing the area of 'artistic methods' and arts-based research approaches in management studies that are described as most promising because they offer a medium that can capture and communicate the felt experience and something of the tacit knowledge of organisations (Taylor and Hansen, 2005: 1224). Dance can be used, and is already increasingly used as a productive form of inquiry by researchers that deploy movement to generate and analyse data on embodied, aesthetic and transitory interaction in organisational life. In this vein, dance can also be used as a presentational form to transmit research findings. Dance is also used as an arts-based intervention to work with organisational members.

Dance Studies

Dance studies is a rather young discipline. In higher education dance studies are offered through the arts and humanities departments, often developing out of the young discipline of performance studies that has its roots in literature studies and languages. Dance theory is a fairly new field of studies from the second half of the 20th century, comprising philosophy, movement analysis and description, and sociological approaches regarding the role of dance in society and culture. Dance studies has developed through broad interdisciplinary attention given to the discipline. Robotics engineering, psychology and medicine have used theories and concepts from dance studies to explore human movement and social interaction. Cultural studies have pushed the boundaries of the discipline to consider dance as a culturally shaped bodily practice with movement influencing concepts of subjectivity and gender in society (Desmond, 1997). At the same time as scholars from other disciplines look into dance studies, dance scholars themselves have broadened the scope of their inquiry beyond art institutions, aesthetic assessments of dance, auteur studies of dancers and choreographers, and historical studies, and have considered dance as a socio-cultural practice, focusing on questions of agency articulated in specific choreographic practices of communities, groups and subjects. With the integration of dance as practice in schools and other social contexts, dance research moved towards a more active exploration of diverse approaches to dance-making. Dance scholars also put more emphasis on the aesthetic and kinaesthetic experience, pointing to the critical potential of dance as an embodied social practice. In this context, choreography is increasingly applied in scholarly, political contexts and in individual contexts, for example as a tool for self-exploration. The broadened focus of the dance discipline from aesthetic judgment to aesthetic experience, understood as the experience of the sensing body, may well have contributed significantly to the increased interdisciplinary scholarly interest in dance.

Because of its interdisciplinary nature, dance studies offers a promising addition to management and organisational research including leadership studies. I shall now further describe the development of the dance discipline, opening a range of doors that connect dance and organisation studies. It needs to be said that dance is looking back on a complex history and relationship between practice and theory, with a multiplicity of exchanges and transmissions and resistance towards categorisation (Brandstetter and Klein, 2013). This book on dance and organisation is a contribution to the on-going process of rethinking and de-thinking questions of dance and theory, depositioning and repositioning, ordering and dis-ordering dance, theory and organisation.

The aesthetic turn in the 1990s in organisations studies was long preceded by developments in the performing arts disciplines, in cultural studies and the humanities. These disciplines underwent a 'performative turn' that brought the performative act and the aesthetic experience into focus. This development gained momentum several decades ago when the discipline of theatre studies along with dance studies shifted its emphasis from an analysis of what happened on the stages in the arts world towards the theatrical processes in social life. Dance studies, similar to performing arts scholarship, stood in a tradition of an evaluation of staged performances, often with reference to a strong historical narrative. American dance scholars (Desmond, 1997) came to consider dance as a socio-cultural practice, focusing on questions of agency and bodily movement in the social realm. Studies in dance today, rather than decoding dance as an art-work, focus on the 'aesthetic experience' that is a part of a culturally shaped, bodily practice. Rather than focusing on dance conventions and styles, this view capitalises on the aesthetic experience that is related to movement in space, the bodily and affective co-presence of actors and spectators that goes beyond intellectual interpretation processes (Siegmund, 2013).

Theatre studies similarly became studies of the performance, which is expressed in the label "performance studies" that also includes dance.

Theatre practice has seen a turning away from the script as the alleged basis of the performance, which is driven simultaneously by developments in society as well as developments in the world of the theatre. In postdramatic theatre (Lehmann, 2006), also referred to as postmodern theatre, the text is often fragmented and dispersed into a collage and montage, emphasised is the aesthetic experience, the theatrical moment of the performance. Performers are materiality rather than mimetic imitation, whereby movements in a cultural context are imitated, not representing fictional characters but presenting something, generating meaning by bodily presence. This focus on the aesthetic dimension is shared with aesthetic approaches in organisation studies.

Of relevance in this context is that dance and theatre performances are a 'co-present encounter', characterised through a bodily co-presence of actors and co-actors (spectators). Performances come into being by the bodily co-presence. Spectators are not regarded as mere observers making sense of what they see and hear or 'interpreting' or 'decoding' it, but are considered as co-players, contributing to the creation of a performance by participating through their physical presence, their perception and responses. Fischer-Lichte (2008: 38) speaks of "shared bodies—shared spaces" to illustrate how this co-present situation depends of the aesthetic and kinaesthetic experience and the materiality of the body. In the context of what often is referred to as the "aesthetics of the performative" (Fischer-Lichte, 2008), the aesthetic perception and interaction and the impact of such co-created performances became more important and also are used in this book to explain interaction in organisations. Valuing processes of interaction between those who are co-present also leads to a consideration of, on the broader level, issues of change and dynamics in social structures, how they emerge, are challenged, negotiated and resisted.

With the performative turn, scholarly attention in the humanities extended beyond the consideration of artefacts such as the score in music or the text in the theatre. The focus on the aesthetic experience has provided theory to access other worlds—including organisations. Performance studies from the late 1980s expanded their view beyond the institutional stages into social life and the notion of "performance" was applied to describe and critically discuss phenomena that use theatrical and socio-symbolic forms of expression. These performances take place on the level of everyday culture, in political events, in the world of fashion and in the world of sports (Schechner, 2002; Turner, 1982). Organisational scholars with a background or interest in the performing arts came to apply their knowledge to organisations, highlighting the concept of performance as the important link between theatre and organisations, albeit for long omitting a detailed discussion of aesthetic elements in favour of metaphorical considerations (Chapter 2).

The performative side of culture had been largely overlooked in a society and science tradition, and also in management studies (Strati, 1999), which defined itself as manifest in text and monuments and material artefacts.

A performative understanding of culture extends beyond artefacts and texts, conceiving of culture as social and performative, embodied interaction. Movements of the body, albeit non-verbal and transitory, were in consequence increasingly valued in cultural studies as performative acts and were accorded a different legitimacy for analysis. With the performative turn, scholars came to consider movement practices 'as performance', putting the performative act, the process of production and the agency into focus. Such a view considers the moving body as an agent that produces reality via the performative act. Performance often is understood as derived from the French verb "parfournier" translated as carrying out and accomplishing. The complex relationship of performance and reality came into focus also with the performative speech acts: Building on the performative dimension in the sense of Austin (1963), where "things are done with words" that are not true or false, rather exerting some kind of action, performances were attributed an impact on social practice. Shifting away from true and false, objective or subjective, the focus turned on the perception of things. The goes along with a loss of an objective point of reference, turning reality into a construct of aesthetic experience and interpretation. Moving bodies hence produce reality not only when they dance on a stage and create an artistic performance. They also produce reality in social life, or in organisations: Performing, for example, gendered movements (kinaesthetic politics), employing kinaesthetic empathy through embodied practices of leadership interaction, or when people move in a specific space and create 'social choreographies'.

Defining Dance in Organisations

Building on the previous discussion, dance is seen in this book on "Dance and Organisation" as performative and aesthetic human movement that includes all forms of bodily movement as well as distinct dance moves. Movement occurs in space and time, and often in relation to others, which is obvious but, when emphasised, brings to our attention the spatial, relational and dynamic, transitory (fleeting) nature of this practice. Dance lies in the moment, it constantly evolves, movements do not have a clear end and beginning, rather inducing new actions in a constant dynamic. There is no distinct definition and the meaning of dance is as broad as dance practices that depend on social, cultural, aesthetic, artistic and moral constraints and cover a spectrum from simple to virtuoso techniques, which can be performed for audiences that may be participatory or social. Dance typically is associated with one or multiple bodies moving in a specified rhythmical manner with or without music. While many readers may think of ballet or artistic dance presentations, others have in their mind images of ballroom dancing, pair dancing, aerobics, ravers moving to techno music, professional and amateur dance performances, and an incredibly broad array of everyday movements including a normal walk through the space. Sound and rhythm is also typically related to dance and its non-verbal nature, which makes dance a 'universal language' capable of expressing emotions, ideas and stories, evoking reflection on individual feelings and social understandings ranging from religion and tradition to political, cultural and artistic issues. This form of communication is practiced when people move in a situation of co-presence. We all move constantly, not only our hands and faces, but our bodies and our thoughts change. Interaction can be seen as a constant improvisation when bodies react, mimics adapt and patterns emerge that structure interaction—as exemplified in the dance form of contact improvisation.

The universality of movement has been emphasised throughout all genres of writing and many authors have argued that "life is dance" (Ellis, 1923) because the world is full of continuous movement. Dance as an art form requires no instruments and tools, just the moving body, and therefore is an ancient medium with a long pedigree that helped to communicate content, concepts and emotions and to build a community through the joint experience. Dance has to it a certain universality as moving is human. The book does not wish to literally accord the status of 'dance' to the entire range of human movement as this would conflate different kinds of concepts and activities, and would ignore the legitimacy of the broad practical and theoretical field of dance as an art form. A definition from dance studies is useful here as it includes the cultural dimension and also points towards communication and knowledge: Dance is seen as an auto-motoric, actively generated movement oriented towards an aim, performed by thinking beings, and addressed towards someone perceiving the action and feeling aesthetic responses (Böhme and Huschka, 2009: 8).

Working from such an understanding in this book allows us to refer to dance as human movement as well as an art form, and all the issues that go along with it and have particular value for organisation studies, subsumed under the notions of kinaesthetic politics, kinaesthetic empathy, choreographies, kinaesthetic training and dance as a research method. Such an approach links to dance studies that as a cultural studies approach has expanded and considers movement in social life. From around the late 1960s choreographic investigation challenged boundaries between dance and everyday movement and claimed any and all human movement as potential dance (Foster, 1997: 253). Similarly, we see in organisations today that people interact and collaborate using their kinaesthetic empathy and constituting their identity in social interaction with others and in space and time. The book considers actual dance practices, be it on stage or in practical workshops in organisations, and it also uses concepts and theory from the dance field to advance a metaphorical understanding of organisations 'as dance' and an anti-metaphorical understanding of movement practices in organisations that are choreographies, that are performed and negotiated through kinaesthetic empathy and practice.

The Body in Organisations

Dance studies is a promising addition to organisation studies, which slowly developed an interest in the moving body. Before attending to the body in motion, organisation scholars have made some steps to explore the role of the body, which, historically in organisations and in organisation theory, has played only a minor role. The body has attracted considerable attention in many fields of academic scholarship largely due to the advances of feminist, postmodern, poststructural and psychoanalytic theories of embodiment that are diverse but have in common that they claim all social actors to be embodied actors, and thus seeing experience as necessarily embodied. The body in organisations has seen emerging scholarly interest from around the year 2000 (Hassard et al., 2000) and organisational experience as well is perceived from embodied standpoints whereby sex, gender and race play a role. The body is not viewed as object, but rather as the medium through which social actors have relations to the world and through which they give and receive information. As a primary means of connecting with the world, the body is an aesthetic sense-making resource.

With the moving body being central to dance, the growing fascination with ideas of performativity and the interest in the performing body in cultural studies has boosted dance scholarship over the past decades or so and constitutes a central bridge to organisation studies. Performativity coming from performance and cultural studies and originating in the work of Judith Butler and others at the time, opened a new gate for dance scholarship to contribute to debates in the cultural studies, and a chance for dance research and the tools already developed within dance scholarship to take forward these debates in other fields.

Dance was received in other cultural studies disciplines and achieved contributions to gaps that studies on the body have opened but not further developed. Movement remained an under-analysed bodily practice and was seen as a promising addition to works on the body in other disciplines—a situation that we find currently in organisation studies as well. In cultural studies in the 1980s and 1990s, extant studies' main emphasis was on two- and three-dimensional visual representation (such as film and visual arts) or on large-scale analyses of categories of subjectivity. Desmond (1997: 2) argued that "in these works, the materiality of bodies and bodily movement can sometimes become paradoxically submerged. Dance as an embodied social practice and highly visual aesthetic form, powerfully melds considerations of materiality and representation together." Expanding the agenda of dance studies as a cultural studies inquiry, Desmond (1997: 2) had formulated a range of questions such as:

> How does dance signal, enact, or rework social categories of identity? Since dance takes the body as its primary medium, can it provide a potential utopian site for imagining what a feminist politics of the body might look like? How can dance analysis lead us toward a

consideration of the vast range of social practices built on strictures (sic) of embodiment which form the tissue of everyday enactment, such as how we move in public, play sports, and communicate through an incredibly complex and undertheorized semiotics of the body? How are codified movement systems such as dance similar to or different from other forms of representation such as language or visual representation? What is kinaesthetic subjectivity?

While dance studies for the past decades has worked along these lines of inquiry, organisation studies only a decade ago began to consider 'the body' and has until now only tentatively explored the potential of analyses on the moving body. This also leads to issues concerning the body as a primary medium in organisations, and all kinds of topics that are related to it: Questions relating to identity construction through movement (kinaesthetic politics) need to be considered and linked to gender research in management; hidden structures informing how people move in organisations need to be considered, along with their function as a social choreography. This goes along with kinaesthetic empathy that informs also leader–follower interaction in organisations. Using dance for analysis of embodied movement structures, and the practical application of dance as a training method provides the methods necessary to access these kinaesthetic, transitory phenomena.

   The body in organisation theory has for long played only an unimportant role. In the tradition of the rational organisation, exemplified in, for example, the notion of Scientific management, the body and its behaviours were considered "lower order" that might "impinge" on the "cool rationality" demanded in the workplace (Brewis and Sinclair, 2000). Scientific management, or Taylorism, however has touched on the complex and deep relationship of movements and organising in some ways: In an attempt to improve efficiency human movement was considered, leading to the development of time and motion studies (or time–motion study). Bringing together the Time Study work of Frederick Winslow Taylor with the Motion Study work of Frank and Lillian Gilbreth, this technique aimed to increase industrial output, accounting for the destructive impact of repetitive behaviour, trying to improve and not to reduce industrial workers' mental and physical strength. Differing fundamentally from earlier epochs in Western civilisation where farmers for example performed a wide range of body movements every day, monotonous work process in industrial times posed new challenges to workers. This also was reflected in dance practice that has imitated forms of work, for example in Meyerhold's "Biomechanics" (Law and Gordon, 1995). Motion studies bears some educational aspects with regard to the training of workers. Some of this tradition can be seen in today's movement workshops in organisations, which however put more emphasis on the idea of expression and insight through movement in the tradition of modern dance.

   Building on the understanding of the body as an aesthetic sense-making resource, new challenges arise in contemporary organisations. The shift from manual work to intellectual work with a growing influence of information technology and the service sector in interdisciplinary dance studies has been interpreted as an "erosion of the influence of work on the body" (Alkemeyer et al., 2003: 7). This devaluation of the body in organisations for dance scholars goes along with an increasing valuation of the body in areas of sport, play and styling in modern society (Alkemeyer et al., 2003). From an organisation studies point of view however, an increasing valuation of the body in many areas of work has been observed. The body is a central part in the world of consumption that does not only sell functional products but creates experiences for consumers (Böhme, 2003). Service work for example requires beauty and aesthetic form and the aesthetics of looks also are part of managerial work, for all genders. A valuation of the body, outfit and style also takes place in visual depictions of managers and theatrical management presentations in front of audiences. Many of these bodily norms and appearances in organisational life have been accorded more attention with what has been referred to as an aestheticisation of organisational life.

Despite the attention paid to the body in organisation studies, it has often been theorised as an 'immobile' project, be it a site of discipline, control and resistance in a Foucauldian understanding, or as an instrument of perception from a phenomenological perspective. Researchers in dance and organisation find that embodiment literature has been far less interested in the fluidity and complexity of our physical existence with surprisingly little written about our everyday embodied and kinaesthetic experiences of movement (Huopalainen, 2015). Recently we see more contributions on the moving body in organisations and moving bodies at work, for example when interacting in non-verbal processes in a surgery (Hindmarsch and Pilnick, 2007) and an ever-growing literature on how people perform organisational space. Satama and Huopalainen (2016) are among the first who have focused on movements and micro-level interactions in dance and fashion shows, showing the relationality of embodied agency and also how these movements are able to alter and change established concepts or 'scripts' of interaction.

In today's working conditions, with different forms of movement, identities also change. Bodily movements, essential to our agency and subjectivity, are a central part in our identity construction in the social realm (Desmond, 1997), and also in the organisational world when we perform ourselves at work. These bodily movements are embedded and influenced by invisible structures, by social choreographies, but also are developed through constant co-operation, be it between leaders and followers or within a team or a group (Chapter 5). Todays' bodies often are less occupied than in Taylorist work settings, but, for example in the service sector, need to find their own ways of improvised and flexible interaction beyond 'rehearsed' routines. Many of these performative processes are co-created and negotiated among people, requiring empathy and collaboration. The growing presence of female bodies in organisations, as well as LGBTQs and people from diverse cultural backgrounds have broadened a spectrum of behaviour and deconstructed clear contours of professional habitus—along with, for example, changed approaches to teaching that value cooperation instead of teacher-centred lecturing to a passive student and distanced 'professorial' behaviour.

Bodies in organisations are in many ways set free from external traditional control mechanisms that also provided stability, and now need to rely on many internal activities that achieve the bodily behaviour. Dance research also has debated that bodily movements relate to complicated questions around embodied agency, control, power and resistance. Identities in social life and in organisations are not as stable and inscribed as they traditionally were, but bodies are 'in motion'. The human body, performing, in interaction, and in movement, often is ignored by the social sciences when they take a theoretical and abstract view, but dance studies is well suited to this endeavour. Dance studies emphasises not only transience but foremost the potential of change and dynamics in the mimesis, in creating and performing structures. So the new bodily structures that we see in organisations not only express social and organisational developments deep down in organisations. They also point to opportunities of negotiating change when the moving body is analysed, used as a research tool and trained in arts-based interventions that use movement.

Extant studies on the body in organisation stand in a tradition that focuses on bodily appearance and bodily norms, rather than bodily movement. Bodily movements have been considered somewhat taken-for-granted and treated as routinely and habitually performed and have been largely overlooked. Following an argument made earlier that the aestheticisation of the economy does not only take place on the surface but affects underlying structures (Welsch, 1997), this book develops the idea that the body in today's world of work needs less muscle power but needs to develop new aesthetic capabilities and, with particular regard to dance, kinaesthetic capabilities that can be trained (Chapter 6), namely kinaesthetic politics (Chapter 3) in terms of individual behaviour, kinaesthetic empathy to collaborate and manage interactions through which people relate to each other (Chapter 4) and to the space and to the context in terms of choreographies (Chapter 5).

Knowledge and the Body

Putting the human body, its aesthetic perceptions and its movement into the focus of scholarly research, addresses issues of knowledge that are central to each discipline. Management scholars came to value the aesthetic experience of organisational phenomena, i.e. the sensory experience about which a judgement such as beautiful, ugly, grotesque and comical may be made.

Foregoing the positivist mind–body separation and its logico-deductive thinking, this stream of research draws on interpretive and critical perspectives, claiming that the study of feelings and emotions is not dubious and 'irrational', but that knowledge is strongly influenced by feelings and sensual, embodied perception (Damasio, 1999). This continues Polanyi's idea of tacit knowledge that in organisational aesthetics research is seen as roughly corresponding to sensory/aesthetic knowing that often is contrasted with intellectual/explicit knowing (Taylor and Hansen, 2005: 1213). Knowing can also be divided into experiential knowing (through the immediacy of perceiving, empathy and resonance); presentational knowing (that emerges from experiential knowing through expressive and artistic forms such as dance); propositional knowing ('about' something in terms of ideas and theories); and practical knowing as 'how to' do something as a skill (Heron and Reason, 2001: 183). Important for this book is the distinction between experiential or embodied, tacit knowing as opposed to intellectual, propositional knowing. Positing a connection between all forms of knowing, it is assumed that experiential and presentational forms of knowing are strongly related to the (moving) body, which helps to build a bridge to dance studies. The notion of embodied knowing will be used in this book to refer to knowledge that is 'in the body', although differentiations are also considered that scholars in the field have made.

The concept of embodied knowledge or 'bodily knowledge' can be found in the phenomenology of Merleau-Ponty (1962) who questioned the Cartesian dualism of mind and body. Merleau-Ponty's philosophy has underpinned the work of many scholars in the area of performance studies and in particular dance studies, and has been received in organisation studies. Considering the 'lived body' as a primary means of connecting with the world, embodiment research emphasises the interconnectedness of mind and body, with experience existing in mind and body. Organisational scholars often equate the concept of embodied knowledge with tacit knowledge (Taylor and Ladkin, 2009), and also with aesthetic knowledge as it is derived from sensory experience. Others however have further distinguished between embodied knowledge, aesthetic knowledge and tacit knowledge (Springborg and Sutherland, 2016: 101) to argue that a view on embodied knowledge from embodied cognition in the sense 'knowing how to do something' can be used to develop an argument for dance in management education when it brings into focus learning how to do things that are transferable from 'dance' to 'leadership' (Chapter 6).

Paving the way for an application of dance, scholars in the field have recently begun to draw on theories and findings from neuroscience—in particular theories of embodied cognition. It is posited that human cognition in general is grounded in bodily, sensory experience (Barsalou, 2010), which means that not only aesthetic elements are used as an input of data, rather the body is assumed as the sensory tool that is operating when we are being reflexive. Empirical research in embodied cognition has found that even abstract concepts are grounded in sensory, body-based experiences. This finding has been used to argue that the sensory experience of art, including dance, can develop the sensory, body-based foundation in which managers base their abstract concepts relevant to leadership and work (Springborg and Sutherland, 2016). In this vein, dance does not only advance organisation studies as a theory, rather the embodied, kinaesthetic practice of dance seems promising to develop reflexive forms of action that are indispensable for leaders and for all organisational members that collaborate and interact at work in organisations. The concept of 'tacit knowing' shares with this view on 'embodied knowing' that all knowledge is grounded in sensory experience. It also points to the idea that the consequences of "committing to the use of particular experiences as tools are, at least in part, a journey of discovery, and cannot be predicted at the outset" (Springborg and Sutherland, 2016: 102). This quote relates well to an idea that is promoted throughout the book that dance may have a critical potential residing in its non-discursive nature, not only being transitory and dynamic, but potentially supporting change through interaction and challenge.

The dance perspective capitalises on issues of 'embodied knowing', positing that knowledge resides in the body. This also is referred to as 'somatic knowledge' (Snowber, 2014), and knowledge that is everywhere in the body and its movement and expression, foregoing the Cartesian mind-body divide. In dance studies, Parviainen (2002) for example accepts Merleau-Ponty's (1962) account of perception as the centrality that the lived body plays in our understanding of ourselves and our expression through dance. Perceiving the world through our bodies we lead embodied existences. Dance and bodily movement can be seen as a kinaesthetic expression of our embodiment, with the body and dance being inseparable. The body is not viewed as an object, which means that people are not 'having bodies' rather 'being bodies' (Snowber, 2014: 253). Meaning is created in the body, not solely in the mind.

The idea of embodied knowing—also equated with tacit knowing (Böhme and Huschka, 2009: 11)—is important for dance scholars, who have not only considered dance as a practice that embodies cultural knowledge, but also as a practice that transmits knowledge and culture through bodily movements (Huschka, 2009). The body is a reservoir of knowledge that is expressed and materialised in the moving body and its social and aesthetic practices, in a cultural and historical context. Whereas dance practice is a knowing-how, dance studies as a scientific discipline attempts a knowing-that, notating, interpreting and theorising dance in a social and historical context. Dance is a model for the tacit eloquence of the body (eloquentia corporis) that is not only a creative practice, but a performative act in which people interact to create and access knowledge. A radical separation of practical knowledge (techné) and theoretical knowledge (theoría), which is characteristic for most sciences, cannot and must not exist in dance studies (Böhme and Huschka, 2009: 10). Dance knowledge is tacit knowledge contained by a dynamic, performative act in which actors know more than they can say—organisations also build on these tacit, embodied forms of knowing. In this regard dance studies are particularly suited as a development of organisation and leadership studies that have paid increasing attention to embodied, aesthetic and tacit knowing to better understand how organisational members make sense of what is happening and how they interact.

Dance and Change

Putting the living body into the focus contributes to critiques of reductionist, disembodied orientations that, for example, propagate the 'management' of one's own life and instrumentally orientated action (Hancock, 2009). It challenges disembodied and non-creative practices in which individual and collective bodies and embodiments are neglected, merely seen as constructed or rendered as instrumentalised objects for a utilitarian exploitative practice. In this sense, the book on dance and organisation also links to critical management studies (CMS) that have been considered as a "performative project" that involves "active and subversive intervention into managerial discourses and practices" (Spicer et al., 2009: 538). Although scholars have explored many theoretical underpinnings, the notion of 'performance' in the obvious artistic sense of the term has not been linked to this topic. Critical management studies typically have drawn on other disciplines for new content of theory and practice and this book explores scholarly opportunities when discussing 'performance' not in the managerial sense in terms of output, but as actions of behaving, doing and 'moving'. These aspects are an inseparable component of organisational life, and are frequently related to practices of managerial efficiency but may also be opposing politics, practices and structures if theoretically and practically activated. Analysing movement in social and organisational life links to critical perspectives in dance studies, which has incorporated influences that have changed the humanities, including poststructuralist influences and postmodern theory, psychoanalytic approaches, feminist theories and Marxism. The engagement with conditions of production and reception of cultural practices means considering the social context as well as the historical pedigree of practices, forms and meanings, and their formative and interrogatory relationship to the construction of subjectivity (Desmond, 1997: 4).

Taking seriously and literally the idea of critical management studies (CMS) as a 'performative project' this book makes attempts to link new theories to organisation studies and points to kinaesthetic forms of training and research (Chapter 6 and 7) that can be seen as performative interventions. Exploration is needed of the ways in which critical management studies could implement such a theoretical and literal 'performative' perspective so as to strengthen its critical impact, not to uphold or promote belief in the managerial project as it is, but to bring meaning into 'motion' and to encourage resistance and change in and through theory and kinaesthetic interaction.

The transitory, fugitive and ephemeral nature of dance has always been a challenge for academic studies of dance and movement and has inhibited the development of dance studies into a discipline in its own right (Foster, 2013). Dance however does not only stand for difficulties of storing and analysis, but these characteristics prove to be a particular asset in today's times of constant change and innovation in the business world. Change is typically linked to motion in our thinking: Drawing on our physical and embodied experience, in everyday language 'change' is considered as 'motion': Experiencing the change of a state is often linked to the sensorimotor domain of moving, with changing the location as you move (Lakoff and Johnson, 1999: 52). Dance as a fugitive practice is not only a metaphor for change, rather the practice of movement provides theoretical insight into change—in organisations as well. I suggest that issues of movement in the social context (kinaesthetic politics), interaction mediated through the senses (kinaesthetic empathy and choreography) and arts-based interventions (kinaesthetic training) contribute to change and innovation in organisations.

The dance perspective has a particular strength and potential for exploring dynamic 21st-century organisations and leadership. Dance studies have emphasised the potential of the discipline with regard to change as the central paradigm for modern times (Klein, 2009), but have not expanded their view to consider organisations that also are constantly changing. Movements not only produce structures that are fleeting, but movements permanently create, perform and transform structures. The same applies to knowledge that is dispersed and embodied. Dance brings into our perception the constant creation and decline of these structures, for example also in collaborations in organisations including leader–follower relationships, and points to the plethora of possibilities that reside in these constant mutual negotiations and creations. In this sense, it is no coincidence that metaphors of dance and organisation appeared during the past years, pointing to a need to understand embodied and ever-changing dynamics. In fact, contemporary tendencies have already been conceptually and critically linked back to artistic forms of work that are not static but innovative and ever changing and that are demanded by today's organisations (Boltanski and Chiapello, 2005). Artistic processes, people and products have been brought into organisations to further innovation (Chapter 6). Insights from dance theory and practical dance-based training advance these views on innovation and change.

Dance as a collaborative and sensual, transitory practice more than other arts perspectives bears a strong utopian moment, pointing to the potential for negotiating change in today's times collectively. Movement and transience have long been elements of the modern experience that is widely reflected in artistic practice and in written works. Walter Benjamin has described in his Arcades Project the experience of the flâneur passing through Parisian spaces and experiencing the world receptively. Dance studies is concerned with transience and movement, but not only with the ephemeral that does not last, rather with a dynamic that permanently builds and transforms structures (Klein, 2009: 206). Dance has thus been heralded by scholars in the field as the discipline with a particular and critical potential in modern and postmodern times and indeed seems to be promising in a context of a specific and wider interest in change and mobility today. We are witnessing a general growth in mobility across a variety of areas including world-wide information exchange through the internet, global trade with products being sent around the earth, logistics, and people travelling and refugees migrating across borders, affecting social, economic, political and ecological developments. The rise of mobility, be it the movement of people, things and ideas, in ways that are corporeal, physical, imaginative, virtual and communicate, affects social life and social sciences (Urry, 2007). These developments also affect organisations when organisational processes and work is not static but mobile, requiring employees and their activities to become mobilised as well. While metaphors of flux, flow and fluidity have become popular in this context, many of us have already experienced the frictions and emotional cost that go along with it. The very spaces of mobility are experienced as 'non-places', again pointing back to the body and its existence. Mobilities that are researched include a broad spectrum of phenomena ranging from professional travel, teleworking, home working, mobile information technology to temporary work, project-based work or virtual teams. Studies investigating these developments often go beyond the consideration of a particular work place that is grounded somewhere and turn towards the virtual aspects of work.

Dance studies, albeit fundamentally embodied, addresses these realities as well. This book with a focus on the moving body in organisations starts with the body to explore issues relating to corporeal and kinaesthetic experience, which is ever present in organisational life. It is part of a counter-movement to increasing virtuality and dematerialisation of digital media, a re-concretisation in terms of body, space and time of our culture. This approach helps to value again the embodied side of modern and postmodern culture and points to aesthetic experiences that cannot be digitised but that people want to experience and also negotiate with their bodies. When embodied perception is the basis for action in a performative and constructivist view that does not posit a 'true' reality, this view can improve action in an abstract society by linking it back to aesthetic perception and manipulation that is always part of the process (Böhme, 2003).

The dance perspective, by addressing the embodied, lived experience, allows for many insights into the abstract concepts of change today and in this sense is much more than a counter-movement. In today's times of digitisation and mobility, there seems to be a growing dichotomy between the body and the mind when virtual networks enable work and communication without movement. The practice of dance however points to our bodies and the limitations its poses for us. Dance does not only oppose the fast virtual world with the slow corporeal world, rather points to movement and halt, to kinesis and stasis, not only to acceleration and deceleration but to all nuances. In this sense dance is a valid conceptual lens for thinking and being, also in organisations.

Contemporary trends such as digitisation call for new ways of cooperating and improvising. The embodied practice of dance is a model for many dynamic forms of cooperation. Principles from dance can be applied to virtual forms of work and leadership because dance emphasises the relational and constantly negotiated dimension of leading and following that happens in-between people, and in a space in-between participants that cannot be fully controlled. Dance is something that is transitory and cannot be reproduced, pointing to these spaces and providing confidence and empathy to deal with them. When the body is our basis of understanding our world, it should not recede into the background but it needs to be developed and trained to achieve skilful knowing and doing (Springborg and Sutherland, 2016). The use of dance as an actual practice and training method in this sense helps people discover how to tap into feelings and bodily ways of knowing, inclusive their 'gut-feeling' and their empathy, to guide their decisions and actions, a competence that is particularly important in situations of uncertainty and ambiguity in today's world of business.

Literature

Adler, N. (2006) The arts and leadership: Now that we can do anything, what will we do? *Academy of Management Learning & Education* 5(4): 486–499.

Alkemeyer, T., Boschert, B., Schmidt, R. and Gebauer, G. (eds.) (2003) *Aufs Spiel gesetzte Körper: Aufführungen des Sozialen in Sport und populärer Kultur.* Konstanz: UVK Verlag.

Austin, J. L. (1963) *How to Do Things with Words.* London: Penguin.

Barry, D. and Hansen, S. (2008) The new and emerging in management and organization: Gatherings, trends, and bets, in Barry, D. and Hansen, H. (eds.) *The Sage Handbook of New Approaches in Management and Organization.* London: Sage, 1–10.

Barsalou, L. W. (2010) Grounded cognition: Past, present, and future, *Topics in Cognitive Science* 2(4): 716–724.

Biehl-Missal, B. (2011) *Wirtschaftsästhetik. Wie Unternehmen die Kunst als Inspiration und Werkzeug nutzen.* Wiesbaden: Gabler.

Biehl-Missal, B. and Fitzek, H. (2014) Hidden heritage: A Gestalt psychology approach to the aesthetics of management and organisation, *Gestalt Theory: An International Multidisciplinary Journal* 36(3): 251–266.

Böhme, G. (2003) Contribution to the critique of the aesthetic economy, *Thesis Eleven* 73(1): 71–82.

Böhme, H. and Huschka, S. (2009) Prolog, in Huschka, S. (ed.) *Wissenskultur Tanz: Historische und zeitgenössische Vermittlungsakte zwischen Praktiken und Diskursen.* Bielefeld: transcript, 7–24.

Boltanski, L. and Chiapello, E. (2005) *The New Spirit of Capitalism,* trans. G. Elliott. London: Verso.

Brandstetter, G. and Klein, G. (eds.) (2013) *Dance [and] Theory*. Bielefeld: transcript.

Brewis, J. and Sinclair, J. (2000) Exploring embodiment: Women, biology and work, in Hassard, J., Holliday, R. and Willmott, H. (eds.) *Body and Organization*. London: Sage, 192–214.

Carr, A. and Hancock, P. (ed.) (2003) *Art and Aesthetics at Work*. New York: Palgrave Macmillan.

Damasio, A. (1999) *The Feeling of What Happens: Body and Emotion in the Making of Consciousness*. New York: Harcourt Brace.

Desmond, J. (ed.) (1997) *Meaning in Motion: New Cultural Studies of Dance*. Durham and London: Duke University Press.

Ellis, H. (1923) *The Dance of Life*. Boston: Houghton Mifflin.

Fischer-Lichte, E. (2008) *The Transformative Power of Performance: A New Aesthetics*. London and New York: Routledge.

Foster, S. L. (1997) Dancing bodies, in Desmond, J. (ed.) *Meaning in Motion: New Cultural Studies of Dance*. Durham and London: Duke University Press, 235–258.

Foster, S. L. (2013) Dancing and theorizing and theorizing dancing, in Brandstetter, G. and Klein, G. (eds.) *Dance (and) Theory*. Bielefeld: transcript, 19–32.

Hancock, P. (2009) Management and colonization in everyday life, in Hancock, P. and Tyler, M. (eds.) *The Management of Everyday Life*. London: Palgrave Macmillan, 1–20.

Hassard, R., Holliday, R. and Willmott, H. (eds.) (2000) *Body and Organization*. London: Sage.

Heron, J. and Reason, P. (2001) The practice of co-operative inquiry: Research 'with' rather than 'on' people, in Reason, P. and Bradbury, H. (eds.) *Handbook of Action Research: Participative Inquiry and Practice*. London: Sage, 179–188.

Hindmarsh, J. and Pilnick, A. (2007) Knowing bodies at work: Embodiment and ephemeral teamwork in anaesthesia, *Organization Studies* 28(9): 1395–1416.

Huopalainen, A. (2015) Who moves? Analyzing fashion show organizing through micro-interactions of bodily movement, *Ephemera: Theory and Politics in Organizations* 15(4): 825–846.

Huschka, S. (ed.) (2009) *Wissenskultur Tanz: Historische und zeitgenössische Vermittlungsakte zwischen Praktiken und Diskursen*. Bielefeld: transcript.

Klein, G. (2009) Das Flüchtige. Politische Aspekte einer tanztheoretischen Figur, in Huschka, S. (ed.) *Wissenskultur Tanz. Historische und zeitgenössische Vermittlungsakte zwischen Praktiken und Diskursen*. Bielefeld: transcript, 199–208.

Lakoff, G. and Johnson, M. (1999) *Philosophy in the Flesh: The Embodied Mind and Its Challenge to Western Thought*. New York: Basic Books.

Law, A. and Gordon, M. (1995) *Meyerhold, Eisenstein and Biomechanics: Actor Training in Revolutionary Russia*. Jefferson, NC: McFarland.

Lehmann, H. T. (2006) *Postdramatic Theatre*. London: Routledge.

Linstead, S. and Höpfl, H. (eds.) (2000) *The Aesthetics of Organization*. London: Sage.

Merleau-Ponty, M. (1962) *Phenomenology of Perception*, trans. C. Smith. London: Routledge and Kegan Paul.

Parviainen, J. (2002) Bodily knowledge: Epistemological reflections on dance, *Dance Research Journal* 34(1): 11–22.Riach, K. and Warren, S. (2015) Smell organization: Bodies and corporeal porosity in office work, *Human Relations* 68(5): 789–809.

Rippin, A. (2013) The human touch versus 'silver-handedness': The importance of the haptic in organizational life, *International Journal of Work, Organisation and Emotion* 5(4): 357–368.

Rowlinson, M. and Hassard, J. (2011) How come the critters came to be teaching in business schools? Contradictions in the institutionalization of critical management studies, *Organization* 18(5): 673–689.

Satama, S. and Huopalainen, A. (2016) 'Bring down the controlled movements!'— Exploring the possibilities of and limitations on achieving embodied agency in ballet and fashion, *Culture and Organization*. DOI: 10.1080/14759551.2016.1151424.

Schechner, R. (2002) *Performance Studies: An Introduction*. London: Routledge.

Siegmund, G. (2013) Aesthetic experience, in Brandstetter, G. and Klein, G. (eds.) *Dance [and] Theory*. Bielefeld: transcript, 81–88.

Snowber, C. (2014) Visceral creativity: Organic creativity in teaching arts/dance education. In Piirto, J. (ed.) *Organic Creativity in the Classroom: Teaching to Intuition in Academics and the Arts*. Waco, TX: Prufrock Press, 253–266.

Spicer, A., Alvesson, M. and Karreman, D. (2009) Critical performativity: The unfinished business of critical management studies, *Human Relations* 62(4): 537–560.

Springborg, C. and Sutherland, I. (2016) Teaching MBAs aesthetic agency through dance, *Organizational Aesthetics* 5(1): 94–113.

Strati, A. (1999) *Organization and Aesthetics*. London: Sage.

Taylor, S. and Hansen, H. (2005) Finding form: Looking at the field of organizational aesthetics, *Journal of Management Studies* 42(6): 1211–1231.

Taylor, S. and Ladkin, D. (2009) Understanding arts-based methods in managerial development, *Academy of Management Learning & Education* 8(1): 55–69.

Turner, V. (1982) *From Ritual to Theatre: The Human Seriousness of Play*. New York: Performing Arts Journal Publications.

Urry, J. (2007) *Mobilities*. Cambridge: Polity Press.

Weick, K. E. (1967) *The Social Psychology of Organizing*, 2nd ed. Reading, MA: Addison Wesley.

Welsch, W. (1997) *Undoing Aesthetics*. London: Sage.

2   Dance as a Metaphor

Art Metaphors

This book on "Dance and Organisation" does not only add a missing piece to a canon of works that have applied arts analogies to the business world, referring to 'organisations as theatre', 'organisations as jazz' and 'leadership as an art'. The integration of theory and practice of dance does much more: It makes accessible transitory and embodied elements in organisational life that cannot easily be described or analysed. Dance is more than another trendy metaphor for organisations when it considers all kinds of kinaesthetic practices, referring to what goes on in-between moving bodies, spaces and people, in situations that cannot be fully controlled, are fleeting and in motion. Centring around the body and constant change, dance studies is a discipline with considerable potential in today's dynamic times.

In this chapter, I will elaborate on the emergence of the rather young dance analogy in the context of the longer practice to employ arts metaphors in organisation studies. This approach is used as a way to describe the development of the dance perspective from a mere analogy towards an interdisciplinary approach that can be used to theorise social and organisational movement practices, that are further discussed as kinaesthetic politics (Chapter 3), kinaesthetic empathy (Chapter 4) and social choreographies (Chapter 5). The discussion of the metaphor also is the gate to contemporary forms of kinaesthetic training (Chapter 6), when dance is practically applied as movement exercises for leadership and organisational development and as an arts-based research method (Chapter 7).

The emerging interest in dance and organisation can be linked to the exploration of art metaphors that have been used as a heuristic tool in management research over the past decades. In contrast to a view on metaphors as nonessential literary figures of speech or derivative concepts of minor importance, the role of metaphor in organisational theorising has been valued (Cornelissen et al., 2005; Morgan, 1980). In organisation theory metaphors of animate being, systems, as well as evolutionary, warfare, machine and culture metaphors prevail. Some metaphors have attracted scholarly attention for decades, for example the 'organisations as theatre' metaphor. The application of judgmental rules or heuristics in relation to metaphor has been suggested, so that researchers could be able to select metaphors that help to explore new ground beneath beaten paths that are interesting and plausible, yet not innovative. I shall use research on metaphor in organisation as a reference point to think through some of these rules to assess the value of the dance metaphor and to make the argument that innovative insights can be gained when digging deeper into dance theory and embodied, kinaesthetic practice.

Organisations can be understood in different terms and in innovative ways when applying metaphors that juxtapose concepts. When these concepts previously were not cognitively interrelated, new views can emerge. The application of the metaphor of the machine for the organisation for example suggests that employees function like 'gear wheels' in a large, hierarchical system in which the output can be optimised by using some sort of 'leverage' and by raising the 'pressure'. Employees are likened to mechanical parts with specific functions and skills, being replaceable and to be exchanged when 'broken'. In this view, rationality is the basis for making decisions, and emotions, relationships and subjectivity of individuals seem to be of no relevance.

Metaphors from the world of arts on the other hand put much more emphasis on contemporary models of work that value individuality, creativity and dynamic processes, exploring the idea that management is not a science, but 'an art'. Managers have been linked to all kinds of artists, from sculptors to painters and actors (Taylor and Hansen, 2005: 1219), which highlights their creative and human-centred approach that goes beyond standardised rational routines of managing. Many arts analogies have been applied to organisations, referring for example, to 'organisations as theatre' (e.g. Mangham and Overington, 1987) where employees play their 'roles' on a 'stage' in front of 'audiences'. Organisations have been compared to jazz bands (e.g. Weick, 1998) that improvise, communicate non-verbally, and 'swing' or 'flow'. These metaphors underline aesthetic issues and also go beyond the hierarchical structure, accounting for employees values and beliefs that are informed by emotions and personal relationships that pertain to the informal side of organisations. The dance metaphor further emphasises these aesthetic aspects by bringing into focus the kinaesthetic dimension of bodily movement, empathy and the existence of invisible, transitory and embodied structures, as well as many elements that are related to it.

Looking back on organisational research, it becomes obvious that certain periods have called for specific metaphors. For example, the metaphor of the organisation as a 'machine' is representative of the times of Scientific Management. The 'systems' root metaphor that includes concepts such as 'environment', 'contingencies', 'barriers', 'inertia' and 'responses', emerged in organisational scholarship and practical management language at around 1955 when 'systems' thinking as a whole was salient (Barley and Kunda, 1992). Writings on organisational 'culture' with ideas of 'sub-cultures' and 'climates' only emerged in the organisational canon in the 1980s when concepts of work have changed to include ideas of self-actualization and subjectivity in work. This principle influencing the application of metaphors, the availability heuristic (Cornelissen et al., 2005: 1566), refers to straightforward and easy ways to access ideas and then combine them with 'organisation'.

We have witnessed a steady trend over the past decades to compare contemporary work models to 'art' and leaders and managers to 'artists' (e.g. Taylor, 2012). So it seems like a natural development that the theatre metaphor emerged, valuing performative, theatrical and emotional aspects over rational and scientific underpinnings of organisational life. Scholars still have struggled with theatre theory that often is simply not available. Meisiek (2004) for example has explained what "catharsis" actually means and what the different interpretations of the term encompass, and knowledge about established categorisations of theatre including epic and postdramatic theatre and different approaches to 'acting' also needed to be established (Biehl-Missal, 2010; Höpfl, 2002). We have seen this with other art metaphors as well, when for example techniques of improvisation as a structured approach and genres of jazz needed to be explained and discussed with reference to organisation (Weick, 1998). With other art metaphors being around, the emergence of dance seems a logical continuation of this trend in management and organisational research in an increasingly dynamic and changing organisational word in the 21st century. Dance has a particular potential despite and because of digitization and virtual work, as new capabilities are required that reside in the body, relating to new forms of empathy, interpersonal cooperation, embodied knowing and the management of uncertainty and dynamic and fugitive spaces in-between that are the topics of dance studies.

Emergence of the Dance Metaphor

Dance as metaphor for organisations is a more recent perspective appearing in the late 1990s and gaining momentum only after the year 2000 (e.g. Atkinson, 2008; Chandler, 2012). Looking back on organisation studies' history, dance and movement however has a longer pedigree that is rooted in studies on the physicality of work and the body in organisation. The complex and far-reaching role of movement in organisations is for example reflected in the works of Frank and Lilian Gilbreth (1917), who developed ideas of Frederick Winslow Taylor on time-and-motion studies that were concerned with employee productivity standards: Employees' repetitive tasks were broken into small steps and the time and sequence of movements when performing the task was observed to identify and then eliminate wasteful motion.

While not going into further detail on time and motion studies, it can be noted that the important aspect to consider for the metaphor of dance and organisation resides in the more literal structural similarities between the two concepts. Exploring such literal similarities that would have been over-looked otherwise is one way to approach metaphor in organisation studies, when it evokes images and invites new thinking about parallels (Tsoukas, 1991). Early publications on the dance metaphor (Atkinson, 2008: 1081) have built on the basic premise, that "management is frequently concerned with the 'means' of movement of an organisation and its people from one place-in-time to an 'other' place in-time in the achievement of some 'end' of economic and/or social value". Following this view, studying organisa-tional movement in contemporary 'ad hoc' organisations would mean to include dance theory as organisation studies currently lacks the vocabulary to sufficiently capture lived, complex and dynamic movement interactions (Huopalainen, 2015: 827).

Choreography is about organising moving bodies in space and time, and these processes are indeed central to organisational management. Going beyond the management of a factory and personnel planning, in services industries, for example restaurants, many routines in fact are choreographed and rehearsed. Fashion shows as well very literally depend on how fabrics and styles are presented on moving bodies. These bodies in the creative industry move in ways that are not as free and spontaneous as one could expect, but strictly scripted and controlled, in a manner not that far away from the organisation of factory workers' bodily movements (Huopalainen, 2015: 843).

These examples have already suggested that using dance as a lens on organ-isation quickly extends far beyond literal studies of movement in spaces, into a consideration of social structures. The view taken in this book follows a flexible approach to metaphors, further exploring how "through assertions that subject A is, or is like B, the processes of comparison, substitution and interaction between the images of A and B [are] acting as generators of new meaning" (Morgan, 1980: 610). Going beyond comparing or likening the target to the source, new meaning is generated through interactive processes of 'seeing-as' or 'conceiving-as', effectively moving beyond an antecedently existing similarity between the concepts conjoined within it (Cornelissen et al., 2005: 1551). The dance metaphor hence goes beyond a composition of meanings that can be found in either the target or source concepts, but includes reference to particular practices and influences that lead to a more specific and stable understanding of previously hidden aspects of 'dance' in organisations, revolving around kinaesthetic politics, kinaesthetic empathy and choreographies in organisation.

Dance as a Metaphor for Leadership

The basis for an interdisciplinary theorising was created when a consider-ation of dance and organisations slowly went beyond the mere metaphor. Dance has become a point of reference in leadership studies in the 1990s, then primarily used as a superficial metaphor. The metaphor of dance made it possible to speak about, for example, leadership in a more dynamic and interactive language, for example when referring to 'steps' that are taken and other forms of 'movement' that lead 'forward' or into new areas. The notion of dance was only used in the title of a book or a paper and deeper meanings of the metaphor were not explored, for example when authors referred to a "Dance of Change", or "The Manager's Dance". Several works loosely refer to businesses being like a dance and Senge and colleagues (1999) for example have linked the notion of dance to corporate change that requires the ability to learn to new "steps" and to "adapt attitudes" and practices. Another example is the EGOS European Group for Organizational Studies 2008 conference theme "Beyond Waltz—Dances of Individuals and Organizations", which used dance as a metaphor to reflect on a broad range of processes in organisations. However, such metaphorical use of dance only draws on the very surface elements of dance.

The application of metaphors to organisations depends on the contemporary availability of knowledge on the field (Cornelissen et al., 2005: 1566). The availability of knowledge on dance has not been very high in the organisational field until the past five years or so, when most parallels that have been drawn are restricted to the most popular and obvious forms of dance involving "steps" for example. Authors such as Stumpf and Dutton (1990) in their paper "The dynamics of learning through management simulations: Let's dance", use dance as a metaphor for various parts of a learning process, but the actual method employed for the course described has nothing to do with dance. Another example is the notion of 'choreography' that pertains to the notation of dance and has for several years been used merely superficially in organisation studies (Scott, 2008: 219), until some efforts have been made to dig deeper into dance theory to better understand aspects of learning and interaction (Rowe and Smart, 2008). Further studies later emerged that pointed to the relevance of movement-related structures and patterns in organisational life and in leadership (Kolo, 2016). Others, like Chaleff (2009: 31), extend the metaphor to emphasise movement, relationship, co-ordination and togetherness in the workplace:

> In the dance of leaders and followers, we change partners and roles [. . .] With each new partner we must [. . .] adjust our movements and avoid others' toes. If we are leading, we must lead, and if we are not, we must follow, but always as a strong partner. We constantly [. . .] improve our gracefulness in a wide diversity of styles and tempos.

Such a view already propagates a quite interactive understanding of leading and following that shares similarities to ballroom dancing, and which has been explored in more kinaesthetic detail years later (Matzdorf and Sen, 2016).

Following the superficial label of 'dance', scholars came to use the metaphor more systematically to discover and highlight important elements of leadership or leadership training, which they found were overlooked in extant literature on leadership. For example, Stumpf and Dutton (1990: 7) write: "Learning through participation in a management simulation has important parallels to a dance. The office environment may be thought of as a dance hall, the participants and facilitators in management simulations as the dancers, and the content as the music." The metaphor is used here to highlight certain themes of relevance, namely, the relationship between a manager's behaviour and the performance of organisations, the relationship between individual actions and the efficiency of teamwork, and the importance of learning to lead through practice rather than through studying texts.

Eventually, scholars have tried to define categories of leadership styles in terms of different dance-forms. Ropo and Sauer (2008) for example contrast practices of ballroom dancing and raving to techno music to suggest further exploration of the relationship between leadership and kinaesthetic experiences of togetherness in dancing. The waltz has been used as an analogy of hierarchical and rational conceptions of leadership, whereas the rave has been used as a model for non-scripted, improvised and continually negotiated forms of interaction between leaders and followers. Scholars using the dance metaphor have soon recognised that future research ought to consider the experience, more specifically, the kinaesthetic experience and embodied dimension that is in the focus of this book.

The language that includes dance in a management context makes explicit underlying ideas of leadership as being related to concepts of movement in a broader sense. In linguistics, the conceptual metaphor (Lakoff and Johnson, 1980) refers to the understanding of one conceptual domain in terms of another. Organisation in this context is understood in terms of the moving body ("dance"). Despite the lack of theoretical exploration of dance in this context, it can be assumed that conceptual metaphors not only shape our verbal existence and communication, but also structure the way we think and act. In this sense, a change in management thinking can be noticed when movement metaphors appeared in the title of books. The occurrence of dance in book titles in the wider management discourse can be interpreted as the expression of a trend in management and leadership practice to acknowledge personal, non-verbal interaction and embodied forms of knowing. These are taken on in scholarly research on leadership that emphasises the embodied, relational and 'aesthetic' dimension (Chapter 4). These concepts also highlight dynamics and change that are immanent in dance as a transitory art form. These motifs, which will be discussed throughout the book, can be seen as emergent in management and leadership theorising when 'dance' appeared as a metaphor.

Turn to Dance Practice and Theory

Following the superficial application of the notion of 'dance', scholars from the year 2000 onwards used the metaphor more systematically to make sense of dynamic forms of human interaction in organisations, emphasising processes of bodily movement, rhythm, themes and variations that also can be found in dance as an artistic representation and social practice. In this vein, Atkinson (2008) explores the concept of an organisational dance by considering human relationships as functions of movement in the time and space of organisations. The manager's task is to synchronise such movement with the rhythm of the organisation, making use of "aesthetic sensibility" (Atkinson, 2008: 1091), to enable organisational members to create new affective perceptions of a reality that is constructed through interaction. Speaking of affects, presence and "dasein", Atkinson (2008: 1083) relates to phenomenology that has become of major importance to scholars working on dance and organisation, taking forward ideas of social construction through movement as 'choreographies' for example (Chapter 5) and a manager's activity as 'kinaesthetic empathy' (Chapter 4).

In a similar vein, scholars filled with more meaning central elements that the dance metaphor initially had pointed to. With regard to leadership for example, dancers and choreographers were interviewed to gain a deeper understanding of the source domain of the dance metaphor and consequently increase their ability to use the metaphor more fully. An example is Denhardt and Denhardt (2006), who questioned dancers (and musicians and other artists) to address six themes of importance for leadership, which are: the interplay of space, time and energy; rhythms of human interaction; communicating in images, symbols and metaphors; improvising with creativity and spontaneity; leading from within; and learning the art of leadership. This turn from dance metaphor towards practice has been taken further by scholars who argue that dance practice, i.e. having managers engage in dance exercises, can be used as 'kinaesthetic training' to teach leadership (Chapter 6).

The application of dance as a metaphor expresses some conceptual ideas of body-based experience and 'movement' in organisations and in leadership as well, where it builds on dance's natural relations to practices of leading and following. While dance in this sense can be considered a useful metaphorical source domain for understanding leadership and followership, the application of the foreign world of dance has been considered a barrier to reflection. Springborg and Sutherland (2016: 99) find the dance metaphor problematic, because metaphors often use a more familiar domain to create understanding of a less familiar domain:

> For most managers (and scholars studying management education) it is reasonable to assume that leadership is a more familiar domain than dance. The use of dance as metaphor may at first glance seem to be inspirational, but it runs the risk of misusing dance as a screen onto which one may project pre-conceived ideas about leadership. Without having substantial, physical experience with actual dance, our ideas about various dance forms are not a good source domain for metaphors of leadership.

This comment points to the low availability of knowledge on the field (Cornelissen et al., 2005: 1566), emphasising the need for theory and some embodied knowing of actual dance practice. While deeper insights into the matter is important, the dance metaphor cannot be simply rejected for mere unfamiliarity. Many other artistic practices in jazz and musical domains, and painting and sculpture, are practices of complex artistic and aesthetic structures and dynamics that in their depth cannot be easily assessed by amateurs. It can be found that those who introduced art metaphors into organisational studies have a special knowledge through connoisseurship, academic studies or personal practice on, for example, the theatre (e.g. Höpfl, 2002; Mangham, 1990), or dance (e.g. Springborg and Sutherland, 2016).

It can be assumed that art metaphors for the broad diversity of organisational scholars and practitioners are areas of the less known, as not all people look back on an arts education or a life of opportunities that enabled them to gather theoretical or practical knowledge of, for example, playing musical instruments, visiting the theatre or practicing professional dance. Still many of these forms are part of social life and practices that involve the body, be it in leisure dancing or joint action in sports and social events. Such an aspect of concreteness also influences the value of metaphor: Concrete source concepts are valuable for organisational researchers in that they are more easily mapped, used and understood (Cornelissen et al., 2005: 1567). Dance is very close to human nature, as a 'universal language' being one of the oldest media of human interaction, involving only the body and its non-verbal expression. Everybody has danced in their lives and is moving their body on a constant basis. Dance's naturalness stands in a tension to codified forms of dance in cultural and social contexts such as ballroom dancing and artistry that carry their own methods, theories and vocabulary. This broadness and also complexity of human movement makes it hard to find a starting point for metaphorical comprehension. Rather than going into the details of codified forms of traditional dances that could be applied as a metaphor to organisation, it seems promising to explore human movement and its kinaesthetic experience.

When dance is seen as human movement and kinaesthetic experience, it may be assessed as coming from a domain too close to organisations, not providing enough distance to function as a valuable metaphor (Cornelissen, 2004: 1566). 'Theatre' for example was seen as not distant enough to the domain of 'organisation', as it is, for example, composed of a collective of humans who interact and perform, putting on a show or creating some sort of spectacle—issues than can easily be associated with organisations. On the other hand, metaphors too distanced also do not find their way into scholarly books, for example 'organisation as chocolate bar' or 'organisation as soap bubble', or have only been trendy for a little while (e.g. 'organisational decision-making as garbage can'). A total lack of correspondence of the domains would result in a metaphor of low value, for example, an 'organisation as a ballet shoe'.

Dance as movement includes ubiquitous human movement in a social context that is an essential part of everyday organisational life with not much distance to organisations. As a term from the area of culture and performing arts, dance however has some productive distance to organisations. Research on dance and organisation does not take a medical approach in looking at everyday movement from a therapeutic, fitness and health perspective, while acknowledging and valuing these issues and their value to organisations. The research presented here recurs on the world of dance to understand kinaesthetic politics, kinaesthetic empathy and social interaction via forms of movement. These aspects so far have not seen much resonance in organisation studies. Bringing in dance theory and drawing on scholarship of different forms of dance such as ballet, the rave or the waltz, the metaphor is able to create some strong and meaningful imagery by relating concepts from more diverse or distant semantic domains, whereby the correspondence between the target and the source concepts with human beings that are moving around can be conceived as quite exact. Interdisciplinary dance scholarship has taken a similar approach when, for example, exploring the gendered movements of bodies on ballet and show stages and using it to increase our understanding of codified movement in social life (Chapter 3).

By filling our understanding of 'dance' with concepts and theories that are apart from everyday movement, the research approach creates some distance between both domains. This allows for projecting and mapping of interconnected relations between previously unrelated concepts that make the metaphor valuable. This approach leads to new frames for researching the world of organisations that would otherwise remain obscure. Coming back to the idea that theories and frames from both worlds are blended, the approach creates new theory on human interaction in organisational life. Rather than staying in the comfort zone by focusing on similarities to make the familiar more familiar, the approach taken here also looks at the new windows that appear when comparing these different worlds. The particular value in the dance approach resides in a development of this correspondence that is developed on the kinaesthetic level, leading to the topics of kinaesthetic empathy, kinaesthetic politics, kinaesthetic training and dance as a research method. Exploring these issues, dance can unfold its potential as a critical discipline in today's organisational word that is about constant dynamics and change.

The Kinaesthetic Dimension

The metaphor of dance and organisation has been extended beyond catchy book titles and comparisons to consider movement interaction between people in space and time. The emphasis on movement, more specifically with the act of setting in motion—kīn(eîn) and the sensual perception of it (aesthesia)—as a kinaesthetic perspective, develops studies on to the sensual, aesthetic experience of organisations. A shortcoming of the linguistic perspective to metaphors, which emphasises the cognitive dimension, is that it does not value the aesthetic dimension of metaphors, although aesthetic, embodied forms of knowing influence how people interact in organisations and also how they interpret and make sense of these metaphors in their minds and bodies. Ways in which people interpret and comprehend metaphors cannot be fully determined by one singly theory, rather depend on the individual's prior knowledge, background and cognitive abilities. They also are not restricted to cognitive processes that are disjoint from corporeal experience of being in the world. Metaphors typically carry with them understandings of our corporeal being and corresponding bodily states (Lakoff and Johnson, 1980). As indicated earlier, 'change' is related to bodily motion and other examples are understandings of directions ('up' and 'down'), touch and effort ('hard') that reflect corporeal experiences and sensual perceptions and have found their way into our language. Art metaphors emphasise the aesthetic experience in organisations that becomes obvious when considering theatrical forms of exchange (theatre), improvisation and non-verbal exchanges (jazz), or forms of 'leadership as an art' that include aesthetic awareness. These metaphors also are understood in ways that draw on embodied forms of knowing when, for example, an individual thinking about the analogy of the organisation 'as jazz band' has experienced musical practice and how it 'feels' to play and improvise.

The conceptual metaphor has implications for the application of the dance metaphor, with dance being about a body moving in time and space. People use their bodily experience to understand not only physical but also abstract concepts, for example when speaking about understanding an idea in terms of 'grasping' an object (sensorimotor experience), drawing on the physical logic of 'grasping' to frame the act of understanding (Lakoff and Johnson, 1999: 45). Neuroscience, which has shown an interest in dance studies as well, support the claim that the popularity of such conceptual metaphors in our everyday language is a sign that we do not only use cognitive facilities but refer to knowing in our entire body, drawing on bodily, sensory experiences to make sense of and act within our environment (Barsalou, 2010). When abstract concepts generally are understood through embodied experience, concepts in organisation studies such as leadership also appear to be informed by an embodied experience, for example of 'leading' and 'following'. Related issues such as 'support' in terms of 'assistance' for example are often framed with regard to the sensorimotor domain as physical support, drawing on the experience of entities and people requiring physical support in order to continue functioning (Lakoff and Johnson, 1999: 52). 'Change' also is linked to bodily motion that brings the moving body and issues such as kinaesthetic politics, kinaesthetic empathy and kinaesthetic training into change processes in organisations. When dance is used not only as a metaphor but as an actual kinaesthetic practice in organisation, for example as movement exercises for leaders, it links to and develops embodied forms of understanding that inform how people interact. This point is for example also made by Springborg and Sutherland (2016: 104) who posit that dance-exercises in organisations can provide new bodily experiences that can support new forms of knowing and doing in the context of managerial work, putting the body into active focus to further the ability of bodily perception. The dance metaphor with its kinaesthetic dimension paves the ground for such practice and theorising.

To think in such concrete ways about dance and organisations, the kinaesthetic dimension of dance needs to be discussed in more detail. The kinaesthetic practice links to everyday movement as an essential practice of existence. Such a perceived closeness between two domains, or insufficient distance, has been assessed as to lead merely to a "re-labeling of the targeted subject with concepts and terms from the source domain [. . .] without offering any new and truly profound insights" (Cornelissen et al., 2005: 1571). In this view the widespread 'organisational identity' metaphor for example more powerfully combines two distant domains that are referred to, i.e. the social world of organisations versus the psychological world of personality and identity formation (Cornelissen et al., 2005: 1567).

The 'organisation as theatre' metaphor from the world of arts however is said to fail to combine the so-called exactness heuristic with the distance heuristic, providing for an 'apt' yet cognitively limited metaphor (Cornelissen et al., 2005: 1570). The metaphor is being considered exact in terms of relations between domains, as the 'social world of organisations' and the source domain of 'performative arts' are both characterised by performativity (Cornelissen, 2004: 710) including human role playing. Elements from the world of theatre such as scripts, characters and scenes, have been transferred and blended with elements of 'organisation', which helped new meaning to emerge in theory that mechanistic metaphors had excluded. The early use of theatre as a metaphor has provided a previously not applied vocabulary of actors, scenes, scripts and so on for exploring organisational life. Many studies in the field have talked about theatrical processes (e.g. Mangham and Overington, 1987; Pine and Gilmore, 1999), also drawing on Goffman (1959) to explore the performative practices of organisational members. Organisations and organisational members are understood as 'performing' to an internal and external 'audience' of customers, colleagues and managers, interacting in a carefully designed space like on a 'stage', and following organisational routines and values like a 'script'.

A shortcoming of these approaches is that they do not analyse in detail the situation of the 'performance' and its aesthetic experience (Biehl-Missal, 2011: 620). This has been seen as an important omission because the concept of performance has been highlighted as the important link between theatre and organisations, with sensory activities being an essential part of what constitutes theatre (Mangham and Overington, 1987: 153). To develop these aspects, analyses drawing on performance studies (Biehl, 2007; Biehl-Missal, 2011) did not use traditional theatre terminology of actors, roles and drama merely to re-label organisational processes, but directly analysed managerial real-life performances 'as performance'. Managers in organisational presentations and most obviously at large-scale events do not 'play' or 'act', but 'perform', they are performers, making use of genuine theatre techniques such as bright lighting and carefully designed settings, and creating an aesthetic experience. In these situations, it is the performance that creates meaning, not a speech manuscript, but the way in which managers act in, and interact with, a specific surrounding. In particular, performance research and theory on postdramatic theatre serves as a theoretical basis for these endeavours. Rather than focusing on dramatic theatre plots and stories, this approach emphasises the performers' and audience's co-presence and the aesthetic situation of performance. Considering dance and organisation with an emphasis not only on the metaphor but on the kinaesthetic dimension, requires an interdisciplinary approach that is pursued in this book, drawing on dance studies and performance studies and integrating concepts, tools and research methods into organisation studies.

Beyond metaphor, book title or catchy conference slogan, interdisciplinary work on dance and organisations has seen its first conference tracks in 2014 and 2016 at the AoMO Art of Management and Organization Conference, followed by a first special issue on "Dance, Organisation, and Leadership", which appeared in the journal "Organizational Aesthetics" (Biehl-Missal and Springborg, 2016). Views in this issue are diverse but concur with the idea that the value of dance for organisation studies resides in the emphasis on the aesthetic interaction and the application of actual dance exercises for organisational development and research purposes. Going beyond the metaphor and the re-labeling of organisational processes as if they were 'dance', it uses the notion of dance to refer to human movement in an organisational context, focusing on dance as an arts-based method in training and research, and including references to theory on dance as a culturally shaped, bodily practice. Leadership for example is not only 'like ballroom dancing', 'leading' other people through space and time while paying attention to the context, but leadership is analysed in terms of body-based dimensions and includes kinaesthetic empathy and continuous co-operation and negotiation between the leader and the follower in ballroom dancing (Matzdorf and Sen, 2016).

The aesthetic perspective counters limitations of the dance metaphor that were voiced in organisational research. As an objection to the dance metaphor, Chandler (2012: 874) found that "the emphasis on physicality is limiting in a world where much work is done sitting in front of a computer screen—requiring little physical movement beyond the keystroke." The dance analogy is in his view still considered to be of some use when exploring work that involves movement and often repetitive movement, and jobs that are not purely sedentary but include movements away from the screen and transitions from computer-mediated to more direct human interaction that might itself be part of the 'dance' of this kind of work (Chandler, 2012:

874). While dance in such a view is taken at face value—bringing us back to the discussion at the beginning of this chapter—an aesthetic approach goes beyond this framework, considering many issues of relevance in modern times of global mobility that not always is virtual, but still embodied. Positing that we remain in our bodies when working and interacting, a kinaesthetic perspective goes beyond the movements of fingers on a keyboard and considers many aspects that pertain to kinaesthetic politics as individual embodiment, kinaesthetic empathy as interpersonal perception, embodied knowing and an abstract understanding of interpersonal co-ordination. On a broader level, a dance perspective valuing dynamics and change contributes to new approaches to manage the uncertain in an increasingly virtual and dynamic nature of organisational life today.

A kinaesthetic perspective also refutes another objection to the dance analogy that is said to be of limited use because dance is largely 'wordless': "Even though movements might have meaning, the dance analogy draws attention away from the actor's written or spoken words and thus risks downplaying the significance of the word" (Chandler, 2012: 875). Dance studies is the discipline that is explicitly concerned with the categorisation, reflection and analysis of bodily movement that takes place in specific constellations (solo, in groups or pairs) in specific settings. Positing that movement has meaning and that meaning, thus, is in motion, it is a discipline that created valuable interdisciplinary contributions because it did not focus on the text and the word as many other disciplines, capturing elements that are fleeting, in motion and often are overlooked. By doing so, dance studies as a cultural studies discipline for the past decades gave much evidence of the relevance of movement. Dance studies have for example explored codified movements on stages that reflect and potentially rework social human movement practices and developed theory on these phenomena, broadening their scope to consider movement in social life, including movement as a form of identity construction (kinaesthetic politics), a mode of perception (kinaesthetic empathy), and as social coordination (choreography). Dance often is referred to as a "universal language", which also becomes obvious in later sections of the book on movement exercises in organisations (kinaesthetic training) and dance as an arts-based research method that bypasses text and word to access embodied forms of knowing. Specific concepts and methods from dance studies for these reasons have been integrated into other research fields, including sociology, and seem to be promising for organisational research as well.

Focusing on movement as a kinaesthetic social practice on the micro-level is the key to contextualise and politicise 'dance' on a macro-level and to answer questions that originate from a metaphorical application of dance to organisations:

> What kind of dance—what steps are involved, what relationships and rhythms? How has it changed over time? How is performance gendered

and what are the gender relations? What physical effects does it have on performers? [. . .] How do movements relate to the space in which they take place and its physical characteristics and artefacts? Is there a choreographer and if so who are they and what relation do they have with the performer? Such analysis leads one to question the extent to which the worker has autonomy in determining the steps taken. We might also ask: What emotions does the dance evoke in performer and in any audience(s)?

(Chandler, 2012: 873)

All these issues addressed here extend beyond the mere metaphor and address kinaesthetic perception and embodied forms of knowing, which are at the focus of dance studies. Dance studies has produced, for example, a large amount of work on human movement in socio-political contexts that expresses, performs and norms gender identities (Chapter 3). The question of movements that relate to the surrounding space also involves the kinaesthetic perception of people. Research on site-specific dance for example is used in this book to discuss how "choreographies" in spaces develop and bring together individuals. The question of a 'hidden choreographer' has been voiced in many metaphorical approaches that use dance, and can be explored in organisation studies by integrating findings from dance studies that have looked at actual movement in social situations that are in fact influenced by hidden norms and structures (social choreographies) (Chapter 5). The coming sections of this book consequently focus on these kinaesthetic dimensions to develop our understanding of many facets of organisations that so far have not been considered.

Literature

Atkinson, D. (2008) Dancing 'the management': On social presence, rhythm and finding common purpose, *Management Decision* 46(7): 1081–1095.

Barley, S. and Kunda, G. (1992) Design and devotion: Surges of rational and normative ideologies of control in managerial discourse, *Administrative Science Quarterly* 37: 363–400.

Barsalou, L. (2010) Grounded cognition: Past, present, and future, *Topics in Cognitive Science* 2(4): 716–724.

Biehl, B. (2007) *Business is Showbusiness: Wie Topmanager sich vor Publikum inszenieren.* Frankfurt: Campus.

Biehl-Missal, B. (2010) Hero takes a fall: A lesson from theatre for leadership, *Leadership* 6(3): 279–294.

Biehl-Missal, B. (2011) Business is show business: Management presentations as performance, *Journal of Management Studies* 48(3): 619–645.

Biehl-Missal, B. and Springborg, C. (2016) Dance, leadership, and organisation: Editorial to the special issue, *Organizational Aesthetics* 5(1): 1–10.

Chaleff, I. (2009) *The Courageous Follower: Standing Up to and for Our Leaders,* 3rd ed. San Francisco: Berrett-Koehler.

Chandler, J. (2012) Work as dance, *Organization* 19(6): 865–878.

Cornelissen, J. (2004) What are we playing at? Theatre, organization and the use of metaphor, *Organization Studies* 25(5): 705–726.

Cornelissen, J., Kafouros, M. and Lock, A. (2005) Metaphorical images of organization: How organizational researchers develop and select organizational metaphors, *Human Relations* 58(12): 1545–1578.

Denhardt, R. and Denhardt, J. (2006) *The Dance of Leadership: The Art of Leading in Business, Government, and Society.* Armonk: M.E. Sharpe.

Gilbreth, F. and Gilbreth, L. (1917) *Applied Motion Study.* New York: Sturgis and Walton.

Goffman, E. (1959) *The Presentation of Self in Everyday Life.* London: Allen Lane.

Höpfl, H. (2002) Playing the part: Reflections on aspects of mere performance in the customer-client relationship, *Journal of Management Studies* 39(2): 255–267.

Huopalainen, A. (2015) Who moves? Analyzing fashion show organizing through micro-interactions of bodily movement, *Ephemera: Theory and Politics in Organizations* 15(4): 825–846.

Kolo, K. (2016) Ode to choreography, *Organizational Aesthetics* 5(1): 37–46.

Lakoff, G. and Johnson, M. (1980) *Metaphors We Live by.* Chicago: University of Chicago Press.

Lakoff, G. and Johnson, M. (1999) *Philosophy in the Flesh: The Embodied Mind and Its Challenge to Western Thought.* New York: Basic Books.

Mangham, I. L. (1990) Managing as a performing art, *British Journal of Management* 1(2): 105–115.

Mangham, I. L. and Overington, M. A. (1987) *Organizations as Theatre: A Social Psychology of Dramatic Appearances.* Chichester: Wiley.

Matzdorf, F. and Sen, R. (2016) Demanding followers, empowered leaders: Dance as an 'embodied metaphor' for leader-followership, *Organizational Aesthetics* 5(1): 114–130.

Meisiek, S. (2004) Which catharsis do they mean? Aristotle, Moreno, Boal and organization theatre, *Organization Studies* 25(5): 797–816.

Morgan, G. (1980) Paradigms, metaphors and puzzle solving in organizational theory, *Administrative Science Quarterly* 25: 605–622.

Pine, B. J. and Gilmore, J. H. (1999) *The Experience Economy: Work Is Theatre and Every Business a Stage.* Boston: Harvard Business School Press.

Ropo, A. and Sauer, E. (2008) Dances of leadership: Bridging theory and practice through an aesthetic approach, *Journal of Management and Organization* 14(5): 560–572.

Scott, R. (2008) Lords of the dance: Professionals as institutional agents, *Organization Studies* 29(2): 219–238.

Senge, P., Kleiner, A., Roberts, C., Ross, R., Roth, G. and Smith, B. (1999) *The Dance of Change: The Challenges of Sustaining Momentum in Learning Organizations.* New York: Doubleday.

Springborg, C. and Sutherland, I. (2016) Teaching MBAs aesthetic agency through dance, *Organizational Aesthetics* 5(1): 94–113.

Stumpf, S. and Dutton, J. (1990) The dynamics of learning through management simulations: Let's dance, *The Journal of Management Development* 9(2): 7–16.

Taylor, S. (2012) *Leadership Art, Leadership Craft.* New York: Palgrave MacMillan.

Taylor, S. and Hansen, H. (2005) Finding form: Looking at the field of organizational aesthetics, *Journal of Management Studies* 42(6): 1211–1231.

Tsoukas, H. (1991) The missing link: A transformational view of metaphors in organizational science, *Academy of Management Review* 16(3): 566–585.

Weick, K. (1998) Introductory essay: Improvisation as a mindset for organizational analysis, special issue: jazz improvisation and organizing, *Organization Science* 9(5): 543–555.

3   Kinaesthetic Politics (Gender)

The public display of bodily motion is an articulation of culture and of social categories of identity and of gender roles. This is relevant, but under-researched in organisational life. Following the discussion on dance as a metaphor and the argument for a perspective that emphasises the kinaesthetic dimension and actual bodily movement, this chapter is on kinaesthetic politics: Starting from the individual and the construction of identity in a social and organisational context through movement, it provides a basis for the subsequent chapters that have a stronger focus on relationships and group coordination, expressed in the notions of kinaesthetic empathy and choreographies. This chapter looks at bodily movement practice as cultural practice and uses the world of dance as a lens for critical reflection and as a source for new theory to be applied on organisational life and to develop research on gender in management. A view on organisational culture that emphasises bodily movement expands traditional logocentric views that have emphasised the importance of verbal language as a carrier of culture and also have valorised the role of artefacts and objects, but have neglected the significance of non-verbal communicative systems and what can be referred to as physical culture that also is created through bodily motion.

The notion of 'kinaesthetic politics' is used here, broadly speaking, to refer to human movement not as 'natural', but as a social or 'political' practice. Advances have been made by cultural studies that have pushed the boundaries of the discipline to consider culture as a bodily practice that is related to dance as an abstraction of physical culture (Desmond, 1997). Moving bodies in organisations and in leadership situations are managed in manifold and also gendered ways, which relate to and result in different experiences of embodied existence in organisations. Performative cultures are not about 'truth' but still they are not false. When dance and movement is a medium, it has an inherent gender-specificity as it is tied to a gendered body in motion. Through the moving body, gender can be done and undone, challenged and changed—in the world of sports, in fashion, in plays and also in organisations. Human movement is not only a result of physical and biological dispositions, rather is considered a result of social influence, which makes movement a 'political' practice, when it confirms, and particularly when it negotiates and changes culture. Dance has been reflected on in terms of kinaesthetic politics as power and possible effects on social order in critical dance studies over the past decade (Lepecki, 2013). Dance as a critical practice capitalises on the dynamic aspect of movement that not only performs and constructs but, as a form of 'kinaesthetic politics' also changes social order that literally is 'in motion'.

The discussion of movement in culture and in organisations is subsumed under the header of 'kinaesthetic politics'. The notion of the political is multifaceted and has been widely debated with regard to dance (Lepecki, 2013). Dance is sometimes perceived as something inherently dissensual, critical and political because of its distinctive epistemological status, its ephemerality and body-based nature: Dance has been considered as predestined for political mobilisation due to its emphasis on the body and its movement, which can demonstrate what language cannot transmit. Dance is a liminal practice permanently at the edge of escaping from its choreographic script, per se in potential 'dissensus' with the social order. Citing these quite broad assertions, scholars have suggested to more specifically ask when, where and how dance practices are dissensual (Barrionuevo Anzaldi, 2013). I shall pose these questions throughout the book with regard to movement in organisations, after having considered dance in the arts as a critical tool for management theorising and development in this chapter.

Dance has been attributed a political potential because it theorises its social context as it practices itself. Choreography for example has been seen as the modality through which dance reflects and theorises the social order and by doing so theorises and activates this relationship (Lepecki, 2013: 154). Following Rancière (2004) dance scholars have often emphasised the political potential of dance in terms of the dissensus, the intervention in the visible and the sayable. This is an important perspective to be further discussed in this section and throughout the book. From an organisation studies point of view, it is worth taking a step back before considering the innovative facet of this term. Dance at first has a normative relation to the social order, when for example mass dances present and perform nationhood, ideologies and political power. On a smaller scale, dance, for example in classical ballet, has transported and performed normative images of gender and race that have been criticised by cultural scholars.

This notion of politics might be interpreted as an embodied practice in organisations that is concerned with dissent, rupture and transformation of normative kinaesthetic practices. Kinaesthetic politics can be seen as a concept of political activity that challenges and changes orders:

> [The] aesthetic is inscribed in political practice—precisely because these practices with their norms, rules and habits already determine sensual perception by socially positioning people, allocating social and political space for them to maneuver [sic] in and thus framing social perception. Exactly therein also lies the political dimension of the physical-sensual,

of movement perception, in other words, the dimension of "kinaesthetic politics": a concept of political activity as the sensual practice of
making cultural and social codes visible and shifting them.

(Klein, 2011: 24)

The practice of dance and movement can be political as a kinaesthetic practice, when it achieves its aim of making visible movements in a different
light and changing them, and making perceivable movements differently.
So the question is how dance and its kinaesthetic politics can operate as an
anti-order, the exception to the 'rules' and 'order' in organisations. Klein
(2011: 25) sees movement as political when it "grates against the reigning
order, norms, habits and conventions—and not only grates against them,
but also changes them." Introducing a critical difference to contemporary
kinaesthetic practices, and enabling a collective development of movement
artistic interventions in organisations (Chapter 6) as well as arts-based
research methods (Chapter 7) have a political potential that does not reside
in its content, but in its form, its aesthetics. In this vein, the study of dance
as well can be a useful addition to organisation theory and also to management education that I will outline in the following sections. The inclusion of
dance as a core element of cultural and educational policy, that dance scholars postulate, along with the documentation as a knowledge culture (Klein,
2011: 24), is the basis for dance as a politics of the aesthetic.

Gender, Culture and Movement

Kinaesthetic politics as a movement politics affects organisations and their
culture. Organisations do not only have a physical dimension, but, as any
culture, can be seen as a physical style system in which humans embody
what it means to be a member of a particular society, group or gender.
Polhemus (1988: 172) describes the relationship of movement and culture:

Culture is not exclusively nor [. . .] even primarily encoded and transmitted by means of words or artefacts. At least in so far as an individual's
first and most rudimentary experience of his or her society is via bodily
manipulation and physical education in its broadest sense, the deepest
and most fundamental foundations of being a member of a particular
society are inevitably corporal. Muscular tonus, stance, basic movement
styles, gestures and so for the once learned are, like any physical activity, remarkably resistant to change and constitute not only the essential
component of personal identity but of social and cultural identity as
well. Furthermore, movement and other physical styles are in any society imbued with symbolic meaning with the result that how we use and
move our bodies is inevitable the occasion for the transmission of all
sorts and various levels of socio-cultural information including, most
importantly, those meanings which exceed the limits of verbal language.

While Mead and Bateson (1942) have in early ethnographic studies shown that being a member of Balinese society requires a specific way of bodily postures, gestures and movements, societies and organisations today are more complex and diverse. Yet still 'Western society' provides many examples of the relevance of physical style. Polhemus (1988: 174) for example refers to the hippies who in the 1960s differentiated themselves from 'straight society' with their 'up-tight' behaviour by their 'laid-back' and 'easy' style. The way of sitting in a chair, walking down the street and leaning against the wall expressed the personal attitude in this clash of cultures. Similar principles can be accorded to organisational members when belonging to an entrepreneurial culture or a traditional corporation, or to the leadership level or to what often is referred to as support staff, who do not only differentiate themselves through clothing and language, but also through their habitus and bodily movements. To be Balinese, to be a Maasai or a hippie—as well as an entrepreneur, a service professional or a leader—is not only to dress, but also to move as one.

Kinaesthetic politics also includes issues of gender that also is constructed through movement. There are two significant categories of experience that inevitable affect an individual's subjective perception of cultural reality: age and gender. Both aspects are reflected in social human movement. While 'young' movement can typically be remembered from the perspective of people of old age, gender is seen as a "primary and insurmountable existential division which must inevitably define cultural experience and the perception of cultural reality" (Polhemus, 1988: 176). Being not only a member of a society, but woman, a man or another gender in a particular society—and in an organisation—also is reflected in and accomplished through movement, which is an experience that is very specific. Feminist scholars have found that gender is delimited by a set of structures and conditions, and movement patterns are part of those structures and conditions that define the feminine and the masculine in the social world. In her pioneering study "Throwing Like a Girl" Iris Marion Young (1980, 1990) has considered movement with regard to gender. In early observations of young people "throwing like a girl", the following is cited (Strauss, 1966, in Young, 1980: 137).

> The girl of five does not make any use of lateral space. She does not stretch her arm sideward; she does not twist her trunk; she does not move her legs, which remain side by side. All she does in preparation for throwing is to lift her right arm forward to the horizontal and to bend the forearm backward in a pronate position. The ball is released without force, speed, or accurate aim. A boy of the same age, when preparing to throw, stretches his right arm sideward and backward; supinates the forearm; twists, turns and bends his trunk; and moves his right foot backward. From this stance, he can support his throwing almost with the full strength of his total motorium. The ball leaves the hand with considerable acceleration; it moves toward its goal.

While the researcher that is quoted attributes difference to sexes but failed to make connections between socially learned movement and gender, Young has broken new ground at the time when linking both. This has been the basis for further research on the modalities of the bodily existence of women and other aspects of their life and experience. Young (1980: 155) has also suggested that the general lack of confidence that women frequently have about their cognitive or leadership abilities is related to an original doubt in their body's capacity. This chapter draws on dance to develop these issues with regard to gender in management research and opportunities for change through kinaesthetic politics.

Performance stages typically mirror society in a variety of ways and it seems worth looking at what is presented to see differently our reality. I shall take a look at the world of dance and recapitulate some of the classic findings to link these to questions of gender in organisations. An understanding about and a 'feeling' for how gender is presented and negotiated through movement on institutional stages, for example in ballet and other dance performances, can inspire us to critically reconsider movement and gender both in society and in organisations.

Dance studies has critically examined the female body on stages. The exposed relevance and large number of female practitioners may also have led to dance's perception as a 'female art'. While a disproportionate number of men can be found in artistic and administrative as well as leadership positions, prejudices towards male dancers and the role of the spectator's gaze have also been considered. In this context, Burt's (2007: 1) book "The male dancer" considers that re-evaluating images of women is different, because celebrating men's achievements in dance always runs the risk of reasserting male dominance, but may also help "to become aware of the conscious and unconscious ways through which dominant ideas are inscribed in dance, [as] a step towards understanding how to create alternative, non-oppressive representations". Female and male bodies in dance are exposed to what is referred to as 'male gaze', a concept from feminist film theory (Laura Mulvey) that has been used in this context. This approach has seen some resistance in dance scholarship as it adopts a spectator-centred approach, different form a choreographer-centred approach that celebrates masterworks (Burt, 2007: xii). A cultural studies perspective however goes beyond the art-work and helps us to build bridges to the organisational world where the gaze is relevant and issues of embodiment as well.

From a gender in management perspective, the idea that dance embodies and negotiates gender ideologies that influence the social world is interesting to follow. Interaction in organisations is framed by the male and also female gaze: In absence of embodied norms for the women leader occupational identity, women were found to monitor themselves and other women, complying with, rejecting and negotiating embodied norms for themselves and other women (Mavin and Grandy, 2016: 1114), thereby limiting ways of being a leader. Dance studies can contribute to gender in organisation research by looking at some examples in which the body in motion has changed gazes and norms. Many extant studies focus on static appearance rather than on movements of the body. When dance is considered a 'universal language', human bodies perform conceptions of gender and speak through movement. Movements are systems which are in many ways different from other forms of representation such as language or visual representation, as they are fugitive, non-verbal and non-discursive. Movement is a complex element in the construction of gender as it is not static, but transitory and difficult to pin down. Despite many important studies on how organisations develop and commodify employee corporeality through aesthetic labour (Warhurst and Nickson, 2009), they focus largely on appearance, rather than considering in detail movements that are performed. Other studies using the theatre metaphor for service encounters are more concerned with conceptual comparisons and external appearances but typically do not account for the ways the body moves. More recent analyses on the aesthetics of managers, however, look in greater detail at how postures and gestures are performed on stage: In management presentations immobile and stable appearances are common that alternate with dynamic steps and reinforcing gestures (Biehl-Missal, 2011: 637). These observations are a step towards an analysis of gendered movement on stages and in organisations.

Such a discussion is situated in an understanding of doing and un-doing gender in organisations (Hancock and Tyler, 2007), with gender being perceived as an activity of managing conduct aligned with normative conceptions of attitudes and activities appropriate for one's sex category. Doing gender is an on-going process in which people interact and use micro-political activities that are perceived as 'feminine' or 'masculine'. These activities include the ways people look, sound and, of course, the way they move. Gender has been conceptualised as a performative act (Butler, 1993). Because of the centrality of the displayed female body in dance practices, dance studies draws on many feminist theories with a strong focus on gender and has developed theory on how gendered identity is constructed through movement and its kinaesthetic perception (Foster, 2013).

Dance studies is a promising addition to gender in management research because it can address those transitory aspects of movement in gender performance that often have been overlooked. Gender research in management has seen immense progress over the last couple of decades but calls have been voiced that future research needs to reveal hidden practices concealed within customs (Broadbridge and Simpson, 2011). Despite a growing interest of organisation research in embodied forms of existence, not only the female body has long struggled to receive appropriate attention, but also its movement is under-researched. Modern organisation is characterised on a refusal of what historically has been seen to be female—the body. Brewis and Sinclair (2000) have described that, influenced by Enlightenment philosophy which assigned reason more to men and bodies to women, in 'rational' organisations bodies and their 'lower order' instincts and passions play little part. The body has long been ignored in organisational design, processes and theorizing, which has been identified by feminist theorists as problematic for women in particular. This area has received growing attention but still demands critical approaches because the female body and its conduct today is exposed to many tacit biased practices in organisational life that include rejection and disapproval (Gatrell, 2013). This also includes the misogynist perception of looks and demeanour that continue to determine leaderships careers, when, for example, in live performance situations such as job interviews male and female participants observe and evaluate particularly the female body and its posture, gesture and movements (Mavin and Grandy, 2016). Many other situations involve assessments of gendered bodies, images and interactions. This section on kinaesthetic politics considers gender, but for the reasons outlined above, puts a particular focus on the female body.

Learning from the Body on Stage

Theorising dance in organisation studies can help to develop a critical understanding of how movement practices express, influence and negotiate body images that are relevant to organisational interaction. Apart from questions of form and style, dance is a kinaesthetic form of politics as it is governed by structures that point to a specific time-based body image in society. While physical culture can be seen as the embodiment of social identity, dance can be seen as an abstraction of stylisation of physical culture. It has been found that dance styles, instead of being arbitrary, constitute a 'natural' expression of the cultural system within which they are found (Polhemus, 1988: 174). What we see on dance stages can thus be a metaphysics of culture or a mirror of society, but is never an objective reflection. Rather dance stages have been criticised for being political in the sense of suggesting 'appropriate' movement patterns that often are gendered and stereotypical (Daly, 1987). Artistic stages can in this vein be considered a looking glass to better understand social developments that crystallise in movement patterns. Contemporary performances also have the capacity to disturb and counteract, to question structures and social practices, when renouncing "the authority of the imposed message, the target audience, and the univocal mode of explicating the world" (Rancière, 2007: 258).

The body in modern dance in particular most clearly reflects contemporary body concepts and also functions as a medium to express, via insecure gestures, falling and contortions, experiences individuals make in today's times (Lehmann, 2006: 163). Dance education includes not only dance making and participation, but also the appreciation of dance. A consideration of what was presented on dance stages can in this sense increase our understanding of the body as a medium that expresses and picks out as a theme human struggles with contemporary phenomena such as speed, technology and body ideals. Dance as an art form is a worthy object of study to theorise relationships between the public display of bodily motion and the articulation of social categories of identity, their transmission, transformation, perception and enactment (Desmond, 1997: 3). These insights also have concrete implications for our understanding of how movement and dance exercises with organisational members can help to get hold of, perform and potentially reconfigure these embodied structures of gender. This also further links to the use of dance as a research method and the analysis of movement in organisations. While organisational research has increasingly attended to the body in organisations, movement that pertains to the body and embodied experiences, not to the seemingly 'rational mind', is still under-researched. In the following sections, I will take a closer look at dance stages to develop some critical ideas about movement in society that can be related back to organisations. This is also useful as the use of dance metaphors in organisations (e.g. leadership as ballroom dance) carry with them an often invisible conceptualisation of embodied relations and gender relations and gendered practice of cultural reality ('leading' and 'following').

While organisation scholars have not looked much into the world of dance, theatre performances and other art forms have already been used as a critical lens on organisations and leadership. For example, Acevedo (2011) draws on art history to show how portraiture reveals the complex dilemmas incorporated within a leader: Comparing a portrait of Pope Innocent X (1650) by the Spanish painter Velazquez and Bacon's study of the portrait (1953), she encounters a cruel, regal and inquisitive depiction as well as a critical illustration of the isolation conferred by the Pope's authority. This approach adds to the exploration of aesthetic expressions as a means of enquiring into organisational leadership. It evidences the potentialities of considering specific artistic expressions, such as portraiture, as heuristic devices towards understanding some of the processes through which leadership is socially constructed (Acevedo, 2011: 46).

Similar endeavours have used the performative arts as a source of critical inquiry. While the two-dimensional artefact of the visual representation does not have to grapple constantly with the materiality of the body, performances are made of bodily movements that only exist in the moment but may convey a strong experience. With regard to contemporary examples and a case of the theatre maker René Pollesch, whose plays show the dark side of work promoted in contemporary organisations, it was proposed that organisation studies should consider such artistic forms more systematically. These artistic forms go beyond extant critical intellectual approaches to organisations as their presentational form provides an aesthetic experience, and conveys both embodied forms of understanding in fuller, richer and stimulating ways (Biehl-Missal, 2013). Pollesch's plays provide a dark impression of role models, communicating through hysteric, fast voices, generating desperation and hopelessness that also is expressed in bodily movements—as a universal language—that often are confined and bound to a restricted area. This is contrasted with many movements of flow when athletes jump across the stages or a protagonist 'stripped off' his shirt and with a naked upper body was 'carried away' by an athletic choir representing the capitalist network, in dollar bill clothing. The aesthetics of the artistic form can 'bring to life' these understandings of work for spectators as well as for organisational researchers in a richer and non-discursive way.

Ballet

Movement in classical ballet is not only what many people perceive as 'oh so beautiful', it rather is a serious form of kinaesthetic politics, reaching beyond the stages into the social perception of movement, gender roles and social roles. Classical ballet has been written about for a couple of centuries now, and to build a bridge to contemporary organisation studies, in this chapter I focus on cultural studies literature that has emphasised ballet's implications for movement as a social and gendered practice.

Dancing in ballet has by transdisciplinary approaches been identified as a "key performer in the construction and circulation of social hegemonies" (Carter, 1998: 195). While female dancers are being praised for 'lightness' and 'airiness' and their sexual aura, researchers have more critically looked at the surface and beyond it to examine how the female body in particular is constructed and deconstructed in dance performances. The patriarchal underpinnings of ballet and gendered ideology have often been overlooked as they are hidden under the veil of 'beauty' that typically is invoked as defence for ballet: The work's beauty makes the performance "feel right", working persuasively on people's understanding and aligning individuals' subjectivity in all its complexity with existing, gendered social order (Daly, 1987). Focusing on this aspect, rather than sketching the history of ballet, the following sections will discuss a couple of issues in movement practices that are relevant for a critical consideration of movement and culture.

Ballet in Western Europe around in the early 19th century was seen a site of ambiguity (Carter, 1990: 206) with a strong feminisation that not only was positive:

> The ballerina was etherealized while her dance technique demanded more and more strength and concealed virtuosity. The ballet itself provoked poetic and impassioned response, yet was also considered a less respectable, and therefore less respected art. Women were put on a metaphorical pedestal but men would be enticed to the theatre so they could literally look up their skirts.

What happened on stages in the Romantic period was ambiguous and has been interpreted as influenced by "confused emotions in regard to women" (Jowitt, 1998: 210): The image of supernatural women has been transported through new techniques, the pointe and flexible dresses. While the stories were told from the male hero's point of view, the airiness of

movements made almost forget that male dancers enabled female movement in the pas-de-deux, attributing to the ballerina a superior position, as
if unrestricted by his codes, and able to drift about on her toes. These images
however portrayed dancers as femmes fatales with erotic force, luring and
tempting the male hero (as the black swan for example or even the peasant
girl Giselle). Attributing some sort of detrimental and seductive impact to
women and their bodies in an old biblical, worn-out tradition lives on in
many aesthetic forms in the world of consumption and organisations (e.g.
Höpfl, 2007).

In the Romantic period, ballet attributed grace and beauty to the female
dancers and strength and action to male dancers. These exaggerated gender
differences via stylised body image and artificial movement attracted critical
voices. Gender differences are seen as an "unabashed hallmark of classical ballet" at every level: costuming, body image, movement vocabulary,
training, technique, pre-feminist narrative and especially the pas-de-deux
structure where female dancers depended on the physical support of male
dancers (Daly, 1987).

Looking at the level of movement performance, a basic application of
an analytic framework such as Laban Movement Analysis (Chapter 7)
helps to understand how the characteristic structure of effortlessness and
lightness is created and how the identity of the female dancer is created.
The first element in this framework is the body, which assumes an erect
and upright position, rather than constantly changing, being bent and
flexed as in contemporary dance. Individual limbs such as feet and legs
move independently in controlled ways, in figures such as battements
and fuettes. The movement is initiated in the legs, the arms remain in
their position, and are not used to generate momentum like in modern
dance forms. The second element of space is unfolded through extended
horizontal and sagittal movement (front to back), which give the ballerina a dominating presence in contrast to male dancers who make less
use of space. Vertical turns and jumps such as jettés and sautés are going
upwards, not downwards with a body touching the floor, and often
make use of the support of the male dancer and contribute to an effect of
'lightness'. This fits to the third category of effort, that is very reduced.
Foregoing the use of body weight for forceful and overly energetic movements such as stamping—which we see, for example, in step dance and
in the practice of Riverdance mentioned in this book—movements are
continuous and not interrupted, with frequent holdings of a pose or the
arabesque. The highly formalised poses and movements require careful
training. Their 'light' impact is supported by highly stylised outfits such
as white ballet tutu that emphasises the female dancer's fragile frame and
naked shoulders and expose long and slim legs.

Gender differences also are transported on the level of the narration,
in addition to the appearance and perception of movement. For example,
in classics such as "Le Sacre du Printemps" (Rite of Spring), initially performed by the Ballets Russes, the narration centres around a young woman,

the 'chosen one' that eventually is obliged to dance to death in the presence of the old men. The ballet "Giselle", which also has been the topic of many scholarly analyses (Alderson, 1986), presents a peasant girl named Giselle who dies of a broken heart after discovering her lover is with another woman, but, in the end, she still summons from her grave to save him from a group of revenging women.

I have used this example to explain kinaesthetic politics that unfolds an impact through its aesthetic form by transporting an ideal of 'female' attitude and behaviour in society, propagating socially charged imagery as a form of the beautiful. Women dominate the stage, while the institutional context of ballet has many issues that a reader can relate to contemporary organisations: The large number of female dancers historically was considerably lower paid than almost exclusively male ballet librettists and choreographers, they were exposed to the male gaze, subject of objectification and sexual harassment. A recent study on the work conditions of dancers still indicated a male dominance front stage as well as back stage, quoting a female dancer criticising that "one famous choreographer [makes] the male dancers carry the female dancers as (if) they were a bunch of chickens" (Satama, 2016: 76). For professionals this requires a considerable emotional and physical effort: Onstage an ideal form of passionate embodied agency is presented that appears supernatural and reaches for perfection. Offstage

Figure 3.1 Dancers in relaxed body postures backstage

Courtesy Minna Tervamäki (photo) and Suvi Satama.

however, the embodied existence of the dancer transforms into something very human, earthly and vulnerable (Satama, 2016: 77).

At this point it is useful to refer to research on the male body in ballet with regard to kinaesthetic politics. Ramsay Burt (2007) has discussed the binary thinking that underpins much of the reception of gendered bodies in ballet, also analysing performances by Vaslav Nijinsky, a Russian ballet dancer and choreographer of Polish descent, heralded as the greatest male dancer of the early 20th century. Nijinsky's roles in ballets like *Narcisse* and *Schéhérazade* are considered transgressive, breaking with the 19th-century tradition that enforced the dominant point of view as male, maintaining heterosexual male norms through keeping male sexuality invisible. Androgynous qualities were ascribed to Nijinsky's dancing, stressing its male power and strength but simultaneously expressing female sensuousness (Burt, 1998: 253). Dance performances such as Nijinsky's *Narcisse* were open to interpretation as an image of the homosexual third sex with its androgynous grace, innocence and unspoiltness, which, however, in the end was punished as a moral fable and thus made acceptable for straight audiences (Burt, 1998: 254). Nijinsky's performances in ballet choreographies of Michel Fokine included both sensual and dynamic expression, hinting at aspects of male sexuality that have not been acceptable, but were positioned within classical or 'oriental' settings far enough removed from contemporary European ones to be a threat to existing conservative gender ideologies.

More generally, the kinaesthetic politics in denaturalizing and deconstructing the representation of female and male gender in ballet dance bears many parallels to deconstructive strategies in the work of later postmodern choreographers at the end of the 20th century, which will be discussed in the following section. The deconstruction of gender binaries as an aspect of kinaesthetic politics is something that feminist scholars have suggested, for example with the tradition of masculine and feminine writing in organisations studies research (Chapter 7). In a context of the gendered nature of expression in organisation studies research that appears to be masculine, rigorous and 'neutral' to appease fears of not-knowing and insecurity, Phillips et al. (2014) suggest a practice of bisexual writing—a writing that challenges masculine orthodoxy by confusing it rather than attempting to replace it with another (feminine) orthodoxy. This relates to delimited gender representation in dance that serves to propose 'stability'—for those who are privileged—rather than letting in the 'non-controllable'. Using the notion of kinaesthetic politics, this book invites to think about the potential of change through movement and dance as a practice that stands for dynamics and cooperation.

Social life is 'in motion' but despite changes of gender roles (and their demeanour) in real life, the choreographies of classical ballet and their gender differences remain untouched for centuries. The heavily choreographed pieces require performers to follow the script and positions and allow little artistic individuality and creative expression. Traditional forms of ballet can be interpreted as a practice in which dancers perform instructions and individual success is achieved through excelling within a given frame. In an interdisciplinary study, Satama (2016) demonstrates the potential of the world of dance as a site of extreme bodily work, emotions and pain, desire and weakness, showing that this is a productive field to generate new insights into embodied agency that we find in comparable forms in today's organisations. Historically, dancers were used as "puppets to be manipulated" in most choreography approaches, and sometimes are included into a more dynamic approach that involves some personal interpretation (Butterworth, 2004: 50). In modern and contemporary choreographies dancers are accorded increasing responsibility and opportunities for improvisation and co-creation. This principle applies to kinaesthetic interaction in organisational life and leadership situations as well (Chapter 4).

Movement in organisations provides opportunities for change but also is constrained. Studies on dance as work have found principles of limited kinaesthetic influence in the work of today's aerobic trainers: Rather than having fun and creating free-style group experiences, a growing trend of standardisation requires them to learn and execute pre-choreographed performances that not only involve steps, jumps and movements, but also shouts and short commandos as well as gestures (Felstead et al., 2007). In this regard, a consideration of classical ballet can help to better understand trends of standardisation, also in other work processes in the service industry in which body movements are increasingly pre-choreographed. Service professionals also are required to reproduce pre-choreographed poses and utterances, but self-directed opportunities reside in their use of kinaesthetic empathy to develop their own social choreographies that are constantly negotiated (Chapter 5).

With regard to pre-choreographed movement it is worth discussing that kinaesthetic politics may reach directly into social life through ballet training. While ballet imagery of the 'ideal' female body, appearing light, effortless and slim may only be a small influence in a society that generally places enormous pressures on everyone to look and act in culturally acceptable ways, being exposed to strategies of disciplining the body has a very direct effect. As Young (1980) has discussed in "Throwing like a girl", gender is produced through practice, when people are doing gender. Gendered bodies are constructed through bodily practice, not solely through watching. Becoming a male soldier for example also is achieved through highly intensive bodily work, when higher ranked officers' movements need to be followed, imitated and embodied through mimesis (mimicked) until being accepted and no more rejected for their brutality perceived earlier (Rieger-Ladich, 2009). Student dancers' bodies in ballet, following Foucault's theory on discipline, can be seen as "docile bodies created to produce efficiency, not only of movement, but also a normalization and standardization of behavior in dance classes" (Green, 2003: 110). Ballet schools that make dancers undergo physical training are a recognised high risk environment for negative body image and eating disorders in adolescents (Abraham, 1996). In aesthetic sports activities, pressure is on both girls and boys who are teased by same-sex peers, with girls also being teased by opposite-sex peers (Slater and Tiggeman, 2011). This has often been related to pressures of being thin and 'light' when practicing this sport, and has directed attention to specific body parts such as bow legs or elevated shoulders also due to the constant view into the mirror as part of the studio practice (Oliver, 2008). On a long-term perspective, the memory shared by many young girls—particularly from before or until roughly the 1980s in basic ballet classes—of being disciplined and being directed to stand at the back behind the skinny dancers in an overstretched mini tutu, might even leave a longer lasting impact.

Ballet as a gendered kinaesthetic practice can be seen as one of many historically and culturally interrelated phenomena that contribute to the doing of gender in today's organisations that oppress and marginalise the female body (Hancock and Tyler, 2007; Höpfl, 2007). The mere metaphor of organisations as a 'ballet' would consequentially attribute to women the role of an employee, lightly and swiftly whirling around, beautiful to look at and communicating emotions mostly non-verbally like in ballet, as practiced historically in jobs such as the 'secretary' or Japanese 'office flower' (Ogasawara, 1998). These positions have seen changes during the decades with changing jobs descriptions mentioning the 'office manager (male/female)' and a broadened responsibility for diverse tasks following strict division of labour. Today such a metaphor would be rejected by most Western employees because of its large perceived distance between source domains ("I am doing 'serious' work and I am nothing like a ballerina").

In an organisational context this historical pedigree and contemporary popular art practice of ballet may also contribute to barriers towards dance and movement workshops in organisations, when women and men do not wish to participate because they feel that their moving bodies don't correspond to "dance" bodies. Wrongly so, as dance practice is a broad field and movement consultants in organisations do not emphasise body images and pre-choreographed steps, rather encourage self-choreographed movement and group cooperation and shared leadership. In comparison to ballet, creative and self-improvised techniques with a less structured approach and the absence of predetermined performance standards have a positive influence on participants. Research on adult dance classes shows that creative, folk, aerobic and ballroom produce a positive change in self-esteem and self-concept that also is related to working with a partner or collaboratively with a group rather than focusing on the individual reflected in the mirror. This links to the use of dance-based methods (Chapter 6) and the use of dance as a research method (Chapter 7).

Modern and Contemporary Dance

Modern dance from around 1900 and postmodern dance from 1960 to the 1970s, forms such as concept dance, new dance and others, as well as contemporary dance have broadened the spectrum of bodily movement in dance, advocating novel methods of creation and integrating personal and social influences. Modern dance has been considered as a kinaesthetic and ideologically grounded critique of and resistance to artistic and social conceptions that are expressed through movement, and has also deconstructed ideals embodied in ballet, such as concepts of 'beauty' and 'femininity'. In contemporary dance, collaborative pieces from the 1990s explored political issues of sexism, feminism, elitism and ideology, in collage structures and non-linear narratives, challenging highly technical dance training, and initiating the link between dance-making and research by including thoughts and reflections of the dancers (Butterworth, 2004: 51).

Emphasising the cultural embeddedness of dance, the consideration of modern dance shows that the development of new ways of physical expression and movement occurred outside traditional structures such as concert halls, as it was initiated by women artists working independently: Dempster (2010: 229) sees early modern dance as a "repudiation of the tenets of nineteenth-century ballet" as an "avowedly female-centred movement, both with respect to the manner in which the body was developed and represented and in the imagery and subject matter employed". While this genre of dance also has been debated in scholarly works for decades in all its facets, this section draws on some selected publications to discuss issues of gender construction through movement as kinaesthetic politics, with reference to some historic examples. These issues so far have been marginally acknowledged in organisation studies (Biehl-Missal, 2015), but will have implications for our consideration of gendered movements in organisations.

The notion of 'modern dance' is used to talk about dance reformers, mostly female, including Ruth St. Denis (1879–1968), Isadora Duncan (1877–1927), Rudolf von Laban (1879–1958) and others. In the early 1900s female dancers created new movements and styles of presentation, breaking with traditional ballet. The genre of modern dance is closely associated with the second generation of modern dancers and their choreographic legacy including Mary Wigman (1886–1973), Doris Humphrey (1895–1958) and Martha Graham (1894–1991). A diverse field of practice, modern dance forms share the conception of the body as a medium and vehicle for the expression of inner and outer forces, with a governing logic that is not pictorial as in ballet, but speaks to the affects (Dempster, 2010: 230). The German dance theatre (Tanztheater) for example—building on Rudolf von Laban, Kurt Jooss and Mary Wigman in the 1920s and also including the work of primarily German choreographers from the 1980s such as Pina Bausch—does not show individuals and their emotions as established and stable, but as fluid and worthy of change, with choreography focusing on the process of the subject. Pina Bausch is in this sense often quoted with the sentence: "I'm not interested in how people move but what moves them."

Contemporary dance builds on many of these techniques still taught today and reflects post-structuralist thought and diversity. The aesthetic practice of dance was broadened through the intervention of body techniques such as Body Mind Centering (BMC) and the integration of movement techniques such as contact improvisation and Asian martial arts into (post)modern dance techniques (e.g. Merce Cunningham), along with a deconstruction of the classical vocabulary (e.g. William Forsythe) (Klein, 2011: 21). When postdramatic forms of theatre (Lehmann, 2006) disrupted the holistic narration and presented sound, silence, movement, fragmented text and the bodies of performers in ways in which they not-acted instead of pursuing complex acting, contemporary dance also changed. Contemporary dance also is not necessarily a narrative art form. Dance defeated existing concepts such as movement as flow by producing interruption, showing unpredictable changes in rhythm, speed and direction. Dance celebrated bodily absence instead of omnipresence that we are used to in other media, dance presented exaggerated slowness in movement instead of dynamic speed that we are used to. Along the paradigm change in the cultural sciences with the performative turn and its critique of representation, issues such as presence/absence, identity, authenticity and authorship became central to contemporary choreography. These approaches address physical reality, pointing to aesthetic and kinaesthetic differences in reality and in perception.

Early modern dancers such as Isadora Duncan for example have discarded the classical ballet's corset and pointe shoes, propagating the liberation of the body, and the female body as well, from outer and external restrictions. Freeing the body from too much clothing that veiled and restricted its movement is an actual and metaphorical liberation. While some of Duncan's performances were seen as relying a bit too much on untainted naturality relied on essentialised notions of identity, they were conforming and contesting at the same time, dismantling the voyeuristic gaze, and shifting representational frames (Manning, 1997).

The merit of modern dance with regard to the history of dance lies in the richness and freedom of gestures and steps, releasing movement from traditional patterns that we see in, for example, classical ballet, medieval folk dance and movement in times of absolutist rulers. Dance has always been a mirror of its epoch and so is modern dance reflective of the energy in the crowded, buzzing cities and the affects of the soul, differing from dance forms that took as a point of reference distinguished and stylised courtly demeanour of the noble class. Duncan has been a coeval to Frederick W. Taylor but did not refer to or know about his endeavours to improve movement in scientific management, her dance rather reflected profound social change in a complementary way. Duncan's movements were considered as "poetic dance", an expression of the soul, that stood in contrast to dance forms such as the ballet with a dramatic plot and holistic action (Laban,

2001: 18). Showing that knowing is dispersed in the body and not resides in the mind alone again exemplifies what dance stands for:

> Movement considered hitherto—at least in our civilisation—as the servant of man employed to achieve an extraneous practical purpose was brought to light as an independent power creating states of mind frequently stronger than man's will. This was quite a disconcerting discovery at a time when extraneous achievements through will-power seemed to be the paramount objective of human striving.
>
> (Laban, 2011: 248)

The idea that movements and attitudes result from inner, embodied experiences can also be found in the Biomechanics as a more systematic approach of actor training developed in the 1920s by Vsevolod Meyerhold, which challenged Duncan's subjective approach. Laban (2001) propagated modern dance education to balance one-sided movement requirements and also to further conscious perception of personal movement impulses. Along with such developments that promoted the interest in the expressive qualities of the body, Duncan woke up people's sense for poetry in movement in modern and rationalist times, showing that the flow and patterns of movement build on inner experiences and structures that cannot be explained rationally. Using dance to express emotions, Duncan in the industrial age challenged the perception of the rational mind as determining force. As a pedagogue, Duncan also was interested in the effects of on-going repetitions and alterations of movement on the inner and external attitudes of the individual. Many of these ideas resonate in dance and movement workshops in organisations in the 21st century and in the theoretical approach that applies dance to organisations and leadership to enhance reductionist and rationalist views and to suggest that movements and dynamics change social interaction. Modern dance can be seen as a form of kinaesthetic politics, which emerged in the era of the industrial revolution, and suggested the expression of embodied knowing and experiences through movement, questioning rationalist views that emerged in psychology, management and society.

Another example of kinaesthetic politics worth mentioning in this book as it makes some references to industrial times and to Berlin, its spirit and decadence, is the dancer Anita Berber (1899–1928) who lived during the Weimar period. Berber also appeared with a dance performance in the film "Metropolis" by Fritz Lang and was painted in 1925 by Otto Dix who recognised her complexity as performer, highlighting her eroticism in a skin-tight, fire-engine-red dress that reveals her body, but still showing the nude-dancer fully dressed and suggesting a more profound understanding of her art (Funkenstein, 2005). Her performances broke taboos with their androgyny and total nudity, and her life with drug abuse and overt sexuality was scandalous. These topics were performed in pieces such as "Cocaine" that suggested pain, horror, hallucinations and paranoia rather than titillation: The dancer threw her body in a monstrous cascade, tormented, agonised (Funkenstein, 2005: 28). Later in the book the argument is made that this historic memory can be seen in site-specific performances (Chapter 5) that situate themselves in a historical discourse of Berlin in economic and political turmoil and overblown decadence described by writers such as Isherwood. Dance is a medium to keep alive and perform a historical bond, also in a context that frees individuals from their pre-choreographed movements.

Going back to dance and gender, more generally modern and contemporary dance takes a critical and resistant position against the ideals of beauty embodied in classical ballet and against its ideology. This form of bodily expression can be seen as subverting the voyeuristic gaze that we have experienced in ballet, projecting essentialised notions of identity, as Susan Leigh Foster (2013) suggests. In this vein, modern and contemporary dance is a form of political resistance because it disrupts these traditional narratives and shows a different aesthetics where dancers do without the over-stylised, "beautiful" ballet movements, and also use their gaze to look at the audience.

Modern choreography refuses mastery over prescribed movements and disrupts traditional and often paternalist narration. Trisha Brown's famous choreography "Watermotor" from 1978 for example is open to a variety of readings. It can be seen as a piece of objectivist dance that focuses on the body movement without references to the world outside, but inevitably also is a reflexive choreography with social references. "Watermotor" has thus been interpreted as opposing highly normatised and suppressive female ballet dancing by positing a new frame to consider female identity construction (Foster, 2013).

Similar to the discussion of ballet, I would recommend the reader to watch the "Watermotor" performance on YouTube, before reading this following brief reflection based on Laban Movement Analysis (see Chapter 7). With regard to the category of the body, in "Watermotor" the performer constantly rotates her arms and legs, as if drawing on the idea of a motor constantly moving in water and within the waves. These movements do not show high effort or expressive energy as in tap dance or aerobics. The low effort however does not come over like controlled airiness known from ballet but rather as indifferent, half-heartedness, playful movement. The dancer refuses mastery of postures but shows her 'indifferent' attitude with movement that does not come from the legs (ballet), but from the centre of the body, interrupted by some expressive efforts when stomping confidently. Arms are used to gain momentum and they seem to give impulses, and are not used for decorative framing of the arabesque. She presents movements that never coordinate the body towards a single action, and mid-ranged movements showing incompatible components and the potential of body parts to be disconnected (Foster, 2013: 59).

The dancer denies the tension, not holding a pose, rather movements remain unaccomplished, constantly going on and going into a new direction and towards a new articulation. While classical ballet shows aerial verticality, modern dance shows a more dynamic relationship with gravity, with falling and recovering, is perceived as floor-bound and inward-looking (Dempster, 2010: 230). The use of space and vertical movement also is less present but the horizontal movement is remarkable with its many constant and unexpected changes of direction.

The dancer follows her own choreography, rather than presenting a pre-choreographed performance. This shows that she is the one who writes her movement and presents her body, in a playful way as if testing movements out for herself, not doing it with much effort for the gaze of the audience. In terms of kinaesthetic politics, she makes appear otherwise hidden gendered structures and performs her way of resistance.

When for the modern dancer, movement as exterior expression is guided by interior feeling (Dempster, 2010: 230), this performance makes visible the experience of being a woman in society through dynamic rotations and changes of direction, through restrained movements that signify an internal struggle with opposing motivations. 'The feminine' is presented here as unstable, fleeting, flickering, transient, a subject of multiple representations, so the shifting quality of body and subject in postmodern dance can be seen as a form of liberation from the 'corset' that delimits women's movement (Foster, 2013). Linking to the vocabulary that is employed in this book, Trisha Brown's presentation conveys a kinaesthetic experience and furthers an embodied understanding for a search of body and identity, which is constantly revolving and rotating and is individually and socially constructed and negotiated.

In this context, I would like to point to re.act.feminism (www.reactfem inism.org), an online archive with collection of videos, photographs and other documents of feminist, gender-critical and queer performance art, a transnational and cross-generational project with works by over 180 artists and artist collectives from the 1960s to the beginning of the 1980s, as well as contemporary positions, including Marina Abramović, Chicks on Speed and many others. The archive shows the relevance of performance art for feminism, its strategies and discourses, and the political potential that centres around movement and performance.

Another example that links kinaesthetic politics and site-specific performance (Chapter 5) is "Lady Gaza" who is dancing in Tel Aviv. Lady Gaza, according to her official fictional biography, is a 33-year-old Catholic housewife from Gaza who regularly comes through an underground tunnel. Her manager is the German artist Naneci Yurdagül (born 1979 in Frankfurt/ Main), who performed with her in the streets of Tel Aviv and at his exhibitions supported by the Goethe Institute. Her movement in space allows her to be present, contradicting the seemingly impossible existence of such a woman, confident and sexualised and from Gaza in this area: "The moment you see that character, it looks impossible. But that's exactly what it's about:

everything is possible," says Yurdagül, a creative and explosive figure himself who deals with performance and multiple identities. Artists show how individuals take their space and claim their ground, performing their personality that may or may not move 'like a girl' (Young, 1990), but always is 'in motion'—towards those who are co-present in the moment and those who hear about it in any other way.

The practice of dance not surprisingly reflects most clearly contemporary concepts of the body: While in classical theatre the dramatic process always occurred between roles, newer, postdramatic forms of theatre have experienced a "self-dramatisation" of the physique whereby the body is more than a signifier, but an "*agent provocateur* of an experience without 'meaning'" (Lehmann, 2006: 162, original italics), generating a particular kinaesthetic experience. Dance expresses principles of postdramatic theatre that does not create an illusion and provides 'meaning', but generates energy, atmosphere and a co-present situation. The body becomes the medium to give form to many contemporary experiences: "[W]hen phenomena that are alien and uncanny to the body are brought to the surface (of the skin): impulsive gesticulations, turbulence and agitation, hysterical convulsions, autistic

Figure 3.2 Copyright "Lady Gaza"

Courtesy Naneci Yurdagül_VGBKBonn 2016 & Galerie Knust x Kunz +, Munich (www.sabi neknust.com)

disintegrations of form, loss of balance, fall and deformations. Just as the new dance privileges discontinuity, the different members (articuli) of the body take precedence over its totality as a Gestalt" (Lehmann, 2006: 163).

This renunciation of the 'ideal' body and its mastery is highly visible in the work of William Forsythe, Meg Stuart and others, when novel postures fill the stage such as falling, rolling about, lying or sitting, contortions, gestures like shrugging one's shoulders, the integration of language and the voice, a novel intensity of physical contact. I have experienced a growing trend also at the 2016 festival "Tanz im August" in Berlin (presented by HAU theatre), with presentations by choreographers and activists niv Acosta and Jaamil Olawale Kosoko who demonstrate that black bodies and black arts matter, and the intersexual artist Silvia Calderoni opposing gender roles on stage. Claire Cunningham's (2016: 25) work is initially rooted in the use/misuse, study and distortion of crutches that she practices as "a self-identifying disabled artist", taking ownership of her disability and her identity constructed through movement. Through the crutches she engages physically with the world, exploring the potentiality of her specific physicality, crafting a unique vocabulary which aims to challenge conventions around virtuosity, classical aesthetic and dance: "We are talking about the language of bodies and there is a whole world of bodies who is not allowed to speak. Dance is an art form, which is most missing these voices" (Cunningham, 2016: 24). Contemporary dance is supposed to include these views and address these issues.

Figure 3.3 Claire Cunningham, "Give me a reason to live", http://www.claire cunningham.co.uk

Photo: Hugo Glendinning

Generally, the deconstruction and re-assemblage of movements, along with the de-training of the dancer's habitual structures and movement patterns, again express that bodies evolve in dialogue with the complex social world:

> The postmodern body is not a fixed, immutable entity, but a living structure which continually adapts and transforms itself. It is body available to the play of many discourses. Postmodern dance directs attention away from any specific image of the body and towards the process of constructing all bodies.
>
> (Dempster, 2010: 235)

These motifs can be experienced in dance performances that reflect trends in real life by deconstructing movement. A constant renegotiation of identity through movement can also be seen in the physical practice of other forms of dance such as contact improvisation. The dancer's identity is not stable and on-going but constantly negotiated in the ever changing context and real-time choreography. Contact improvisation does not provide a set of vocabulary of movements, rather sets parameters for how to move that include weight transfers, 'draining' weight out of one area of the body and 'collecting' it in another. Being sensitive to the body's weight and its movement tendencies allows new possibilities of movement to unfold spontaneously and in co-operation, as expressed in book titles such as "sharing the dance" (Novack, 1990). These aspects also are prevalent in dance forms used for arts-based interventions in organisations (Chapter 6), where participants negotiate their 'stance' towards each other through movement.

Before I end this section, I want to return to the motif of "Throwing like a girl" (Young, 1980). Times are changing and brands like Always, a maker for feminine care products, use more realistic portrayals of women. A Super Bowl commercial for the brand's "Like A Girl" campaign shows differences in how young women, girls and boys perceive the phrase "like a girl", giving a positive and empowered content to what it means to run, throw and do pretty much any activity "like a girl". While the spot still was criticised for not dealing with menstruation, making female fluids appear embarrassing, the ad was perceived as ground-breaking (Berman, 2015) and certainly adds to a contemporary cultural studies perspective on kinaesthetic politics. The motif also is altered in the world of fashion. While in most fashion shows, models' walks are highly stylised and scripted, the brand Comme-des-Garçons propagated a different style: Translating the French meaning of the name into movement, models walk "like the boys" in ways more similar to real life than to what we are used from the catwalk. Clothes and shoes only allow simple movement and the extent of movement the clothes need that come to life in dialogue with the body in motion (Lehnert, 2003: 221). In the ballet "Scénario" created for Merce Cunningham in 1997, the Japanese fashion designer Rei Kawakubo devised scenography, light and costumes in the style of her collection "Body Meets Dress, Dress Meets Body". While many issues informing movements already are deeply embodied, clothing as an external layer of the body functioned as an obvious limitation and determination of movement.

The internalisation of movements also became the theme for performances that use slow motion. This topic links to initial observations about dance as a paradigm for modern times with everything in fast flow. For example, in Robert Wilsons work, very slow movements are employed not for the visual effect but for the kinaesthetic effect. Theorists find that "when physical movement is slowed down to such an extent that the time of its development itself seems to be enlarged as through a magnifying glass, the body itself is inevitably exposed in its concreteness" (Lehmann, 2006: 164). Motoric perception becomes alienated when actions such as walking, standing, changing positions vertically remain recognisable but still appear changed. Putting these movements and their imperfection—not their embodiment of classic ideals like in ballet—under the looking glass exposes the spectator's voyeuristic gaze onto the performer. Again this emphasises that living bodies are different from technological and virtual perfection, but still living bodies whose movement in dance exposes today's suspicious expectations.

With regard to virtuality the choreographies of William Forsythe do not, as in classical dance, originate from a body centre, rather body parts have different tempi resulting in de-centred and multiple centres of gravity, extending the movement radius into immaterial worlds. The performances oppose experiences of virtuality by presenting and emphasising human bodies and their movements, trying out opportunities of transformation, of real presence of survival (Odenthal, 2005: 27). Contemporary dance is not about re-presentation of stories, rather the emphasis is on perception, on immediacy and co-presence, which is the core of performance. Performance for Forsythe is a 'machine of sensual education' to access and question aesthetically and kinaesthetically contemporary times (Odenthal, 2005: 30). The body, and the gendered body, is shown as an unstable, constantly evolving and transient phenomenon. The body in dance takes a position towards the other's gaze and contemporary challenges such as virtuality, audio-visual stress and everyday mechanisation of the human body. In many modern dance forms, performers subvert the audience's gaze by not fulfilling expectations and changing patterns of movement, encouraging spectators to think about what else is possible.

Literature

Abraham, S. (1996) Characteristics of eating disorders among young ballet dancers, *Psychopathology* 29: 223–229.

Acevedo, B. (2011) The screaming Pope: Imagery and leadership in two paintings of Pope Innocent X, *Leadership* 7(1): 27–50.

Alderson, E. (1986) Ballet as ideology: Giselle, Act II, *Dance Chronicle* 10(3): 290–304.

Barrionuevo Anzaldi, F. (2013) Pitfalls of 'the political': Politization as an alternative tool for dance analysis? in Brandstetter, G. and Klein, G. (eds.) *Dance [and] Theory*. Bielefeld: transcript, 159–166.

Berman, J. (2015) Why that 'like a girl' Super Bowl ad was so groundbreaking. *Huffington Post*. http://www.huffingtonpost.com/2015/02/02/always-super-bowl-ad_n_6598328.html (Accessed 1 Aug 2016).

Biehl-Missal, B. (2011) Business is show business: Management presentations as performance, *Journal of Management Studies* 48(3): 619–645.

Biehl-Missal, B. (2013) 'And if I don't want to work like an artist . . . ?' How the study of artistic resistance enriches organizational studies, *Ephemera: Theory & Politics in Organization* 13(1): 73–87.

Biehl-Missal, B. (2015) 'I write like a painter': Feminine creation with arts-based methods in organizational research, *Gender, Work & Organization* 22(2): 179–196.

Brewis, J. and Sinclair, J. (2000) Exploring embodiment: Women, biology and work, in Hassard, R., Holliday, R. and Willmott, H. (eds.) *Body and Organization*. London: Sage, 192–214.

Broadbridge, A. and Simpson, R. (2011) 25 years on: Reflecting on the past and looking to the future in gender and management research, *British Journal of Management* 22(3): 470–483.

Burt, R. (1998) Nijinski: Modernism and heterodox representations of masculinity, in Carter, A. (ed.) *Dance Studies Reader*. London and New York: Routledge, 250–258.

Burt, R. (2007) *The Male Dancer: Bodies, Spectacle, Sexualities*, 2nd ed. New York: Routledge.

Butler, J. (1993) *Bodies That Matter: On the Discursive Limits of 'Sex'*. London: Routledge.

Butterworth, J. (2004) Teaching choreography in higher education: A process continuum model, *Research in Dance Education* 5(1): 45–67.

Carter, A. (1998) Locating dance in history and society, in Carter, A. and O'Shea, J. (eds.) *Dance Studies Reader*. London and New York: Routledge, 193–195.

Cunningham, C. (2016) Destructed contemporary. Interview: Gustavo Fijalkow. *Magazin im August* 22–25. http://magazinimaugust.de/2016/08/06/claire-cunningham-deconstructed-contemporary-2/ (Accessed 1 Aug 2016).

Daly, A. (1987) Classical ballet: A discourse of difference, *Women & Performance: A Journal of Feminist Theory* 3(2): 57–66.

Dempster, J. (2010) Women writing the body: Let's watch a little how she dances, in Carter, A. and O'Shea, J. (eds.) *The Routledge Dance Studies Reader*, 2nd ed. London and New York: Routledge, 229–235.

Desmond, J. C. (ed.) (1997) *Meaning in Motion: New Cultural Studies of Dance (Post-Contemporary Interventions)*. Durham, NC: Duke University Press.

Felstead, A., Fuller, A., Jewson, N., Kakelakis, K. and Unwin, L. (2007) Grooving to the same tunes? Learning, training and productive systems in the aerobics studio, *Work, Employment and Society* 21(2): 189–208.

Foster, S. L. (2013) 'Throwing like a girl?' Gender in a transnational world, in Butterworth, J. and Wildschut, L. (eds.) *Contemporary Choreography. A Critical Reader*. New York: Routledge, 53–62.

Funkenstein, S. L. (2005) Anita Berber: Imaging a Weimar performance artist, *Woman's Art Journal* 26(1): 26–31.

Gatrell, C. (2013) Maternal body work: How women managers and professionals negotiate pregnancy and new motherhood at work, *Human Relations* 66(5): 621–644.

Green, J. (2003) Foucault and the training of docile bodies in dance education, *Arts and Learning Research Journal* 19(1): 99–125.

Hancock, P. and Tyler, M. (2007) Un/doing gender and the aesthetics of organizational performance, *Gender, Work & Organization* 14(6): 513–533.

Höpfl, H. (2007) The codex, the codicil and the codpiece: Some thoughts on diminution and elaboration in identity formation, *Gender, Work & Organization* 14(6): 619–632.

Jowitt, D. (1998) In pursuit of the sylph: ballet in the romantic period, in Carter, A. and O'Shea, J (eds.) *Dance Studies Reader*, 2nd ed. London and New York: Routledge, 209–219.

Klein, G. (2011) Dancing politics: Worldmaking in dance and choreography, in Klein, G. and Noeth, S. (eds.) *Emerging Bodies: The Performance of Worldmaking in Dance and Choreography*. Bielefeld: transcript, 17–28.

Laban, R. von (2001) *Der moderne Ausdruckstanz in der Erziehung*, 5th ed. Wilhelmshaven: Heinrichshofen-Bücher.

Laban, R. von (2011) Modern educational dance (1948), introd. by Ann Carlisle, in McCaw, D. (ed.) *The Laban Sourcebook*. London: Routledge, 237–256.

Lehmann, H. T. (2006) *Postdramatic Theatre*. London: Routledge.

Lehnert, G. (2003) Mode als Spiel. Zur Performativität von Mode und Geschlecht, in Alkemeyer, T., Boschert, B., Schmidt, R. and Gebauer, G. (eds.) *Aufs Spiel gesetzte Körper: Aufführungen des Sozialen in Sport und populärer Kultur*. Konstanz: UVK Verlag, 213–228.

Lepecki, A. (2013) Dance and politics, in Brandstetter, G. and Klein, G. (eds.) *Dance [and] Theory*. Bielefeld: transcript, 153–158.

Manning, S. (1997) The female dancer and the male gaze: Feminist critiques of early modern dance, in Desmond, J. C. (ed.) *Meaning in Motion: New Cultural Studies of Dance (Post-Contemporary Interventions)*. Durham, NC: Duke University Press, 153–166.

Mavin, S. and Grandy, G. (2016) A theory of abject appearance: Women elite leaders' intra-gender 'management' of bodies and appearance, *Human Relations* 69(5): 1095–1120.

Mead, M. and Bateson, G. (1942) *Balinese Character*. New York: New York Academy of Sciences.

Novack, C. (1990) *Sharing the Dance: An Ethnography of Contact Improvisation*. Milwaukee: University of Wisconsin Press.

Odenthal, J. (2005) Die Entmythisierung der Welt: Versuch über William Forsythe, in Odenthal, J. (ed.) *Tanz. Körper: Politik*. Berlin: Theater der Zeit, 27–31.

Ogasawara, Y. (1998) *Office Ladies and Salaried Men: Power, Gender, and Work in Japanese Companies*. Berkeley: University of California Press.

Oliver, W. (2008) Body image in the dance class, *Journal of Physical Education, Recreation and Dance* 79(5): 18–41.

Phillips, M., Pullen, A. and Rhodes, C. (2014) Writing organization as gendered practice: Interrupting the libidinal economy, *Organization Studies* 35(3): 313–333.

Polhemus, T. (1988) Dance, gender and culture, in Carter, A. (ed.) *The Routledge Dance Studies Reader*. London and New York: Routledge, 171–179.

Rancière, J. (2004) *The Politics of Aesthetics*. London and New York: Continuum.

Rancière, J. (2007) Art of the possible: An interview with Jacques Rancière, *Artforum* (March): 256–269.

Rieger-Ladich, M. (2009) Lektionen in symbolischer Gewalt: Der Körper als Gedächtnisstütze, in Alkemeyer, T., Brümmer, K., Kodalle, R. and Pille, T. (eds.) *Ordnung in Bewegung: Choreographien des Sozialen. Körper in Sport, Tanz, Arbeit und Bildung.* Bielefeld: transcript, 179–195.

Satama, S. (2016) 'Feathers on fire': A study of the interplay between passion and vulnerability in dance, *Organizational Aesthetics* 5(1): 64–93.

Slater, A. and Tiggemann, M. (2011) Gender differences in adolescent sport participation, teasing, self-objectification and body image concerns, *Journal of Adolescence* 34(3): 455–463.

Strauss, E. W. (1966) *The Upright Posture: Phenomenological Psychology.* New York: Basic Books.

Warhurst, C. and Nickson, D. (2009) 'Who's got the look?' Emotional, aesthetic and sexualized labour in interactive services, *Gender, Work & Organization* 16(3): 385–404.

Young, I. M. (1980) Throwing like a girl: A phenomenology of feminine body comportment motility and Spatiality, *Human Studies* 3: 137–156.

Young, I. M. (1990) *Throwing Like a Girl and Other Essays in Feminist Philosophy and Social Theory.* Bloomington: Indiana University Press.

4 Kinaesthetic Empathy (Leadership)

A Phenomenological Approach

Movement practices in the sense of 'dance' are constitutive practices in social and organisational life that form relationships and interaction. The previous section has discussed that movements are not only a mere representation of social identities and gender, rather a form of kinaesthetic politics that has an effect on those 'embodied minds' who are present, watch and interact. Moving means to engage with performative aspects of social orders and this leads us to a reconsideration of leadership. While many studies over the past decades have come to consider leadership as an embodied form of interaction, the kinaesthetic, movement-related dimension remains under-researched. In this chapter, I will in greater depth discuss the role of movement in leadership practices that are embodied, and will draw on the concept of kinaesthetic empathy from dance studies, linking to phenomenological approaches to leadership. Kinaesthetic empathy refers to processes of taking-in, or tuning-in to others' movements and bodily expressions.

Leadership theory has long said that bodies do not matter until more and more researchers have taken into account the materially lived world of leadership and their bodies. Within the context of aesthetic approaches to organisation, leadership studies came to focus on the sensual aspects and the living body of leaders that has generally been considered an 'unwanted and unwelcome guest' (Hansen et al., 2007: 553) in this research tradition. Perspectives that turn to the body and embodiment in the practice of leadership, extending leadership theory towards a more situational, relational and integral understanding of leading and following, parallel other studies on the body in organisations as a reaction to various shortcomings and limitations of conventional organisational discourses that have marginalised or objectified the body. Living bodies are seen as tangible media through which various forms of leadership practices are enacted, negotiated and even resisted.

This development started from a consideration of the surface aspects of the bodies. Following an impression management approach (Goffman), scholars have considered the outer body as an expression of identity and have for example analysed managers' presentation on official photography and the values they tried to express via clothing, mimics and posture. From this starting point researchers soon came to take into account the aesthetic dimension of leader–follower interaction, as also discussed in publications that did not only compare leaders to theatre actors but referred to the relationship between performer and audience, the atmosphere and intra-relation between both groups.

Leadership increasingly came to be understood from a phenomenological perspective as an embodied process, in which leaders and followers engage in an exchange of physical, visual and aural clues (Ladkin, 2013). Bodily gestures and postures, facial mimic, tones of voice and other forms of expression are part of an embodied practicing of leadership, which also includes aesthetic sensibilities and competencies (Springborg, 2010). This is obvious in many areas of service work that require a permanent situative co-ordination between those who interact. For example, care workers need to see and feel what is going on, not proceeding along a strict plan, but engaging in a dialogue between bodies. This also holds true for the range of service workers or those that perform 'aesthetic work', when responding to others and to atmospheres, be it waiters, sales staff or university lecturers. These mute forms of coordination happen without direct bodily contact, and can also be found in the world of arts, when chamber orchestras or jazz musicians (Barrett, 2012) play together, improvise and perform—and predominantly in the practice of dance when bodies through kinaesthetic empathy coordinate a situation.

This addition to traditional concepts of leadership is seen as a necessity in today's complex and dynamic economy catering to human needs and desires, demanding and allowing for personal subjectivity and emotionality at work. Conceiving of aesthetics in Baumgarten's tradition as sensual perception and the interlinked forms of aesthetic and sensory knowing and felt meaning of objects and experiences (Hansen et al., 2007: 545), such approaches inquire into leaders' capacity to motivate employees and to what is felt by the individuals who are in contact with them. This helps to re-integrate material, bodily qualities and lived experiences for a re-embodied leadership as relational and emerging event (Küpers, 2013: 336).

Leadership studies that follow a phenomenological perspective to re-assess and revive the relevance of bodily processes and embodied realities of leadership and followership are not a return to pre-modern longing for corporeal unity. Rather they are useful in today's digitised world. Such an approach links the "embodied sensorium of practice to contemporary forms of sense-making, for example in cyberspace, with its tele-presences and multimedia applications" (Küpers, 2013: 348). Facing the complexities of current leadership practices, it remains important to recognise that not all what is involved in them can be grasped. As leadership today is placed in increasingly complex, often paradoxical or dilemmatic individual and collective organisational settings, the extension of leadership studies is increasingly relevant as it emphasises that practices of leadership happen "in and through the very in-between of leading and following" (Küpers, 2013: 348), not in a linear or hierarchical line in a dichotomy of leader and follower. Based on Merleau-Ponty's understanding of embodiment and practice, leadership is by Küpers (2013) interpreted as "an emergent process of the inter-practice of leading and following."

Considering leadership as embodied practice from the perspective of dance studies, shows how practices are shaped by bodily processes and an embodied responsiveness, which addresses in-between improvisation and co-created spaces that also exist in virtual or remote forms of leadership and co-evolve within a multidimensional nexus of organisations. Focusing on the co-created nature of leadership that is accessible through the embodiment gate may help to develop more suitable forms of practicing leadership that are human-centred and sustainable, rather than only instrumentalist. The view presented here can help to facilitate a more relational, co-creative understanding of leader- and followership.

Phenomenological perspectives have offered conceptions of leadership as an embodied material and relational practice. The advanced phenomenology of Merleau-Ponty (1962) provides for many researchers a valuable gate for approaching and interpreting bodily and embodied practices as well as the creative interplay of leading and following in everyday organisational life. The phenomenology of the body puts a focus on the body and the embodied experiences of an individual in relation to other human beings and objects and the physical environment. The body is conceived of as the centre from which human agency unfolds, which makes a leader–follower relationship not a social or discursive construct, but a phenomenon that is perceived through our bodies. A leader–follower relationship is thus not only experienced through the body in the place of thinking and speaking, but also created and negotiated through embodied experience. Such a perspective seems useful for leadership studies as is can be seen as a critique of approaches that "assume the body must be understood as either as passive object (corpus) or as subject as extension of the mind; instead of seeing it as constituted by both as a living body ('Leib')" (Küpers, 2013: 337). Conceiving of practice and agents as first and foremost embodied and its practitioners as primarily corporeal beings, leads to a conception of a co-created, embodied practice of leadership:

> Following the outlined phenomenological understanding of the nexus between embodiment and practice, human beings involved in leadership and in followership can be interpreted as 'body-subjects-in-action', whose embodied experience connects them to their life-world in specific times, places and socio-cultural contexts. As such, embodied leaders and followers as practitioners are comported intentionally, movingly

and responsively towards a socio-material and joint, co-created world, while their experiences open up to inexhaustible, but meaningful and creative possibilities.

(Küpers, 2013: 339)

Emphasising the idea of embodied interaction, in this area of organisational research, a range of advances have been made to develop the dance perspective. In the last years a number of practitioners books were published on "dance of leadership" as well, including views on the rhythm, energy and 'flow' of leadership that relates to the aesthetics of dance. Ropo and Sauer (2008: 560) for example use the traditional dance, waltz and the postmodern dance experience of raves to "challenge traditional, intellectually oriented and positivistic leadership approaches that hardly recognize nor conceptualize aesthetic, bodily aspects of social interaction between people in the workplace." Many scholarly publications in this area see leadership as socially and bodily constructed through the senses (Hujala et al., 2016), emphasising the corporeal nature of social interaction in leadership. Dance theory and the concept of kinaesthetic empathy develops this approach by adding and exploring the kinaesthetic dimension of leadership.

In the next step, I will present further thoughts on the kinaesthetic feedback loop, followed by a comparison of leaders and actors in the context of 'leadership as an art' that point to the necessity of an increased aesthetic and kinaesthetic awareness. This is an aspect that resonates with the issue of 'kinaesthetic politics' and emphasises a leader's bodily presence. More detail is then provided by referring to studies on conductors and DJs. Leadership is framed as a relational, co-created process embedded in physical interaction among leaders and followers.

The Kinaesthetic Loop

To better understand embodied processes in leadership situations as well as the in-between and co-created spaces that also exist in all forms of leadership, a consideration of the kinaesthetic dimension and an inclusion of dance theory is useful. Dance studies as the discipline primarily concerned with human movement and its impact can help to develop our understanding of the kinaesthetic dimension in leadership situations and, beyond this, points to the improvised, relational and co-created spaces in leadership interaction that emerge and cannot be fully controlled.

Studies on leadership as an embodied practice have pointed to the kinaesthetic level of shared human experience where the relation and connection to others is achieved and negotiated through engaging with somatic cues (Ladkin and Taylor, 2010: 69). Zeitner and colleagues (2016: 178) suggest that becoming an "embodiary" leader involves a "greater sensual awareness of people in a group and their kinesthetic impact on each other", which can be developed through reflected practice and training.

Such an awareness or empathy for kinaesthetic elements has been emphasised in studies that have looked into the world of music where interaction happens non-verbally through complex relational processes and bodily perception, for example between conductors and musicians and between a group of musicians, including jazz players. The concept of kinaesthetic empathy from dance studies (Parviainen, 2002) has been used in this context (Gilling, 2014: 115; Ropo et al., 2002) to describe processes of taking-in, or tuning-in to others' movements and bodily expressions.

The kinaesthetic sense, which has been discussed from the 1880s and which is a rather complex and not singular matter, has also been considered an addition to the five senses mentioned by Aristotle (Fabius, 2009). Kinaesthesia (from kinesis, Greek for motion, and aesthesis, for sensation) is defined as the ability to feel movements of the limbs and body. Kinaesthesia has been identified "as arising from sensory stimulations via receptors in muscles, tendons, joints, skin, vestibular apparatus, eyes, ears, and also from an interior knowledge of motor commands", relating to perceptions of balance and equilibrium, the motion of the body and the limbs and their position, and force and exertion (Longstaff, 1996: 42). When watching dance, people experience kinaesthetic empathy when they feel they are participating in the movements they observe, and experience associated feelings and states. Kinaesthetic empathy in dance studies means that other people's movements are not only perceived visually but corporeally sensed: Spectators of dance do not only react to the visual component of dance but perceive it as a kinaesthetic phenomenon in the entire body, experiencing related feelings and ideas, participating in movement even if they are distant (Foster, 2011).

Dance, albeit strongly visual, is not only perceived through the eyes, rather is perceived aesthetically with different senses and through the entire body. Dance scholar Ann Daly (2002: 307) has argued: "Dance, although it has a visual component, is fundamentally a kinesthetic art whose apperception is grounded not just in the eye but in the entire body." Fabius (2009: 331) describes the contradiction that dance "is created through the experiences of moving bodies while primarily accessed visually by its spectators". The experience is not only for the eyes, but for the entire body, with spectators possessing the ability to feel movements of the limbs and body. Going away from a more ocular-centric approach to choreography in the 18th and 19th centuries, newer forms of dance have emphasised the kinaesthetic experience. The preoccupation with the sensual, kinaesthetic experience of the moving body has influenced contemporary choreographers who employed new artistic strategies, challenging the dominance of the visual in dance performances. Focusing less on body image, body language and representation, the dynamic connections and the on-going feedback between bodies has moved into focus. For example, the choreographer Boris Charmatz uses the obstruction of sight to emphasise perception through the body as the pivotal element of the performance, encouraging the spectator to ponder about the role of kinaesthetics and sensual perception in choreography.

The choreographer William Forsythe shows improvised decision-making, when the dancers' experiences of their moving bodies contribute to making the choreography in the very moment (Fabius, 2009: 340). Kinaesthetics assumes a central role in the production of the choreography, so that audience members to not focus on body images but take part in the kinaesthetic experience. This idea of kinaesthetics and improvised choreography not only applies to the world of dance, but also to the social world where individuals do not assume pre-defined postures but negotiate how their bodies move through space in social choreographies (Chapter 5) and behave in leader–follower interaction.

Actor in the Theatre

When thinking of movement and leadership, the former Microsoft CEO Steve Ballmer may come to mind. In a performance labelled "monkey dance" that went viral as an online video, the manger paraded on stage, jumping and dancing, ending with the enthusiast shout: "I love this company, yay!" While this is a very explicit and simple example of dance and leadership, I shall develop ideas that more generally emphasise the relevance of movement and experience with regard to leadership, starting with a consideration of stage performers.

Movement is a factor widely recognised that influences how an audience reacts to a leader or a speaker on the business stage, or a performer in the theatre. Charismatic leaders typically adopt animated body movements, employing not only verbal forms of expression to communicate, but also moving theirs arms and legs, adopting different postures and mimics. For this reason, studies on leadership and charismatic leadership in particular have compared leaders to actors onstage. Theatre art and leadership have in common strong performative components and there is a tradition of comparing organisations to theatre and leaders to actors. Leadership has been considered as a performing art and it has been observed that organisational life is increasingly becoming theatrical and performative in character, underpinned by a prevalence of theatrical practices that also are used by corporate leaders for creating compelling performances. Theories of acting underlying the dramatistic genre provide insights into behaviour in organisations (Höpfl and Linstead, 1993) and such approaches gain importance in today's aesthetic economy with an increase of theatrical situations that aim at manipulating impressions.

In this context, studies inspired by Goffman's (1959) theories have described the impression management skills charismatic leaders need for executing their 'role' and for giving convincing 'performances' to an 'audience' of followers and organisational stakeholders. As described elsewhere (Biehl-Missal, 2010: 280–281), charismatic leadership theories use impression management (Leary and Kowalski, 1990) as a common point of reference to describe leadership as an activity that regulates information about the self, the organisation and other entities primarily for other people. It has been suggested that the use of theatrical techniques can help leaders to bolster their image of competence, building follower belief and commitment in pursuit of a vision. To achieve this, leaders need to act coherently and consistently, showing sensitivity to followers' needs, values and expectations, portraying themselves in positive ways (Gardner et al., 2005). Studies have analysed the convincing choice of metaphor and gesture and powerful oratory, and have confirmed that in staged presentations leaders use a range of theatrical techniques such as bright light, impressive stage design and persuasive rhetoric to convey such positive, controlled and reassuring impressions.

In a publication that compares leadership 'as an art' with the presentation of heroes on theatre stages (Biehl-Missal, 2010), I have illustrated that aesthetic features do not alone turn leadership into an art. Rather than suggesting simple improvements for leadership development, theatre instead may offer critical ideas about aesthetic interaction. Theatre does not provide leadership ideals but teaches us about anti-heroes, about personalities who are discomforting, yet contentious and problematic. Theatre protagonists are not portrayed positively, 'heroic' or at their 'best' but as lacking both control and confidence. Leaders are the epitome of drama and over the millennia the stage has made fools of kings, capitalists and communists rather than praising them. Examples of problematic or undecided 'heroes' include Shakespeare's manipulative "Henry V" who uses rhetoric and symbols to build up appearances; and Hamlet, who ponders about "to be or not to be", about whether it is worth to "suffer" or "to take arms". Sophocles' Antigone ponders about her inability to make decisions and to 'manage' her destiny, delivering long unassertive meandering streams of thought about her decision to oppose family law and state politics. The aesthetic form reflects and exposes the darkness of political argumentation. Galy Gay in Bertolt Brecht's "Man Equals Man" is an 'untragic hero', who cannot say no, who does not remain faithful to himself but easily adopts ideas and change. He is not an ideal of focused attitudes and opinions and Brecht shows how individuals get influenced and seduced by the system and by ideologies that they often accept without resistance or reflection.

On the level of content, theatre presents a fundamental disrespect for tenability and positive affirmation, it can 'play down' seriousness and articulate the dubious, and on the aesthetic level, it can confront social expectations and in a subtle fashion can touch and irritate audiences. Exposing heroes' weaknesses, the constraints of role-playing and the fact that appearances are deceiving, theatre can encourage audiences to question and possibly reject charismatic leaders and the organisational systems that surround them. Theatrical situations have a sensual and kinaesthetic impact on bodily co-present audiences via interplay of the text and performative techniques such as hysteric, hasty or inhibited speech, and distanced or restricted gestures.

'Leadership as an art' through this lens includes critical interaction through increased aesthetic awareness particularly from the viewpoint of followers. This is an aspect that resonates with the issue of 'kinaesthetic politics' that runs through the book. Embodied leadership links both fields of organisation and theatre as it is precisely the bodily co-presence of actors and spectators, the shared aesthetic situation, which constitutes theatre (Fischer-Lichte, 2008: 38). In the next sections, further examples of embodied leadership will be presented, emphasising an embodied dialogue between leaders and followers.

Conductor and Orchestra

The concept of kinaesthetic empathy has been used in studies on leadership and conductors. The metaphor of the conductor at first sight however is a rather traditional model highly symbolic for a strong (male) individual 'setting the tune' and directing others, and does not seem to fit dynamic 21st-century organisations. Leaders have compared themselves with orchestral conductors when leading large groups of strong and individualist personalities working together. Indeed, a conductor leads such a group without verbally telling them what to do, enabling their interpretative intent to co-create a symphony. But the metaphor has much more to offer when the kinaesthetic dimension is considered. Due to the strongly visual and authoritative nature of the image, the invisible kinaesthetic processes, the physicality and interactive nature of the non-verbal communication between a conductor and musicians was ignored for long.

Recent studies put an emphasis on the relational processes between conductors as leaders and the orchestra members. The music conductor often has been reduced to a charismatic figure whereby the interactive nature of the musical performance has been overlooked. Going beyond an understanding of a conductor orchestrating the musicians, Koivunen and Wennes (2011) put the interaction into focus. This is a large step forward from the popular metaphor of a conductor as a hero and a holder of control and power, towards an understanding of leadership not as a possession held by an individual, but as a relational, embodied process between leader and followers. Conductors engage in relational leadership processes with the musicians through mutual listening, aesthetic judgment and kinaesthetic empathy. The aspect of kinaesthetic empathy comes in when "conductors communicate their ideas and interpretation of the music by physical gestures and movements", for example with the right hand showing the beat and the left hand suggesting phrasing and intonation, whereby "facial expressions, the eyes particularly, also convey cues to the musicians about how the particular piece of music should be played" (Koivunen and Wennes, 2011: 62). These relational processes are non-verbal, as language could not convey the same message bodily movements could, when perceived in relation to one self, so that the ensemble follows the conductor with body movements and kinaesthetic empathy.

Drawing on phenomenology and applying the concept of the embodied subject to a conductor, Gilling (2014) in his study on orchestras employs ideas of kinaesthetic empathy to discuss that leadership is not a disembodied activity, but a co-created process embedded in physical interaction among colleagues. Gilling (2014: 121) has found a kinaesthetic connection when orchestra musicians engage in empathic observation of facial expressions and postures and physically relate to the conductor. The conductor's upbeat gesture, occurring in silence, is one of the most obvious kinaesthetic activities, and vital to the whole music-making process. It does not only convey an idea about speed and dynamic volume, but also abstract ideas, such as the sound quality the conductor is looking for (Gilling, 2014: 116). Other bodily expressions such as breathing and eye contact allow for responses and empathetic interaction, which also extends to the musical instrument that stands in a direct relation to the organist's body. These exchanges of gaze and gestures as expressions of interest and the mutual reactions point to a reversibility in a leadership context.

Kinaesthetic empathy and the auditory, visual and gestural information given and received by individual musicians in the orchestra drives leadership and collaborative coordination. The continuous kinaesthetic exchange has been referred to as a "cyclical kinaesthetic loop" (Gilling, 2014: 116). Musicians in an orchestra physically relate to each other and influence each other. For example, physical energy is also transmitted through forceful, abrupt or gentle bow strokes that relate to a conductor's gestures and also influence her or his physical activity. The rhythm as an underlying vibe holds the music together, and in an orchestra is produced by those who play the relevant parts, while the conductor and others shape the melody. In this setting, each musician is accorded some form of authority and influence:

> This then affects how each musician 'makes sense' of their situation and 'gives sense' to colleagues, as section players will contextualise what they see from the front stands according to what they see and hear in their immediate vicinity and act accordingly. Every musician, whether player or conductor, is therefore involved to one degree or another in followership, as they 'make sense' and leadership, as they 'give sense' to those around them.
>
> (Gilling, 2014: 125–126)

Leadership and followership in such as situation is dispersed and shared. Leadership exists and becomes in the spaces between all of the performers co-operating. Pointing to the intra-spaces (Küpers, 2013), such an approach again highlights the importance of the relational dimension of leadership and of kinaesthetic empathy when humans interrelate through bodily presence—when they act through their bodies on others. Gilling (2014) shows that through an on-going kinaesthetic loop, the orchestra performs and brings to life the musical event. The co-constructed leadership situation is experienced not only in the mind but expressed through bodily action. Such a study on orchestras showed that for all leaders it is important to develop kinaesthetic empathy: "The leader who understands the empathetic connections that lie within the physical fabric or organizational activity at any level will [. . .] be able to harness the powerful creative energy that is released when valued individual contributions become unified collective action" (Gilling, 2014: 131).

DJ and Dancers

Dance studies can be applied to develop the idea of the existence of a cyclical loop that is perceived through the body and that drives collaborative coordination. The analysis of a situation in which people dance even better shows that such a loop not only is perceived through the body but generated kinaesthetically through movements of the full body that cannot be observed in other settings such as orchestras. To illustrate this, I shall draw on a study on DJs and the leader–follower interaction that is co-created through a kinaesthetic dialogue (Biehl, forthcoming). What exists on the stage in dance or theatre or between the DJ booth and the dance floor can be described as a 'feedback loop': in typical theatrical situations, the performance is brought forth by and made forceful by a self-referential and ever-changing feedback-loop (Fischer-Lichte, 2005: 111). There is something going on between stage and audience in the space that is co-created in the very moment by all those who are present. Activities such as leading, managing, teaching and, after all, DJ'ing are relational activities. For DJs it is not just about mixing tracks into each other, but about the art of "mixing music with people", and making them 'move' at a party or a rave (Biehl-Missal, 2015: 6).

The performance is not only created by the actions of the person on stage, but also influenced by the other participants' response to it—a dimension that cannot be fully controlled. When watching dance or listening to an orchestra, many of these responses ranging from utterances to mimics and small gestures influence the overall atmosphere, while on a dance floor the atmosphere is palpable to a greater extent. Peter Brook (1968) describes how an "empty space" becomes the lieu of performance when people are present and fill the room with a co-created atmosphere that is distinctive and changes in every performance, depending on all sensually perceptible responses, often vaguely referred to as the 'mood' of the people present or the 'energy'. The space itself also has an influence on how the interaction is perceived (Chapter 5). When speaking of leadership dispersed between participants, such a view emphasises the space in between all actors in which something is created.

The notion of 'co-presence' is used in performance studies literature as well as in phenomenological perspectives on leadership (Küpers, 2014: 340), to emphasise the embodied perception in a shared situation where the audience is not passive but active. The power of a co-present situation is to address participants not as rational beings but as 'embodied minds'. This is also reflected in studies that emphasise the need for leaders to stay with their senses and aesthetically make sense of what happens around them

(Springborg, 2010). I have already made the point that such an approach also is useful to other leadership situations that may also happen virtually because the view emphasises the relational and constantly negotiated dimension of leading and following, also referred to as the inter-practice (Küpers, 2013), and the space in-between participants that cannot be fully controlled. Dance is something that is transitory and cannot be reproduced, pointing to embodied structures that are hidden, personal and difficult to access.

Developing the ideas on kinaesthetic empathy and the kinaesthetic loop between leaders and followers, I will discuss more evidence on living bodies that serve as tangible media through which leadership practices are negotiated. I will turn towards the rave that early studies on dance and leadership have heralded a prime forum of inquiry as it is a collective, co-created and dynamic activity (Ropo and Sauer, 2008: 560), with blurred boundaries and spontaneous interaction (Chandler, 2012: 871). The consideration of the rave with non-choreographed modes of interaction in greater detail shows the situational and responsive nature of a shared leadership interaction.

The consideration of a techno DJ as a musical artist (Biehl, forthcoming) who 'manages' a crowd and literally makes people 'move'—and in return is being 'moved' by the mass—has developed other studies that use artists as an inspiration for leadership. Extant publications compare leaders to actors and other artists, and traditionally refer to arts that do without much body-movement through the space such as painting, sculpting or are metaphorical without considering the actual kinaesthetic experience generated through movement. Different from charismatic leaders or some superstar DJs, 'underground DJs' who do not provide a pre-recorded product but chose the music during their set as a reaction to the atmosphere and audience, co-create something with the audience in a feedback process in a shared situation that is influenced, negotiated and determined through movement. Studies on conductors go beyond the dichotomy of the "lion tamer" or the "priest" to show the co-creation of a musical event in which "musicians are immersed with conductor as primus inter pares" (Gilling, 2014: 114). Studies on DJs have also shown that the obvious visual dichotomy between what is often referred to as "digital shamans", "maestros" and "priests" is deceiving, pointing to a more interactive embodied leadership interaction. The overall situation, be it the symphony or the party, emerges from a co-created embodied interaction. Leadership appears to be a shared activity with possibly reversible roles of leading and following, driven forth by a kinaesthetic feedback loop.

In my study, DJs interviewed have emphasised that for their performance they value the closeness to the audience, distancing themselves from celebrity figures on high stages that may reflect images such as 'God is a DJ.' The following image is made with a new 360° photo apparatus and its round allocation of agents visualises the concept of the feedback loop and shared

Figure 4.1 Norman Nodge, Dance Tunnel at Autumn Street Studio, London
Courtesy Michael Hornbogen Photography

situation rather than suggesting a dichotomy of a leader (on stage) and followers (on the floor).

DJs find that the best feedback is when the crowd keeps dancing, and
express their effort to make people move, improvising the choice of music
in the very moment. Kinaesthetic empathy is relevant here as DJs themselves
consider their job a "bodily form of communication". In a club setting,
the feedback loop occurs between the dancing crowd and the DJ as well as
among individuals on the dance floor, as a relational process that is mediated not only by vision, but by kinaesthetic empathy. DJs generally perceive
the dancing crowd not as individuals but as a moving mass and connect
kinaesthetically to the overall 'energy' and atmosphere.

Embodied leadership situations have been considered a dialogue that is
created by movement and gestures (Bathurst and Cain, 2013). As in other
leadership situations, people on the dance-floor seem to value and also further a kinaesthetic connection, mimicking immediately when DJs raise their
arms or make certain gestures, expanding the kinaesthetic feedback loop. In
an auto-ethnographic addition to my study on DJs, I performed live onstage
as well and caught myself dancing behind the DJ desk, realising that the
room started mirroring and feeding back my movement (lifting arms makes
the crowd cheer as well), which made me move even more because I wanted
them to dance and have a good party (Biehl-Missal, 2015: 6). DJs in general
react to a felt pressure to move and to build up eye-contact. In the interviews
that were conducted, a DJ reports his interpretation of mute dancer's gazes:
"Ey DJ, we love what you played, but if you don't look at me next time you

can stay at home!" DJs believe that some dancers want to be guided and 'led' through movements, and try to build up eye-contact.

Responding to this perceived pressure, DJs use movements for 'crowd management', making efforts to connect to the audience, but consciously employ restricted movement. For DJs expressive dancing is only possible with pre-recorded sets, whereas mixing requires the hands to be on the sound devices and mixer. My study that interviewed DJs showed that they reject too much movement, referring to celebrity DJs' dancing as "egomaniac", like a "clown" or "jumping jack". Rather they aim to show some form of embodied serious commitment: It is not about ecstatic dancing to a specific tune, but about "showing that you are giving everything, that must be conveyed (. . .) to pump the crowd so that they commit as much as I do" (Biehl, forthcoming). A female DJ asserted that she is particularly cautious and refrains from expressive movement that typically is known from celebrity DJs that are mostly male, rather restricts herself on twisting records and building up eye contact. This is reflective of kinaesthetic politics and relates to the gendered nature of leadership, including the lack of female embodied role models in organisational leadership that puts additional pressure on women. It has been discussed that standardised movement behaviour is used in other work situations in the dance field, such as aerobic training, to make them more manageable. DJs as artists however do not follow pre-choreographed routines but develop their movements according to their kinaesthetic experience in the interactive situation. This resonates an idea that popped up at different instances in the book: Movement in leadership situations today is not as pre-choreographed as it appears, rather individuals, like in modern and postmodern dance, find their own ways to negotiate the interaction, using their kinaesthetic empathy and relate to their audience of 'followers'.

These forms of leading and following are related to embodied forms of knowing. DJs' choice of music is improvised in situ and legitimised verbally by brief assessments of "it just fits", which still leaves room for surprises when dancers do not react enthusiastically to what the DJ has considered a "sure killer of the floor". Embodied knowing about this practice is difficult to verbalise, as explained by a female DJ:

> You feel the dancing and the atmosphere (. . .) whether you speed up or build down your programme, when you realize, oh, some are tired now . . . I feel it, not consciously, and I know exactly where to start from . . . when I register people are 'soft', I won't do hard core techno, but when I realize, this is what they want—or the previous DJ failed to do— . . . then I jump right in and pull it through.

The mixing practice also is a result of year-long training, with more experienced DJs being more confident that they would be able to relate to the dance floor. Interaction in this case is to a large part kinaesthetically mediated, going beyond a visual perception of the dancing crowd or a rational choice of music to reacting to bodies in motion. As indicated earlier, DJs do not only aim to make people dance, fuelling the kinaesthetic feedback loop, but also play tunes that purposely disrupt the flow. Techno DJs may mix rock or reggae tunes into their set, breaking kinaesthetic patters of raving if dancers co-operate and change their movements, contributing to a transformation of the co-present situation. Challenging audiences has been related to forms of 'leadership as an art': For example, the comparison of leaders and actors showed that the artists on stages do often refrain from meeting expectations. Such approaches of 'artistic' character help to generate innovation in the situation.

Not delivering what is expected was related to authenticity by DJs: "I am being a bit egocentric here, I play what I like, because what moves me I can transfer—to make other people move". Assuming that the kinaesthetic feedback loop works better when the DJ is fully committed to the music—which may be perceived through kinaesthetic empathy—not only emphasises the relational component but echoes ideas about authentic forms of leadership (Ladkin and Taylor, 2010) that may also reflect contemporary ideals of desired personal fulfilment in work.

Overall the analysis of a situation that involves dance shows many details in the kinaesthetic dimension of embodied leadership that other studies have not considered, and highlights the socially interactive and transitory nature of the situation as well. Going beyond the obvious appearance on the visual surface, which suggests that DJs—and other leaders—perform a hierarchical or charismatic model of leadership, studies on DJs put even more emphasis on invisible and fugitive elements of leadership through an exploration of kinaesthetic empathy, highlighting the co-created nature of the interaction. This posits the leader's body within an embodied and kinaesthetic network that are organisations.

The dynamic nature of leading and following is further emphasised in practical workshops (Chapter 6). The use of movement workshops for leadership development in practical ways develops these ideas, when enhancing embodied understandings of 'leading' or 'following', and furthering an understanding of leadership as a co-created and relational process. The idea also resonates in studies that used dance as a research-method (Chapter 7). The kinaesthetic interchange as negotiated in dance has for example attracted Hujala and colleagues' attention (2016) when they performed an 'invitation to dance' with their invisible, imaginary bosses. Performing the perceived interaction, stumbling and wobbling for example expressed an individual's frustration with poor leadership, while an aggressive tune subverted hierarchy and dominance, prompting the participant to consider different leadership strategies. The researchers find that followers, too, have power in the construction of the leader–follower relationship: The follower can actively withdraw from the relationship, fade unconsciously into a passive object or choose to be the initiator (Hujala et al., 2016: 23). This emphasises the role of the follower as an active partner in the relationship—as a co-leader, bearing responsibility for the leadership interaction.

Performance studies has emphasised that in an aesthetic interchange driven forward by a feedback loop, participants can experience themselves as subjects who have the power to influence others and whose actions are influenced by a collective interaction (Fischer-Lichte, 2005: 111). The subject in this sense is neither autonomous nor other-directed, but bears some responsibility for a situation that she or he has not created, but co-created. The analysis of the 'rave' points to opportunities for resistance and change, when people are 'not moved' or refuse 'to move'. Other analyses of dance interactions also point to the negotiated nature of leading and following. The dance perspective goes beyond common leadership research that view leaders as exceptional individuals and followers as an audience and an uninteresting mass. It brings into our perception the constant creation and decline of these structures, as well the plethora of possibilities that reside in these constant mutual negotiations and creations.

Literature

Barrett, F. (2012) *Yes to the Mess: Surprising Leadership Lessons from Jazz*. Boston: Harvard Business Review Press.

Bathurst, R. and Cain, T. (2013) Embodied leadership: The aesthetics of gesture, *Leadership* 9(3): 358–377.

Biehl, B. (forthcoming) Making 'people move': Embodied leadership in the work of techno DJs, *Research Note*.

Biehl-Missal, B. (2010) Hero takes a fall: A lesson from theatre for leadership, *Leadership* 6(3): 279–294.

Biehl-Missal, B. (2015) Let me entertain you? Some reflexions on the professor as a DJ, *Organizational Aesthetics* 4(1): 4–8.

Brook, P. (1968) *The Empty Space*. London: Penguin.

Chandler, J. (2012) Work as dance, *Organization* 19(6): 865–878.

Daly, A. (2002) *Critical Gestures: Writings on Dance and Culture*. Middletown, CT: Wesleyan University Press.

Fabius, J. (2009) Seeing the body move: Changing ways of seeing the dance. Kinesthetics and choreography at the end of 20th century, in Butterworth, J. and Wildschut, L. (eds.) *Routledge Reader in Contemporary Choreography*. London: Routledge, 331–345.

Fischer-Lichte, E. (2005) *Theatre, Sacrifice, Ritual: Exploring Forms of Political Theatre*. London: Routledge.

Fischer-Lichte, E (2008) *The Transformative Power of Performance: A New Aesthetics*. New York: Routledge.

Foster, S. L. (2011) *Choreographing Empathy: Kinesthesia in Performance*. London and New York: Routledge.

Gardner, W., Avolio, B., Luthans, F., May, D. and Walumba, F. (2005) 'Can you see the real me?' A self-based model of authentic leader and follower development, *The Leadership Quarterly* 16(3): 343–372.

Gilling, D. (2014) From Mahler to the movies: Physical empathy in orchestral leadership, in Ladkin, D. and Taylor, S. (eds.) *The Physicality of Leadership: Gesture, Entanglement, Taboo, Possibilities.* Bingley: Emerald, 109–134.

Goffman, E. (1959) *The Presentation of Self in Everyday Life.* London: Allen Lane.

Hansen, H., Ropo, A. and Sauer, E. (2007) Aesthetic leadership, *The Leadership Quarterly* 18(6): 544–560.

Höpfl, H. and Linstead, S. (1993) Passion and performance: Suffering and the carrying of organizational roles, in Fineman, S. (ed.) *Emotion in Organizations.* London: Sage, 76–93.

Hujala, A., Laulainen, S., Kinni, R., Kokkonen, K., Puttonen, K. and Aunola, A. (2016) Dancing with the bosses: Creative movement as a method, *Organizational Aesthetics* 5(1): 11–36.

Koivunen, N. and Wennes, G. (2011) Show us the sound! Aesthetic leadership of symphony orchestra conductors, *Leadership* 7(1): 51–71.

Küpers, W. (2013) Embodied inter-practices of leadership—phenomenological perspectives on relational and responsive leading and following, *Leadership* 9(3): 335–357.

Küpers, W. (2014) To be physical is to 'inter-be-come': Beyond empiricism and idealism towards embodied leadership that matters, in Ladkin, D. and Taylor, S. (eds.) *Physicality of Leadership, Gesture, Entanglement, Taboo, Possibilities.* London: Emerald, 83–108.

Ladkin, D. (2013) From perception to flesh: A phenomenological account of the felt experience of leadership, *Leadership* 9(3): 320–334.

Ladkin, D. and Taylor, S. (2010) Enacting the 'true self': Towards a theory of embodied authentic leadership, *The Leadership Quarterly* 21(1): 64–74.

Leary, M. and Kowalski, R. (1990) Impression management: A literature review and two-component model, *Psychological Bulletin* 107: 34–47.

Longstaff, J. S. (1996) *Cognitive structures of kinesthetic space reevaluating Rudolf Laban's choreutics in the context of spatial cognition and motor control,* Doctoral dissertation, City University, London.

Merleau-Ponty, M. (1962) *Phenomenology of Perception,* trans. C. Smith. London: Routledge and Kegan Paul.

Parviainen, J. (2002) Bodily knowledge: Epistemological reflections on dance, *Dance Research Journal* 34(1): 11–22.

Ropo, A., Parviainen, J. and Koivunen, N. (2002) Aesthetics in leadership: From absent bodies to social bodily presence, in Parry, K. and Meindl, J. (eds.) *Grounding Leadership Theory and Research: Issues and Perspectives.* Greenwich, CT: Information Age Publishing, 21–38.

Ropo, A. and Sauer, E. (2008) Dances of leadership: Bridging theory and practice through an aesthetic approach, *Journal of Management and Organization* 14(5): 560–572.

Springborg, C. (2010) Leadership as art—leaders coming to their senses, *Leadership* 6(3): 243–258.

Zeitner, D., Rowe, N. and Jackson, B. (2016) Embodied and embodiary leadership: Experiential learning in dance and leadership education, *Organizational Aesthetics* 5(1): 167–187.

5 Choreography (Collaboration and Space)

The notion of choreography is central to the dance discipline and has different definitions that revolve around movement, embodied practice and collaborative work. In organisation studies it is particularly promising to apply choreography not as a metaphor, but to consider actual forms of movement co-ordination and collaboration on a micro-level and choreography as an ordering structure and framework on a macro-level. Such an approach is able to explore issues that earlier studies on dance and organisation have pointed out, for example the idea that movements may be connected in ways that cannot be accessed with extant organisational theory:

> [M]ovements may not be highly scripted, elaborate or individualized. Rather than individuals being the focus it makes sense to focus on the movement of a mass, to the beat of the machine. However, the emotional side of this is important, too—the mass may come to feel they are moving in common. There is a we-ness and an emotionally charged atmosphere.
>
> (Chandler, 2012: 871)

Choreography in this chapter is used to explore ways of collaboration, with bodies that are co-ordinated and 'inscribed' through previous experiences and embodied forms of knowing and influenced by the space in which they move. With regard to issues such as kinaesthetic politics and kinaesthetic empathy the central argument of this book is further developed that dance and movement as a transitory practice builds on and expresses tacit and embodied forms of knowledge that are permanently negotiated, presenting opportunities for dynamics and change. In a first step, the interaction between people will be discussed as a social choreography, followed by the consideration of space that influences a site-specific choreography.

The notion of choreography originally relates back to the chorós (Greek) and chorus (Latin), denoting the defined place in which dance was performed. Choreography also includes graphós, graphein (Greek: writing, originally: scribing) in terms of inscription and writing. Dancing is writing in the space, inscribing the space not with letters but with ephemeral scriptures created through dance movements, appearing and disappearing—with the 'graphic', albeit fugitive, character of dance linking to media of explicit knowledge such as notation, language and images (Böhme and Huschka, 2009: 12).

Choreography is used here in the broad sense of the organisation of movement in time and space (Etchells, 2013), reflecting the understanding that choreography does not have a single definition, and is open to be used in ways that highlight different aspects of the choreographic process, product or profession. This is for example shown in the work of Corpus (2015) who have assembled many contemporary views on choreography that extend the original definition of choreography. Originally choreography is used to refer to the notation of movements in a dance performance, from the late 17th century onwards, which could be read by others and thus be re-performed, archived and studied, and has also been used to refer to the creation of dance from the late 18th century.

The practice of choreography in dance has seen a trend towards collaboration over the past hundred years. In modern dance practice, choreography has developed from hierarchical processes that we know from ballet or other pre-choreographed genres such as folk and social dances, into a collaborative practice (Klein, 2015). In classical ballet, a more traditional form of hierarchical leadership is executed, when steps and positions are delimited by style conventions and the structure of the music. The choreographer Kolo (2016: 44) finds that: "Similar to a Fordist organization, [in ballet] the aim is precision and variation on purpose or by mistake is to be avoided, leaving no space for individuality and creativity to the performers or workers." Depending on the dance form however, the interaction between the choreographer and the dancers has become increasingly cooperative.

An example of contemporary collaborative practice is William Forsythe who in a performance called "Bouncy Castle" made the audience the sole participants and let them create their own movement performance in an inflatable jumper. With regard to collaborative work with the dancers, Forsythe (in Odenthal, 2005: 24) once spoke of leadership as shared with performers: "All I am giving to dancers are my thoughts and not the results. I do not tell anybody what to do, I only tell them how to do it. I have created the right conditions, but movements manifest through the dancers themselves." Following the idea of choreography as co-created, Pirkko Husemann (2009) has analysed the work practices of Xavier Le Roy and Thomas Lehmen and also found that the idea of writing (graphein) in the space (choros) today does not see a sole choreographer as the author, rather promotes an understanding of the choreographer as an artist that works in relation to the dancers and to the collective. Choreography in this way can be a critical practice by probing new ways of interaction (Husemann, 2009: 138), and could also be an inspiration for studies on organisations.

The notion of choreography with regard to interaction has already been applied in the organisational world. Service processes and multi-dimensional business processes share with dance choreographies that they are performed with and through moving bodies and are transitory. Web-processes today are used to design, document and implement these choreographic processes, for example Business Process Modelling Notation BPMN 2.0, administered by the Object Management Group (Kolo, 2016: 37). One of the first choreographic process modelling software programmes is called "Let's dance". In this context, choreography refers to the interaction of different processes, which are controlled by different process owners and not one authority (these are called "Web Service Orchestrations"). Choreography is related to bottom-up, self-organising practices of collaboration. Such a self-organising nature of the interaction stands in a direct relation to studies that consider human interaction as a social choreography.

Social Choreographies

Choreography is considered in interdisciplinary dance theory beyond the world of dance as a form of communicating through movement, leading to an understanding of choreography as a way of moving in a social context. Choreography is not another metaphor, allegory or an image for social interaction, rather choreography is the very matter, the matrix, of social interaction denoting "its disposition and manipulation of bodies in relation to each other" (Hewitt, 2005: 11). This perspective builds on the notion of kinaesthetic politics, when movements are not 'natural' but support the social order or have the potential to change it. Such a view of choreography also is of particular value for organisation studies as it allows to access in new ways behaviour in organisations.

The notion of 'choreography' that refers to the organisation of moving bodies has already been used in organisation studies, albeit mostly metaphorically to point to some form of hidden influence that informs how people's bodies move and interact. For example, in keeping with a former EGOS conference theme "Beyond Waltz—Dances of Individuals and Organizations", Scott (2008: 220) has asked for the one who is "choreographing" individual's dances like a puppet player in organisations and society, looking for hidden influences on people's interaction. Following interdisciplinary dance theory rather than using dance as an analogy helps to understand what these hidden influences are and that they are performed and negotiated through kinaesthetic practices.

'Choreography' can be understood in terms of humans moving together, being influenced by social, cultural and also organisational rules. Choreography in this sense has been applied to explore human movement outside dance performances in everyday life. An interdisciplinary dance studies perspective considers social orders—as well as organisational orders—as 'choreographies', which emerge not in a stable, but in a dynamic and per-formative process through co-created and mutually influenced interaction of human bodies and things in space and time (Alkemeyer et al., 2009: 7). In the practice of dance as an art, interactions take place that mostly are choreographed and scripted to a higher degree, but which also are of relevance to the performance of social orders and the positioning of human actors within these choreographies. The perspective of dance studies is help-ful to understand how not only dancers, orchestra members, DJs and others interact through kinaesthetic empathy, but how organisational members, including leaders, service professionals and academics, draw on forms of knowing that reside in their trained and socialised bodies as the prerequisite for successful coordination.

Considering human movement practices not only suggests that there is someone like a puppet player making people 'move' (Scott, 2008: 220), but points to embodied influences that interdisciplinary dance studies in par-ticular account for: Movements in the social world are commonly not only reflecting but also reproducing social structures, convention and meaning, so it is worth considering the kinaesthetic mechanisms in place between par-ticipants. Similar ideas are voiced by organisational scholars that see move-ment as a dialogue between bodies that produces and preserves knowledge (Slutskaya and De Cock, 2008: 856). Related is Bourdieu's (1984) account of the habitus as a structured, structuring structure: Agents have incorpo-rated practical principles within their habitual, typical corporeal schema by way of immersion in human movement practices. In less regulated work situations, it is worth considering actual kinaesthetic practice that is con-stantly performed and negotiated, albeit being linked to established move-ment practices, tacit structures or 'choreographies'. These 'choreographies' are not explicit in rules and regulations, but are perceived through the body and are trained through bodily practice and constantly performed through movement interaction.

An example is research on teaching and lecturer–class interaction, in which teachers negotiate their 'positioning' (Pille, 2009). Literally, the posi-tion of the body in the classroom was found to influence students, who react to postures and gestures that they were accustomed to through other teach-ers as part of the specific organisational culture. For example the established teacher's authoritative crossing of the arms in a central space in front of the blackboard lead to silence and attention, whereas the young training teacher's efforts to attend to individual students while moving through the space led to a dissolution of the silent situation with students talking and moving as well.

Teacher training in a specific organisation can be seen as an indoctrina-tion that starts with the body and its movement (Pille, 2009). Training on the job serves to create an embodied knowing about the social choreogra-phy and is a rehearsal of practices that are 're-member-red' as movements of the extremities ('members') (Brandstetter and Völckers, 2000). Leadership and authority in this view is not determined by individuals' charisma for example, but is created through the mastery of the social choreography. This resonates the earlier discussion of the DJ-dancer interaction when dancers expect music artists to respond to and give kinaesthetic signs that drive forward the kinaesthetic feedback loop. Dance theory points to the relevance of embodied knowing to be able to perform such a social choreography.

Embodied knowing in other literary works also is related to the limbs and movements, for example in Marcel Proust's "A la recherche du temps perdu" episode with the cobblestone at Piazza San Marco: In the court of the Hotel de Guermantes the protagonist's foot steps on a stone, which then slightly moves under the weight, as did a stone many years earlier at the public square San Marco in Venice. The memory of the journey surprisingly and suddenly emerges as a mémoire involontaire with compelling liveliness. Paralleled is this in Proust's Madeleine episode when memory is triggered by the senses of smell and taste. The biscuit as well as the stone as an external object is more than a carrier of memory:

> Our memory, which we possess as beings equipped with a human mind, exists only in constant interaction not only with other human memories but also with 'things,' outward symbols. With respect to things such as Marcel Proust's famous madeleine, or artifacts, objects, anniversaries, feasts, icons, symbols, or landscapes, the term 'memory' is *not a metaphor but a metonym* based on material contact between a remembering mind and a reminding object. Things do not 'have' a memory of their own, but they may remind us, may trigger our memory, because they carry memories which we have invested into them, things such as dishes, feasts, rites, images, stories and other texts, landscapes, and other 'lieux de memoire.'
>
> (Assmann, 2008: 111, original italics)

From the dance perspective, it can be emphasised that the memory resides in the entire body and is brought to consciousness through movement and contact with the stone in this example. The memory does not reside in the stone or the mind, rather is dispersed through the entire body and can, as in this case, be triggered by one of the moving limbs. With regard to the original meaning of choreography as 'writing', choreographies 'inscribe' the body and leave traces that are memorised. Researchers from different fields have explored questions concerning memory, acknowledging that cognitive and bodily memory are not independent, but whereas the cognitive memory deletes constantly, the body doesn't forget (van Imschoot, 2010). Turning this the other way round explains the potential of dance as a research method (Chapter 7), when movement can bring to the surface knowing that resides in the body.

Co-creating the Choreography

Choreographies in organisational settings today however are not only about 're-member-ing' pre-scripted choreographies, but increasingly about self-directed or co-created choreographies. It has been argued that contemporary work cultures are characterised through a deconstruction of the disciplinary influence on the body that was prevalent in disciplinary societies (Alkemeyer et al., 2003: 7). This observation further speaks for the dance discipline that came to emphasise kinaesthetic experience and collaboration over theatrical representation. Not only in Fordist environments, movements were regulated, but also in banking and academia clearly contoured professional habitus were common with specific routines of bodily behaviour, attitudes, mimics and gestures. Many areas of work are not any more dominated by a traditional habitus that typically was achieved through a long-ranging integration into the work process, be it through training on the job measures followed by a life-long existence in a similar environment in which performative practices are produced and reproduced. People once referred to as a "bankier"—a word of French origin—often saw themselves in a tradition of the noble tradesman ("ehrbahrer Kaufmann" in German), with whom today's global investment bankers do not seem to have much in common despite of the dark suit, not in ways of moving, interacting and ethical thinking. In the Western academic world, the male white professor in brown tweet jackets, with glasses and a cigarette still is around in some universities, but higher education has seen changes with an increasing cultural and gender diversity and corresponding kinaesthetic politics. The historically grown professional habitus becomes less important in a globalised work force, with increasing mobility of products, work and people, and new career profiles emerging. Overall, with the decline of the habitus, interpersonal coordination becomes increasingly important.

In service work, standards of impression management and pre-choreographed routines, including habitual ways of appearing (e.g. Witz et al., 2003) appear to be partly substituted by participants employing kinaesthetic empathy to negotiate their own ways of interaction. Demonstrating a heightened empathy and ability to cooperate, which we also know from sports practice and dance, people re-adjust and re-member their own body in relation to others. Evidence was found in a forthcoming study I did with Christina Volkmann and a choreographer and students from a hotel school. We observed a connection created and negotiated through kinaesthetic empathy, which is something that participants improved during training on the job or had already developed during the time they interacted and worked together:

> Especially when you work with someone a long time, I think good teamwork is sort of knowing what your colleagues do without even looking. Like in the restaurant service, I know it is being very aware of

what your team members are doing around you, just being able to kind of function without thinking too much about it, and it just being very smooth, like the dynamics of the team. (. . .) So it's not when you're in a set job, generally after an amount of time you would really have a really good team dynamic or whatever with your colleagues.

Emphasising the element of routine achieved over time through kinaesthetic training, participants said that movement coordination exercises were "easier with your friends", as they felt "more comfortable", having "a different connection from people you don't really know". On participant spoke about enhancing the 'reading' of others: "I think it helps when you know someone; because if you know them quite well, you can kind of read each other better." Moving bodies stand in a dialogue or a kinaesthetic connection and create a network:

> I think you know each other's natural body movements, like how they react on a day-to-day basis; and if you know that, you can pick up on the smaller body movements that indicate what they're going to do. So it's maybe not instinct, but the fact that you know each other better. You pick up on the little things, whereas if you're doing it with someone you don't really know, you don't know almost like their little twitches that say they're going to do something, unlike you do with your friends where you know everything that they're going to do.

What is described here not only resembles the rehearsal of a dance routine, but is a social choreography. What can be seen here is an em-bodi-ment (when an influence is being incorporated, 're-member-ed' and becomes part of the bodily movement). Beyond this, participants through daily training develop their kinaesthetic empathy and understanding of the interaction that they found complicated and stressful when starting their job, and are able to coordinate each other and to improvise in work situations. Even if the space, service routines and verbal and non-verbal interactions are to some degree predefined, agents deploy their own kinaesthetic empathy to co-create the situation and develop their choreographies.

Social choreographies are influenced, but not finally determined through organisational norms and roles, they are not stable but constantly performed, and 'in motion'. Movements are commonly not only reflecting but also producing and reproducing social choreographies, so it is worth considering in detail these kinaesthetic exchanges between participants and forms of power and politics that inform collective agency again and again. Moving means to engage with performative aspects of existing orders and possibly changing them. A dance perspective points to ways in which these choreographies can be subtly altered, for example by going beyond the theatrical framework of representation and the sociological concept of the habitus, pointing to collaborative, co-created exchanges. These ideas need to be further explored by future research and are already taken on in practical trainings (Chapter 6). I shall now turn to the relevance of movement in relation to space, further discussing choreography as the co-created production of a social reality.

Site-Specific Performance

Choreographies are collaborative practices in which people use their kinaesthetic empathy and embodied understanding to coordinate their actions. In this sense, choreography can be applied beyond the world of dance to the social world and to organisations. While these social choreographies are negotiated between human agents, it is worth taking into account the choreographies people develop as a reaction to space and to other people moving in the space. In this section, I shall look at organisational spaces and their impact on people's movement and interaction and the resulting 'performance' of space. Early studies on dance and organisation have asked for research on how "movements relate to the space in which they take place and its physical characteristics and artefacts" (Chandler, 2012: 873). Integrating dance studies that have examined the impact of space on movement is promising, as organisation theory has shown an increasing interest in space but has only tentatively explored moving bodies in space and their relation to a specific site.

Organisational scholars have demonstrated a considerable interest in the materiality of space, but have paid only little attention to the moving body in the space (Dale and Burrell, 2008). Theorising the representative function of organisational space, earlier studies have explored architectural features that, for example, give banking buildings respectability and continuity, or express to the public who the corporation is and what it stands for. Organisational symbolists posit that architectures' impact can "influence our perception of reality, to the point of subtly shaping beliefs, norms and cultural values" (Gagliardi, 1996: 575). Following these insights, architectures and artefacts have been viewed not just as a system of signification operating in organisations but primarily as vehicles of aesthetic experience. Examples range from coffee shops, sports bars and boutiques to all kinds of flagship stores and shopping malls world-wide. These also have been discussed as ideological instruments that, like a lotus drug, make people "numb" and turn them into sedated consumers (Murtola, 2010). Emphasising the interactive dimension, marketing research has also provided many examples of atmospheres in which consumers resist and negotiate these atmospheres (e.g. Biehl-Missal and Saren, 2012). A dance perspective develops this view, showing that the atmosphere is not created by the space alone, but is co-created by the space and people, and people's moving bodies.

The diverse body of research on organisational space has already tentatively pointed to movement, positing that the nature of the space influences people's bodies and behaviour, whereby the 'generative building reflects movements, not static conditions', with the architecture being 'the choreography of movements' (Kornberger and Clegg, 2004: 1106). Whilst these authors use choreography as a metaphor without providing more detail on how to work with this broad term to analyse organisational space, a dance perspective can apply deeper insights on choreography to understand how the body moves in the static space, responding to and interacting with a space. Adopting a dance perspective allows to conceptualise the space as not only being in the 'in the air' within a stable architectural frame, but as being 'in motion'.

In the 20th century—the era of space as per Foucault—the definition of choreography has changed to include a more topographic understanding of arranging and ordering bodies in space and time (Klein, 2015: 19). Choreography originally includes a consideration of the space as the defined place in which dance was performed, as expressed in the notion of chorós (Greek) and chorus (Latin). Dance traditionally is situated in a specific place, with chorós being the lieu for bodies in motion that is placed and framed (Böhme and Huschka, 2009: 12). Taking into account the site-specific dimension and developing the discussion of choreography as interaction between moving bodies that are inscribed by social structures, an understanding of choreography as moving together in an organisational space is developed in this section.

Such an approach fills a gap in studies on organisational space and cultural studies that have conceived of the space and the architecture as a medium, but have neglected the role of the moving body. Routed in the belief that our culture is a written and text-based culture, which primarily shows in texts and monuments, including buildings, corporate architectures and even sites of remembrance, the performative side of (organisational) culture has often been insufficiently valued. Sociologist Jan Assmann (2008: 111) has in this context emphasised the role of the performing body and its movement as a medium, building a bridge to cultural memory that exists in the forms of narratives, songs, dances, rituals and symbols, and "requires for its actualization certain occasions when the community comes together". Components of culture existing in disembodied form thus require, for re-embodiment, not only institutions such as monuments and spaces, but also dances and performances that function as a medium, bringing to life and performing these spaces. Through movement in a space embodied, tacit knowing is explicated and transmitted kinaesthetically, with performers in their bodies knowing more than they can verbally express (Böhme and Huschka, 2009: 11). Organisational culture consequently also exists in site-specific choreographies, i.e. people's movement through the space that is transitory and non-discursive, but still is part of what makes our social interaction. An awareness of this issue can be seen in contemporary office buildings that encourage movement, circulation and conversation, going beyond mere decorative and symbolic aspects of architecture.

Particularly suited for an exploration of how people move in an organisational space is the concept of site-specificity from dance studies, which has considered the relationship of space and place and movement: Site-specificity posits a specific, aesthetic interdependence between the materiality of space, its context and people's movement (Kloetzel and Pavlik, 2009). The medium of dance and human movement serves to express, transform and embody the experiences and interactions with the site (Hunter, 2005: 368). This perspective emphasises that the experience of spaces is generated not through the architecture and the materiality alone, but through people's movement and interaction within the space. In this view, people are not only influenced by the space but co-create the space through their movements. The site influences the movements that people are likely to perform, and people's movements also 'perform' the space in a mutually re-enforcing process of creation. In such a process, participants through kinaesthetic experience also generate an embodied understanding of the space and their relation to it.

An understanding of the space influencing people's movement and social role has been voiced in dance studies, with Gabriele Klein (2015: 20, translated) considering choreography as "omnipresent in social spaces as an aesthetic paradigm, e.g. in the design of gardens and parks, urban planning, traffic infrastructure, architecture, . . . or in the organisation of mass events like military parades, party congresses, pop concerts or soccer games". An example for the influence of an environment on behaviour as a movement performance are the walks of King Louis XIV and his crowd in the park of Versailles, which were choreographed and based on detailed instructions on steps, body rotations, gestures and the direction of gaze of other strollers (Kolesch, 2006: 107). The material frame suggests and enables movements that are then performed and which create a kinaesthetic experience and embodied understanding of a social order.

The concept of site-specificity from dance studies posits a specific sensual interdependence between the space, its context and people's movements (Kloetzel and Pavlik, 2009; Pearson, 2010). Shifting the focus away from the stable and visual aspects of space towards movement with its embodied and fugitive nature acknowledges the dynamic and complex nature of organisational spaces.

Theatre director Peter Brook (1968: 57) in his book "The Empty Space" has once written that an empty space is open to all kinds of possibilities, is 'magic' because invisible ideas can be understood there through sharing experiences, through physical presence and interaction. While any space can be filled with a special atmosphere (Böhme, 1993), site-specific work explicitly integrates the characteristics of the space into the creation of the atmosphere. Avoiding the decontextualisation of blank theatre space, site-specific work is "informed by the smallest details of the sites in which it exists; it celebrates, and sometimes interrogates, a site" (Kloetzel, 2010: 136). Artists move beyond the entrenched Cartesian dualism and into a phenomenological one by focusing on the lived bodily experience of place.

Site-specific dance and performance is associated with performances that take place outside a decontextualised theatre space, in a specific space that is the reference point. In site-specific performance, there is no 'fourth wall' separating stage and audience like in classical theatre, but performers and audience co-create the experience that bears a specific relationship to the site. The specific atmosphere, physicality and tactility of the location helps to communicate values of a culture to the audience. Beyond this, site performances do not only entice people to experience sites aesthetically, but to perceive them as cultural locations in a nexus of personal stories and interpretations. Mike Pearson (2010: 42) uses the term "archaeology", with site performances offering an archaeological reading of a site, exposing audiences to a rich layering of cultural knowledge and connecting them to the space in a different way. Site-specificity emphasises that the material frame of the surrounding architecture with its historical, social or aesthetic function provides hooks for people who open themselves up to the space and embrace the space and engage in a dialogue with the space. Site-specific dance in this sense turns places whose history and relevance may often be in the dark into places replete with rich histories and memories (Kloetzel, 2010: 135). In times of globalisation and increasing homogenisation, the local places still serve as a touchstone, and site-specific work is relevant and transferable to organisations that are active globally but also use space in different ways to connect to environments.

Dance studies is a field that focuses on dynamics and change, also specifically in social choreographies and when spaces are 'performed'. The mimetic practice is an appropriation and a bodily reproduction and a new construction of reality that is non-discursive and that also offers the potential of innovation towards past and presence. Kinaesthetic practices that precede and parallel cultural memory transmitted via text and words provide an interesting area for the re-embodiment and re-negotiation of culture within and through organisational spaces.

In organisational contexts, as well as in artistic site-specific performances, the moving body is used as an instrument for introspection and reflexion, and the engagement with the site allows to challenge interpretations and meanings of the space. Illuminating different perspectives and amplifying marginalised voices asks questions such as: Whose history of this place is accurate? Is the use and understanding of the place beneficial for a community? (Kloetzel and Pavlik, 2009: 5). As in other contexts, these artistic performances do not give easy answers but enable audiences to play with their own associations and develop their own interpretations through what they have experienced when watching, witnessing and reacting to the movement. Addressing participants in kinaesthetic ways, a site-specific performance opens up opportunities to experience space in novel ways and to uncover deeper meanings of it. The site-specific performance is seen as a "translation of place that heightens our awareness of surroundings", as a result of a "reading" of place on physical, sensual, intellectual and emotional dimensions (Kloetzel and Pavlik, 2009: 2). In this regard the site dance genre is considered to offer a "high level of hope for the human-environment relationship", functioning as both a model and a guide for future human-place exchanges (Kloetzel and Pavlik, 2009: 124).

The notion of site-specificity can be transferred to organisations not only when artists use corporate spaces to present a choreography, but also when organisational members, relating to the space and its context, create an atmosphere that is site-specific and create a kinaesthetic experience that informs their embodied understanding and thinking. Their everyday movements in organisational space can be compared to those of performers in a site-specific performance as they can be seen as dynamic responses to the site and the space that are phenomenological responses, born of being in the moment and open to the here and now of the site phenomenon (Hunter, 2005: 374). In addition to this, the concept of site-specific performance also links to forms of kinaesthetic training (Chapter 6) and research methods (Chapter 7) when organisational members use dance as an arts-based method to express and give form to their embodied knowing about work issues, creating a performance that is specific to their organisation. Site-specific dance practice is in this sense referred to in a range of examples to access issues of power and culture that are linked to a space. In this chapter, I shall address different settings, including examples of how artists engage with organisational space in form of an uninvited artistic intervention. The idea of social choreography is developed with regard to collective dancing and movement in several spaces ranging from pragmatic collective movement in a museum to ecstatic dancing in a techno club.

The Lived Space and the Non-place

Through movement, spaces change and people change as well. Organisation studies have mostly considered space, but not people's movement in spaces. The concept of site-specific performance develops approaches to space that use phenomenology. Bachelard (1969) and Lefebvre (1991) are referenced in studies on site-specific dance and have been used in organisation studies as well, as these writings are concerned with the complexity of experiencing space and place. A broad range of elements including sensory, cognitive, spatial, ideological, historical and psychological factors play together and influence our perception. These elements overlay the 'organised space' that has been planned and executed by architects, interior and exterior designers, and engineers, who distributed of objects, symbols and people within a physical space to ensure order and control. Such deliberate constructions of space give material form to functional aspects and attempts to control certain settings and behaviours. Spatial planning is the outcome of the dominant relations of production, it represents the dominant spaces in any society (or mode of production) (Lefebvre, 1991: 39).

The notion of 'lived space' (Lefebvre, 1991: 39) denotes the phenomenologically experienced space of 'inhabitants' and 'users' overlaid with imaginary and negotiated spaces, going beyond the deliberately planned architectural elements. Rather than simply filling the space according to the intentions of the planners, people's living actions always go beyond what is intended, suggested or imposed. People engage with the physical space through all kinds of behaviours including movements. This has also been referred to as spatial practice (Lefebvre, 1991: 38), the realm in which spatial planning and lived experiences in the space occur and also may challenge each other.

Site-specific performance as an engagement with the planned space may emphasise, challenge and distort aspects of lived experience that relate to the space by questioning links between people's action and the space and its context. Amplifying these issues through spectacle, site dance aims to engage participants in a dialogue. It opens up a discursive space that reveals the power structure inherent in the site and people's lived experience in the space, illustrating the potential dynamics of the site in new ways.

Most site-dances refer to the planned or organised space and illuminate these spaces in new ways, bringing out different layers of experience of these settings and furthering an exchange between the site and the people concerned with or affected by the site. Audiences typically are challenged to consider the role of particular places in historical or social events, or the role of a place as a background for human achievements and failings. In the lived space resides a potential for resistance against dominant spheres, which is emphasised by dance.

To illustrate how the 'lived space' is performed beyond the 'planned space', I will give some examples that relate to the concept of the non-place (Augé, 1995), as a space of homogenised corporate culture. The term refers to spaces that are not specific to a certain local and social context, but can be found anywhere and are designed to be passed through or consumed rather than appropriated. Non-places are sites through which people pass or travel, for example airports, shopping malls, supermarkets, hotels and superhighways (whether for information or vehicles) and other sites that people hurry past. Those spaces retain little or no trace of people's engagement with them, the venues could be anywhere, and remain anonymous.

Artists from different fields have begun to critically explore such empty corporate spaces. The painter Verena Landau for example (Biehl, 2007) has chosen as non-places annual shareholder meetings and her six-pieced edition "pass_over" deals with the passing over of shareholders from the world outside into empty and cold atmospheres where space, time and identities seem to be annihilated. Not only outer appearances become unified, but people's bodily movement also is depicted as restricted and diminished. Landau's series shows large halls and deserted staircases leading down, illuminated by white, sterile light that does not relate in any way to the time and season outside. A single person standing on a staircase gives an idea about the loneliness of people in the system. People don't gather socially, walking alone, are observed by security personnel, directions are predetermined and

Figure 5.1 Digital Photomontage "pass_over02" from Verena Landau's Edition
        pass_over (2006)
Courtesy of the artist

limited. The lack of personality and individuality, also in movement, is dotted by only small signs of resistance, a walk against the flow, a colourful outfit, a constrained face.

These shareholder meetings became a place of artistic resistance when performers intervened and invaded organisational space. Rimini Protokoll, a group of theatre directors, used Daimler's 2009 Annual General Meeting as a ready-made event and constructed it as a theatre play entitled "Hauptversammlung". Two hundred theatre spectators were embedded, against the will of the company, into the carefully staged event. Participants in their feedback emphasised the relevance of their experience of space, using the metaphor of a 'bath' in the mass (Biehl-Missal, 2012: 221) that referred to an embodied understanding of organisational interaction and power, created through different material and performative elements in situ.

Capitalism has constantly reconstructed relations of space, also via the acceleration of the turnover of capital—for which stock markets and shareholder meetings are representative. Non-places are associated with a global rise in mobilities that do not only take place on the corporeal level but extent to global trade, capital streams and information technology, and require people to become mobile as well (Augé, 1995). Site-specific work with movement in such a space in many ways connects conceptually to global trends and their effects on people's bodily and local existence.

Another example of resistance in corporate non-places is Reverend Billy and the Church of Earthalujah, who invade retail spaces and also banks with semi-ironic preacher performances. The performance activist Bill Talen has been sentenced to jail for initiating theatrical preacher performances in his role of 'Reverend Billy' in front of Disney stores where he appeared with a Mikey Mouse crucified to a wooden cross, and in Starbucks stores, which he criticised as 'theatrical environments' that disguise the exploitation of workers including coffee farmers and baristas (Biehl-Missal, 2013: 83). Artistic critique goes beyond an intellectual message, residing in the aesthetic experience created through singing and shouting performers that interrupt capitalist ideology and sterile consumption atmospheres (Biehl-Missal and Saren, 2012).

Reverend Billy and Savitri D. with the Church performed a political ritual called "Naked Grief" in the lobby of Deutsche Bank in Barcelona, Spain (D. and Talen, 2011). The participants started weeping dramatically, Savitri disrobed and Reverend Billy implored the "God of Deutsche Bank" to stop

Figure 5.2 Reverend Billy from the Church of Life After Shopping attempting to exorcise bad loans and toxic assets from the Bank of America ATM in Union Square, New York City

By Jonathan McIntosh—Own work, CC BY-SA 3.0, https://commons.wikimedia.org/w/index.php?curid=6719064

investing in CO_2-emitting coal-fired power plants. Coal was poured over the head and shoulders of Savitri with the crowd singing "Earthalujah!" The performance is site-specific as it invaded a corporate space, creating a lived space full of symbols and other interpretations, putting the moving body in the centre. The dramaturge deliberately used her naked body to refer to the 'mother (earth)', through the aesthetic experience of the performance providing a different understanding of the impact of global coal industries on human beings and the aliveness of human protest. I recommend that readers look online for the pictures (for reasons of copyright), while a similar protest is shown below.

The strategy of disrupting clean organisational space can also be seen in a performance by Melanie Kloetzel (2010) called "The Sanitastics". It took place in the homogenised, corporate landscape of the Walkway System in Calgary, Canada, a closed and tunnelled space with fluorescent lights, video-surveillance and temperature control consisting of a series of pedestrian bridges that pass over busy streets over several miles. The 'in-between', travelling nature of bridges made the artists ponder about their role in the city, and brought up multiple questions of identity: Who were we in such a place of conformity? Among the business suits and random shoppers, who stuck out? (Kloetzel, 2010: 140). Dancers explored the space by occupying parts of bridges, through movements that did not progress linearly through the space interrupting the flow of traffic, and highlighting the incessant and uniform movements of the non-place. They dressed in bizarre costumes and distributed organic litter that was then cleaned in an act of a performance—pointing to the strangely antiseptic, unnatural landscape into which the corporate workers insert themselves daily (Kloetzel, 2010: 140). The movement of travel as a linear movement from one end of the space to the other was interrupted by performers lingering and resting. These disruptions pointed to questions of the power of urban planning and its impact on people's daily lives and further opportunities of change through movement.

Bodies in the site-specific works speak of human existence and pose critical questions: Choreographer Stephan Koplowitz (1999) for example took on ideas from Taylor and Gilbreth's early motion studies in organisations in a site dance "Kohle Körper" ("Coal Bodies") inspired by the physical design, the purpose and history of the Kokerei Factory in Essen, in the former coal mining area of Germany. Dancers' bodies are rubbing and grinding against the historic coke ovens, embracing them and jumping against these objects of everyday work. Making efforts to surmount a 50-meter-long groove "like mice in the cage", dancers express a mix of feelings about work from devotion to aggression, including "neurotic movement patterns amongst the coke ovens [that] speak of human powerlessness" (Albrecht, 1999). A critique of monotonous industrial labour that challenges the bodily but renders numb the mind is performed. Movement-based site work, due to its focus on process and impermanence, can critically engage audiences in ways that question the use of the site and its impact on people.

The idea of adding more meaning to a place can further be illustrated by an example of site-specific dance that shows how personal and cultural history can be linked to the topography. The director Louise Ann Wilson, having lost her sister of a brain tumour, has chosen the title "Fissure" to refer to the limestone landscape in Yorkshire Dales, England, and also to the similarly looking groove separating the two cerebral hemispheres of the brain. Participants and dancers walk along on uneven ground, dancers move in and within the cracks of limestone, using the same choreographic material but producing different movements that are not fully synchronised. This has been interpreted (Hartung, 2014: 9) with regard to informational units that are not processed in the same ways by different parts of the brain when being affected by a tumour, and also as a metaphor of emotions, moving through the body. Movement also is a pars pro toto when attention is drawn to the living body that does not function the way it is expected to. This performance illustrates how metaphor in dance works and also draws attention to the connection of embodied knowing and movement, which is central to the book. Participants have entered "a strange borderland between inner and outer world, an inside turned outward (and vice versa)" (Hartung, 2014: 12). In the performance, these issues are not verbalised as a rational argument, rather they are transmitted via the kinaesthetic experience of moving over and standing on the uneven ground, watching and participating in the dance.

Memory Place and Museums

A strength of site-dance is to turn non-places, organised spaces or natural spaces into places of meaning for the society and for those who participate—as illustrated by the previous examples. The concept of 'non-place' (Augé, 1995) stands in contrast to Pierre Nora's (1989) idea of a 'memory place', encompassing geography, historic contexts, symbolic connotations, collective memory and identity. Site-dance in this regard moves a place towards a 'memory place' that stands in a tradition that is brought back to life, for the moment of the performance and beyond. In this section, I shall look at research in the field of museum studies that links to organisation studies and has started to consider not only the organised space but the 'lived space', i.e. people's movement in the space and the resulting experience. Moving through a space affects what people think of the space, of themselves and their culture. Site-specific movement in a museum is a social choreography that is 'political' in the sense of kinaesthetic politics as it serves the purpose of creating an embodied understanding of the individual and society, its relation to the past and present.

Museum studies, similar to marketing and organisation studies in today's aesthetic economy (Böhme, 2003), have increasingly valued the atmosphere in spaces. Museums have become more people-centred, emphasizing visitors' experiences (Henning, 2006: 91), while historically, many of the 19th-century museums were crowded, chaotic and dark, remaining incomprehensible to many visitors. Museums today not only serve to conserve and display art, history, technology and other topics, rather they try to "mass produce and retail 'unique experiences' that are phenomenologically real" (Hein, 2000: 80). These experience can be seen as a co-creation of visitors moving in the space. In this sense, organisational spaces are not only 'like a theatre' with a carefully styled scenography, rather spectators co-create the atmosphere through actual movement in a choreography. Relating to the notion of kinaesthetic empathy, visitors, by creating a site-specific performance, are doing something that is similar to what Böhme (2003: 73) has described as aesthetic work, and can be referred to as 'kinaesthetic work': People perform movements that endow spaces with an atmosphere that is a corporeally perceived quality of feeling. This kinaesthetic practice creates an embodied understanding of the present and the past, which is not produced by the space alone.

Architectures in museums invite specific movements that tell stories and create an embodied understanding of the context. Scholars have in this regard critiqued museums as fundamentally ideological institutions, with the space producing a certain kind of citizen. In museums the use of itineraries served to control movement of visitors who in turn corporeally follow the narration: Movement of visitors typically is channelled, slowed down and 'ordered', bringing them on a 'respectful' distance towards artefacts and suggesting a humble attitude towards the nation and its history (Bennett, 1995: 181). A contemporary example of itineraries is the BMW museum in Munich, Germany. Moving on ramps that connect the locations of the exhibition, mobility and movement in motor sport and technology are not only symbolised but experienced through the moving body (Biehl-Missal and vom Lehn, 2015: 246). 'Rolling' through the space smoothly and effortlessly, visitors can embrace the tidy and spacious arrangement of ramps that is reflected in the sleek and polished automobiles that are not only rationally perceived as special and valuable, but sensually and kinaesthetically experienced in the joy they propose in ideal conditions of driving—without however giving space to ponder about alternative, ecological and more sustainable forms of (public) transportation.

Providing the material basis for a site-specific performance, museums encourage visitors to create a choreography by moving through the space and in relation to each other. A prominent example that provides an embodied understanding of history is the Jewish Museum in Berlin, with its postmodern part by Daniel Libeskind. Referring to a piece on the atmosphere in this museum (Biehl-Missal and vom Lehn, 2015: 249), I shall elaborate on movement in particular. The space can be seen as physical provocation for the visitor, offering stairs with varying numbers of steps, floors that are tilted horizontally and torn vertically, as well as hallways in which the ceilings narrow down. The bodily movement of visitors becomes an endeavour of 'balancing' their personal understanding of German-Jewish history, of 'finding a position' within this historical context literally on the bodily level in the space and in their minds as well. The movement is not only specific to the site, but relates to and incorporates the historical context and the history of Jews and other groups that were murdered by the Nazis in Germany. Moving through the 'garden of exile' for example, visitors struggle with the tilted floor that stands in an angle to the outer space, corporeally suggesting an understanding that the exile for German Jews remained difficult and always required efforts to adjust.

The museum has hollow void spaces with walls of bare concrete, standing separate from the rest of the building. Daniel Libeskind explained that the voids of the museum refer to that which can never be exhibited when it comes to Jewish Berlin history: Humanity reduced to ashes (Stiftung Jüdisches Museum Berlin, 2013). Being exposed to the naked walls and cold space that is narrow but high, the subject slows down movement, stands still and is attentive, almost feels pressed down by an imaginary weight. The art work "Shalechet" (Fallen Leaves) by Menashe Kadishman fills one of these voids, the Memory Void, with countless small 'screaming' faces made of the silent and cold material of iron. Visitors are allowed to move through this installation. Walking over the metallic faces fills the space with a cold cling-clang sound that may provoke associations of the industrialised murder that progresses with a rhythmic tone, in this case driven forward by the movement of the visitor. The uneven floor forces visitors to bow down their head, looking at the screaming faces, so as not to tumble. Movement

Figure 5.3 Jüdisches Museum Berlin
Photo: Ernst Fesseler

is slowed down, a corporeal 'attitude' of shame and sadness is created as a site-specific performance.

Choreographies are in museum spaces created by individuals in the space and also permanently negotiated among visitors. Researchers in the field have shown that visitors move through spaces, kinaesthetically reacting to other people's body language, postures, movements and corporeal involvement (Biehl-Missal and vom Lehn, 2015: 250). Building on sociological accounts of the interaction order, where all those visitors present in the space monitor each other's conduct and create an environment of mutual observation and observability (Bennett, 1995), the kinaesthetic negotiation of this practice has moved into the focus of analysis. Video-based studies of people's interaction in museums indicate that the exhibition experience is a practical achievement produced by people present in interaction, in the space and around the works of art (vom Lehn, 2013). Visitors respond to but also resist efforts to organise the space, complementing and altering the atmosphere in a form of 'kinaesthetic work' within the material frame provided by museum managers, designers and curators. When visitors move from one exhibit to the next, they transform their bodily arrangements in the space, interacting with their kinaesthetic empathy:

> Visitors manage to accomplish their concerted onward movement without, or with only little, talk by reacting to their aesthetic perception of the situation. They monitor, often from the corner of the eye, other visitors' "state of involvement" with the exhibit and notice changes, for example in posture, that suggest they might be ready to move on. When [. . .] a visitor turns to the right and moves away from the exhibit she is looking at with a friend, the latter may treat that bodily turn as an invitation to leave and align with that invitation by taking a step backward and turning his upper body to the right. In other cases, visitors feel encouraged to bring their engagement with the exhibit to a close when other people arrive in the locale.
>
> (Biehl and vom Lehn, 2015: 250)

Such a silently negotiated choreography includes all those who are present in the space. It has also become apparent that, for example, children's small and fast steps when running around in the space disturb the slow routine of other individuals. Visitors, for the practical purposes of gaining access to the works, may use different movement strategies that have been described in the media as well: For example, visitors stand behind a crowd viewing a painting and wait for a gap to open into which they then "sprint", or they "use a stroller as a weapon to get close to paintings" (Berkow, 2006). These strategies when deployed as part of a traditional museum visit would be sanctioned. Sprinting into gaps, barging right through the crowds or slipping under people require accounts that explain the unusual conduct. These accounts help normalise the situation in the museum and highlight that the prime purpose of the visit is the encounter with original works of art; whilst 'normally' they would integrate into the overall choreography, the situation of stress requires them to deploy unusual techniques and break out of the overall choreography.

The Techno Club

Moving bodies perform a social choreography that also is specific to a site, creating an embodied understanding of social life in present and in past. This idea already is echoed in contemporary choreographies and dance research: Matthias (2015) for example posits that urban spaces are a permanent choreography, in which inhabitants use their physical senses, kinaesthetic empathy and a shared physical knowledge of urban surroundings to respond to the interpersonal dynamics and create a "groove" that is specific to particular cities. Developing this idea, I shall refer to a study in which I explored a techno club as an organisational space that links past and present, creating a collective understanding through movement and dance (Biehl-Missal, 2016).

Human movement and dance is non-discursive but nevertheless existent as an important medium of social and cultural practice (Klein, 2004: 250). Creating an embodied understanding and collective, cultural memory, dance has played a role in many societies (Assmann, 2008: 112), and has also been attributed a strong social function when commemorating the most important event in recent German history: the Fall of the Berlin Wall in 1989. Twenty-five years later, an increasing number of books appeared that relate techno music to German identity and history, with the embodied rave allegedly anticipating a mental reunification of Germany (e.g. Denk and von Thülen, 2012). The emerging techno movement that 'took place' in Berlin is linked to this moment in time (Klein, 2004: vii).

Literature on site-specific dance stresses strong links between performance and tradition, with dance unearthing the memories linked to place and creating links between grand narratives and particular sites (Kloetzel and Pavlik, 2009: 27, 28). What goes on in techno clubs such as Berghain can be conceived of as a site-specific performance. The practice of dance in the techno club is related to narratives and the site of Berlin in many ways. The techno club Berghain resides in an impressive architecture (Rüb and Ngo, 2011) and has been labelled "the best techno club in the world" by many voices ranging from the *New York Times* to *DJ Mag*. Its particular embeddedness in the social and historical tradition of the formerly divided and radical Berlin is celebrated in popular media, for example *The New Yorker* (Paumgarten, 2014) and the *Rolling Stone* (Rogers, 2014). The club building, a neo-classical heating power plant from the 1950s, is situated between the East (the Friedrichshain quarter) and the West (Kreuzberg) and therefore named Berghain, symbolising the reconciliatory function of techno music and dancing that is said to have reunited Berliners from East and West (Denk and von Thülen, 2012). Berghain draws on its historical tradition and strengthens its existence through what Bell and Taylor (2011: 6) refer to as continuing bonds between the past and present: Rather than positioning the past as something other, distinct and separate from the present, the organisation and the crowd maintain relationships with the past and recreate a temporal relatedness through aesthetic practices in the space.

People's dancing and movements in a techno club can be compared to those of dancers in a site-specific performance as they can be seen as dynamic responses to the site and the space that are phenomenological responses, "neither objective or subjective, (but) borne of being in the moment and open to the here and now of the site phenomenon" (Hunter, 2005: 374). The medium of human movement in such a site-specific performance functions as a means to give form to experiences and interactions with the site, no matter whether the body is in an explicit artistic or another cultural context. Choreographer Meredith Monk emphasises that for site-specific work she listens to what the space is saying to her (Kloetzel and Pavlik, 2009: 45). Ravers too, like professional dancers and other leisure dancers (Klein, 2004: 163), and people moving through an organised space like a museum, react consciously and unconsciously to spatial features and the social or organisational context and generate new understandings that are perceived not solely cognitively but through the body.

Figure 5.4 Berghain techno club in Berlin, guests lining up in the morning hours
Photo: Author

Monuments provide a material focus through which we are able to experience and co-create our understanding of presence and past. In Berghain, the internal room structure, with some small and intimate spaces and other big and massive spaces, has been described by architects as an "Ermöglichungsarchitektur" ("architecture of enabling") (Rüb and Ngo, 2011: 146), emphasising that space does not only exert control but also provides opportunity. The space does not have many dead ends, even restrooms being transitional spaces. The design facilitates constant movement and circulation of guests, encouraging less predictable interaction and encounters, which also are part of the social choreography in this case. Many other examples of organisations are well-known where buildings are specifically designed to encourage spontaneous conversations and exchange, for example expressed in Steve Job's opinion on the Pixar building. In the techno club are several kinds of hidden and sparsely illuminated spaces, including darkrooms, which are populated during the weekly 36-hour parties that spill into Monday mornings. These motives stand in the traditions of a city with a history of post-world war depression, poverty and inflation (Biehl and vom Lehn, 2016): They evoke Berlin's intriguing 1930s subculture, portrayed by popular writers such as Christopher Isherwood, the bohemian city in a world on the very brink of ruin. Contemporary artworks (Berghain, 2015) influence the atmosphere such as Wolfgang Tillman's sexualised body photography and Piotr Nathan's 25-meter Panorama "rituals of disappearance" in the basement foyer reminding of the ritual feast, the maelstrom of music.

On the dance floor techno music echoes the architecture's industrial connotations and stands in the mix with history, with techno as a post–cold war folk music inclusive to everyone, and resident DJs reflecting on their East-German pedigree (Nodge, 2014). Dancers move as an element of the mass to the four-to-the-floor beat, stomping in strict time, often bare-chested. Dancing as a mimetic practice (Klein, 2004: 245) not only mimes and expresses the rules and practices of a community, but also performs, keeps alive and constructs anew a specific Berlin narration through the medium of the body and its movement.

The site-specific dance articulates and rehearses contemporary social conditions and reaches beyond the space of the organisation into society—again functioning as a form of kinaesthetic politics. The 'industrial badassness' that is in the air, and forms of unrelenting, solitary raves (Paumgarten, 2014), and the vibe that rave studies refer to (St John, 2009: 93). Opposing the capitalist version of time of many other European cities with decadent, weekend-long parties (Rogers, 2014), allows people to be part of an alternative experience. Different contemporary conditions are rehearsed and practiced, when, for example, dancing is not heteronormative and gendered, and not centred around DJs celebrating hierarchy and fame, and diverse behaviours can unfold in a space that opens up opportunities.

When people's bodies perform movements and interact in an organisation with its space and artefacts, this keeps alive and gives persistence to social choreographies as structures that are non-discursive, invisible and that may exist within or alongside explicit norms. With regard to corporations today, also at the circulation of staff between offices and in halls, and at the tempo and rhythm of walking and steps in an organisation can be considered a performance of culture. Traditions and culture through these media are transmitted, performed and kept alive, like in dance and human social movement (Cohen Bull, 1997). This means that movements and literally trodden paths as embodied forms of organisational culture would also inhibit change and restrict 'progress' (from the Latin word: progredere, moving forward). Dance studies as a critical perspective looks at these non-discursive practices and envisions opportunities for change. The following section of the book will consider forms of kinaesthetic training that address these implicit choreographies that may be site-specific and informed by kinaesthetic empathy, and are constantly negotiated between people. The last section of the book looks into dance-based research methods that allow researchers to access these embodied understandings of an organisation.

Literature

Albrecht, K. (1999) Mensch, Arbeit und Maschine, Getanztes Kokerei-Projekt in Essen. *Neue Ruhr Zeitung*, 27 August. http://www.pact-zollverein.de/medien/_deutsch/_pdf/presse/ps1999/kokerei_rez.pdf.

Alkemeyer, T., Boschert, B., Schmidt, R. and Gebauer, G. (eds.) (2003) *Aufs Spiel gesetzte Körper: Aufführungen des Sozialen in Sport und populärer Kultur*. Konstanz: UVK Verlag.

Alkemeyer, T., Brümmer, K., Kodalle, R. and Pille, T. (eds.) (2009) *Ordnung in Bewegung: Choreographien des Sozialen. Körper in Sport, Tanz, Arbeit und Bildung*. Bielefeld: transcript.

Assmann, J. (2008) Communicative and cultural memory, in Erll, A. and Nünning, A. (eds.) *Cultural Memory Studies: An International and Interdisciplinary Handbook*. Berlin and New York: de Gruyter, 109–118.

Augé, M. (1995) *Non-Places: Introduction to an Anthropology of Supermodernity*, trans. J. Howe. London: Verso.

Bachelard, G. (1969) *The Poetics of Space*, trans M. Jolas. Boston: Beacon Press.

Bell, E. and Taylor, S. (2011) Beyond letting go and moving on: New perspectives on organizational death, loss and grief, *Scandinavian Journal of Management* 27(1): 1–10.

Bennett, T. (1995) *The Birth of the Museum: History, Theory, Politics*. London: Routledge.

Berghain Ostgut GmbH. (ed.) (2015) *Berghain: Kunst im Klub*. Berlin: Hatje Cantz.

Berkow, I. (2006) Sometimes, viewing art involves breaking a full-court press. *New York Times*. http://www.nytimes.com/2006/03/29/arts/artsspecial/sometimes-viewing-art-involves-breaking-a-fullcourt-press.html?_r=0 (Accessed 1 Sep 2016).

Biehl, B. and vom Lehn, D. (2016) Four-to-the-floor: The techno discourse and aesthetic work in Berghain in Berlin, *Society* 53(6): 608–613.

Biehl-Missal, B. (2007) Aesthetics of emptiness: Verena Landau's pass over reflects the cold atmosphere of shareholder meetings, *Aesthesis* 1(2): 80–85.

Biehl-Missal, B. (2012) Using artistic form for aesthetic organizational inquiry: Rimini Protokoll constructs Daimler's annual general meeting as a theatre play, *Culture and Organization* 18(3): 211–229.

Biehl-Missal, B. (2013) Atmosphere of the image: An aesthetic concept for visual analysis, *Consumption, Markets & Culture* 16(4): 356–367.

Biehl-Missal, B. (2016) Filling the 'empty space': Site-specific dance in a techno club, *Culture and Organization*. DOI: 10.1080/14759551.2016.1206547.

Biehl-Missal, B. and Saren, M. (2012) Atmospheres of seduction: A critique of aesthetic marketing practices, *Journal of Macromarketing* 32(2): 168–180.

Biehl-Missal, B. and vom Lehn, D. (2015) Aesthetic atmospheres in museums: A critical marketing perspective, in Macdonald, S. and Rees-Leahy, H. (eds.) *Museum Media: International Handbook of Museum Studies*. Hoboken, NJ: Wiley-Blackwell, 235–258.

Böhme, G. (1993) Atmosphere as the fundamental concept of a new aesthetics, *Thesis Eleven* 36(1): 113–126.

Böhme, G. (2003) Contribution to the critique of the aesthetic economy, *Thesis Eleven* 73(1): 71–82.

Böhme, H. and Huschka, S. (2009) Prolog, in Huschka, S. (ed.) *Wissenskultur Tanz: Historische und zeitgenössische Vermittlungsakte zwischen Praktiken und Diskursen*. Bielefeld: transcript, 7–24.

Bourdieu, P. (1984) *Distinction*. London: Routledge and Kegan Paul.

Brandstetter, G. and Völckers, H. (eds.) (2000) *Remembering the Body*. Ostfildern-Ruit: Hatje Cantz.

Brook, P. (1968) *The Empty Space*. London: Penguin.

Chandler, J. (2012) Work as dance, *Organization* 19(6): 865–878.

Cohen Bull, C. (1997) Sense, meaning and perception in three dance cultures, in Desmond, J. (ed.) *Meaning in Motion: New Cultural Studies of Dance (Post-Contemporary Interventions)*. Durham, NC: Duke University Press, 269–288.

Corpus (2015) Theme: What is choreography. www.corpusweb.net/tongue-6.html (Accessed 1 Aug 2016).

D., S. and Talen, B. (2011) *The Reverend Billy Project: From Rehearsal Hall to Super Mall with the Church of Life After Shopping. Critical Performances*, edited by Alisa Solomon. Ann Arbor: University of Michigan Press.

Dale, K. and Burrell, G. (2008) *The Spaces of Organisation and the Organisation of Space: Power, Identity and Materiality at Work*. Basingstoke: Palgrave Macmillan.

Denk, F. and von Thülen, S. (2012) *Der Klang der Familie: Berlin, Techno und die Wende*. Berlin: Suhrkamp.

Etchells, T. (2013) Definition of choreography. *Corpus—Internet Magazine for Dance Choreography Performance*. http://www.corpusweb.net/answers-0107.html (Accessed 1 Jul 2016).

Gagliardi, P. (1996) Exploring the aesthetic side of organizational life, in Clegg, S., Hardy, C. and Nord, W. (eds.) *Handbook of Organization Studies*. London: Sage, 565–580.

Hartung, H. (2014) Fissure(s): Walking/dancing along, across and in-between lines of difference, *Performance Research* 19(6): 5–14.

Hein, H. (2000) *The Museum in Transition: A Philosophical Perspective*. Washington, DC: Smithsonian Institution.

Henning, M. (2006) *Museums, Media and Cultural Theory*. Maidenhead: Open University Press.

Hewitt, A. (2005) *Social Choreography: Ideology as Performance in Dance and Everyday Movement, Post-Contemporary Interventions.* Durham, NC: Duke University Press.

Hunter, V. (2005) Embodying the site: The here and now in site-specific dance performance, *New Theatre Quarterly* 21(4): 367–381.

Husemann, P. (2009) *Choreographie als kritische Praxis: Arbeitsweisen bei Xavier Le Roy und Thomas Lehmen.* Bielefeld: transcript.

Klein, G. (2004) *Electronic Vibration: Pop Kultur Theorie [Electronic Vibration: Pop Culture Theory].* Wiesbaden: VS Verlag.

Klein, G. (2015) Zeitgenössische Choreografie, in Klein, G. (ed.) *Choreografischer Baukasten. Das Buch.* Bielefeld: transcript, 17–49.

Kloetzel, M. (2010) Site-specific dance in a corporate landscape, *New Theatre Quarterly* 26(2): 133–144.

Kloetzel, M. and Pavlik, C. (2009) *Site Dance: Choreographers and the Lure of Alternative Spaces.* Gainesville: University Press of Florida.Kolesch, D. (2006) *Theater der Emotionen: Ästhetik und Politik zur Zeit Ludwigs XIV.* Frankfurt: Campus.

Kolo, K. (2016) Ode to choreography, *Organizational Aesthetics* 5(1): 37–46.

Koplowitz, S. (1999) Kohle Körper. http://www.koplowitzprojects.com/kokerei.html (Accessed 1 Aug 2016).

Kornberger, M. and Clegg, S. (2004) Bringing space back in: Organizing the generative building, *Organization Studies* 25(7): 1095–1114.

Lefebvre, H. (1991) *The Production of Space.* Oxford: Basil Blackwell.

Matthias, S. (2015) Groove feeling: Somatischer sound und partizipative Performance, in Ernst, W-D., Mungen, A., Niethammer, N. and Szymanski, B. (eds.) *Sound und Performance: Positionen, Methoden, Analysen. Thurgauer Schriften zum Musiktheater, Vol 2,* Würzburg: Königshausen und Neumann: 591–607.

Murtola, A.-M. (2010) Commodification of utopia: The lotus eaters revisited, *Culture and Organization* 16(1): 37–54.

Nodge, N. (2014) Crate Diggin': Sounds from East Germany. https://www.fabriclondon.com/blog/view/crate-diggin-norman-nodges-sounds-from-east-germany (Accessed 1 Aug 2016).

Nora, P. (1989) Between memory and history: Les lieux de mémoire, *Representations* 26(1): 7–24.

Odenthal, J. (2005) Paradigmenwechsel im Tanz. Ein Gespräch mit William Forsythe, in Odenthal, J. (ed.) *Tanz. Körper. Politik.* Berlin: Theater der Zeit, 22–26.

Paumgarten, N. (2014) Berlin nights: The thrall of techno, *The New Yorker* 24 March: 64–73.

Pearson, M. (2010) *Site-Specific Performance.* Houndmills and Basingstoke: Palgrave Macmillan.

Pille, T. (2009) Organisierte Körper: Eine Ethnographie des Referendariats, in Alkemeyer, T., Brümmer, K., Kodalle, R. and Pille, T. (eds.) *Ordnung in Bewegung: Choreographien des Sozialen. Körper in Sport, Tanz, Arbeit und Bildung.* Bielefeld: transcript, 161–178.

Rogers, T. (2014) Berghain: The secretive, sex-fueled world of techno's coolest club. *Rolling Stone.* http://www.rollingstone.com/music/news/berghain-the-secretive-sex-fueled-world-of-technos-coolest-club-20140206 (Accessed 1 Aug 2016).

Rüb, C. and Ngo, A. L. (2011) Das Berghain: Eine Ermöglichungsarchitektur, *Arch+, Zeitschrift für Architektur und Städtebau* 201/202 (March): 146–151.

Scott, R. (2008) Lords of the dance: Professionals as institutional agents, *Organization Studies* 29(2): 219–238.

Slutskaya, N. and De Cock, C. (2008) The body dances: Carnival dance and organization, *Organization* 15(6): 851–868.

St John, G. (2009) *Technomad. Global Raving Countercultures*. London: Equinox Publishing.

Stiftung Jüdisches Museum Berlin (2013) The Libeskind building. http://www.jm berlin.de/main/EN/04-About-The-Museum/01-Architecture/01-libeskind-Build ing.php (Accessed 1 Sep 2016).

Van Imschoot, M. (2010) Rests in pieces: On scores, notation and the trace in dance, in Van Imschoot, M., Van den Brande, K. and Engels, T. (eds.) *What's the Score? On Scores and Notations in Dance*. http://sarma.be/oralsite/pages/What%27s_ the_Score_Publication/ (Accessed 1 Nov 2015).

Vom Lehn, D. (2013) Withdrawing from exhibits: The interactional organisation of museum visits, in Haddington, P., Mondada, L. and Nevile, M. (eds.) *Interaction and Mobility: Language and the Body in Motion*. Berlin: De Gruyter, 65–90.

Witz, A., Warhurst, C. and Nickson, D. (2003) The labour of aesthetics and the aesthetics of organization, *Organization* 10(1): 33–54.

6 Kinaesthetic Training (Arts-Based Interventions)

Artistic domains have been used as an inspiration and a practical tool in the world of business, going beyond the mere metaphor of organisations as theatre, jazz bands, orchestras and dance. So-called arts-based or artistic interventions bring people, practices and products from the arts into organisations to help address issues the organisations are facing (Berthoin Antal, 2009: 4). This young field also started to incorporate practices, processes and people from the world of dance. Contemporary choreography generally thrives beyond the art world in an ever-expanding field of applications, including scholarly and political activities (Butterworth and Wildschut, 2009), work with young people (Svendler Nielsen and Burridge, 2015) as well as individual self-exploration (Klein et al., 2011). The use of dance in organisations seems a natural continuation of its historic tradition of exploring social, spiritual and political contexts.

In this chapter I will discuss the practice of dance as 'kinaesthetic training' or arts-based intervention in an organisation. Given the relatively young history of dance-based interventions, I start with a brief consideration of artistic interventions in organisations, and situate dance as a human movement practice in this context, pointing to its particular potential in today's dynamic times. This is followed by a discussion of factors that may have inhibited the use of dance as a practical tool, as well as factors that speak for the use of dance. These more general considerations are then followed by a section on the impact of arts-based interventions. A framework is then used to discuss dance as an arts-based intervention: The matrix draws on the previous chapters and includes a continuum ranging from dance as metaphor to kinaesthetic experience and practice, and another axis that presents more individual aspects of kinaesthetic politics and group aspects that are concerned with choreography.

Arts-based methods in organisations are commonly used to generate innovation, to help members to see more and to perceive things differently, to activate them and to foster collaborative ways of working and personal development (Berthoin Antal and Strauß, 2013). Such an approach stands in a broader context of challenges for leadership and management in the

21st century, where innovative and creative, dynamic and human-centred approaches that commonly are related to the world of arts gained new relevance. Arts-based interventions emphasise embodiment over assuming disembodied and purely cognitive actors, linking to studies on the aesthetics of organisation and the body. These initiatives aim to develop abilities that are linked to aesthetic, sensual perception and forms of working 'like an artist' that are not advanced by methods commonly used in management education and training such as case studies and other tools.

The moving body and its perception is at the centre of dance-based movement exercises. In general arts-based methods comprise, to mention just a few: artists in residence, organisational theatre, theatre workshops, poetry workshops, art collections, workshops with painting or sculpture, music projects and presentations by orchestra conductors or jazz bands, and many more. The wide variety of different forms of arts-based interventions have seen increasing scholarly attention over the past years (e.g. Barry and Meisiek, 2010; Johansson Sköldberg et al., 2016). Also the wider context of these interventions, including the role of the intermediaries who bring together artists and organisations has been explored (Berthoin Antal, 2012). While the use of theatre in organisations goes back to the 1990s, other artistic practices such as music workshops, poetry and painting sessions are also used for more than decade now. Arts-based interventions take a wide diversity of forms and involve all kinds of arts. There are short projects lasting only a few hours, as well as those lasting days, weeks or months.

Dance is the youngest field of practical engagement in this context. Until today few scholars have used the practicality and corporeality of dance as a development and learning tool (e.g. Hujala et al. 2016; Matzdorf and Sen, 2016; Springborg and Sutherland, 2016) while management consultants and dancers (e.g. Kolo, 2016; Ludevig, 2016) have facilitated dance-based workshops for a longer period. Relatively few instances of the applications of dance in leadership programmes around the world have been found until now, but promising assessment for growth of the field has been given (Zeitner et al., 2016). Only for a couple of years now, dance practitioners, choreographers, dance pedagogues and trainers have discovered the world of business as an opportunity to work with people and organisations. Dance-based methods can come in different forms as arts-based initiatives. These sessions must not be confused with dance classes that rehearse steps such as the waltz or samba. Rather, participants move one-to-one, in pairs, or as individuals, through space, performing different exercises and movements. Exercises include dialogue and personal reflection on issues related to work and organisation. Often directed by one or two facilitators with a background in organisational consulting and dance, their variety of pair and group movements, postures, rhythm and improvisation allows participants to physically experience and 'better understand' various scenarios, which stand in a relation to their life in the organisation.

Dance used for organisation and leadership development has deeper roots than obvious at first glance, and is more than just another addition to extant arts-based interventions. Movement is a constitutive element of different social forms of play, all kinds of ceremonies and rituals, of public presentations and, as discussed in this book, interaction in organisations. These interactions do not build on special movement techniques like in dance and in sports, but on kinaesthetic empathy and embodied understanding of the social and organisational context. Historically, the body and its movement played a role in organisations, and as a practical intervention dance in early industrial times was used to develop individuals' movement repertoire that was restricted to simple and repetitive movement sequences. Laban (2011) suggested modern dance education to balance restricted work movement, but also to further conscious perception of personal movement impulses—this idea can be found in contemporary workshops that invite leaders and all organisational employees to 'sense' their impulses and develop individual or group movements employing their kinaesthetic empathy rather than rehearsing specific steps, postures and habitus. The use of dance in organisations today just reflects and responds to contemporary demands.

Dance foregoes the verbal, discursive content and the figurative artefact, is embodied, transitory and fugitive. The particular opportunities of dance in general reside in the non-discursive, in cooperative modes of working, and also in embodiment on the level of kinaesthetic politics (Lepecki, 2013). It needs to be discussed in which ways dance workshops can constitute a site of experimentation for new forms of embodied social interaction in organisations. As early metaphorical works on dance have highlighted, organisational change relates to time, spaces and routines and is affected by abilities such as "walking the talk" that may not only be a dance analogy, but actually depends on the negotiation of many movement-based, timely and spatial interactions and related experiences.

Organisational scholars have already come to suggest that dance-based exercises could "serve well in calling into question and re-constructing the everyday practices and routines which we usually maintain and reconstruct unconsciously in everyday working life" (Hujala et al., 2016: 28). Movement and embodied activities typically create and affirm relationships among social actors, connecting individual actors to a community. This has been established for other dance activities in a social group or leisure crowd where people move in specific ways in relation to each other and to a space (Alkemeyer and Schmidt, 2003: 83). Embodied activities in this sense form relationships in organisations as well and, through kinaesthetic change, may change organisations. In this section, kinaesthetic training is discussed with regard to how people's movement affects their relationship to each other as kinaesthetic politics and choreographies including leader–follower interactions and group collaborations.

Bringing dance theory and organisational practice together leads to a consideration of dance 'as a practice of critique'. The critical potential of dance reveals itself through different kinaesthetic experiences that are facilitated by movement practice, not so much through rational judgment. Husemann (2009: 138) has argued that critique can be practiced through a kinaesthetic mode of working that facilitates other experiences: "Certain artistic methods of working are critical in the sense that they test new forms of community, friendship, and complicity, as well as experiment with new forms of production." The sense of community is of importance here, although community is not the aim, but a precondition for a political practice as an aesthetic activity (Klein, 2011: 24). In experimentally structured spaces of experience alternative social practices can be tried out. Dance-based practices with organisational members create new experiences and access embodied forms of knowing that can be used to work on organisational issues. Engaging with forms of leadership and work hierarchies in order to disarticulate or re-articulate their structure, can influence the tacit and embodied structures in organisations. These social choreographies are performative and emerge in dynamic and practical processes through the interaction of human bodies in space and time, whereby they are influenced, but not finally determined through subjective intentions and organisational norms and roles. The dance perspective inspires us to explore further the ways in which these choreographies can be reproduced as well as altered through embodied interaction.

Barriers and Supporting Factors

Dance is a rather new method to work on organisational issues, and I shall reflect on some barriers that have inhibited the use of dance and some more arguments that support the application of dance. Dance gaining ground only decades after other arts-based practices have been established corresponds with the development of dance as an academic discipline. The dance discipline has been neglected or undermined by a number of elements. They include ephemerality and transience, the perception of dance negatively as a 'female' art, little documentation and social status, and its very nature that is seen as an activity of the body rather than mind, particularly in conservative and religious thinking (Butterworth and Wildshut, 2009: 2).

All of these factors that have inhibited dance practice can be found in organisations: Management is conventionally considered a rational and cognitive issue, whereby bodies and emotions are ignored, and dance workshops were met with scepticism (Hujala et al., 2014). The emphasis on the body in a positivist and seemingly rationalist organisational environment has not particularly helped workshops that centre around the moving body. When rationalist and masculine behaviours dominate organisations and emphasis is on the mind rather than on the body, working with moving bodies is something that may be perceived as divergent.

During my field research I have interviewed an HR manager who reported a failure from a workshop: A group of male managers only hesitantly took part in a "dance workshop" and eventually ended it because of their cultural understanding that two men ('hard guys') must not touch each other and dance together. In ballroom dance exercises that I have participated in myself, I noticed uneasiness of the male dance partner (which in that case went along with increased polite British small talk to diminish embarrassment) when we were asked to assume the basic position with a hand on the shoulder and the back. The issue of touch in ballroom dance exercises has been reported to lead to initial embarrassment, with participants noticing how rare it is for business colleagues to have any physical contact (Powell and Gifford, 2016: 139). Practitioners with regard to this issue often report that it is much easier to work with improvised group movement in business organisations (Ludevig, 2016). The positive aspect of touch however has been expressed with regard to workshops in retirement homes and hospitals, where sometimes the act of touching, along with rhythm and surfacing happiness gets participants to connect with themselves and others (Zeitner et al., 2016: 178).

When using dance, one needs to be aware of a range of preconceptions and traditions of restricting the body. Organisational members and women in particular have internalised tacit forms of oppression of bodies and may feel exposed and threatened through these exercises. Another obstacle to the use of dance-based methods is that bodies in organisations have been silenced and during the long tradition of physical and service work have been employed in many ways that are unsafe and destructive. It is a question of ethics and respect for the human body to critically reflect this tradition and not to further constrain bodies in organisations. Authors point to limitations of dance-based tools, for example participants' hesitations to use physical space and body positions in creative and free ways, as if they felt limited by patters of everyday work. Engaging the body involves participants on a very personal level, evoking a variety of emotions and questions. Whereas joy and passion often emerged in the dance-based interventions, it was reported that participants also experienced fear, anger and frustration, which leads to the requirement to provide a safe environment for employees not only to open up but also to deal with emotions and issues that emerge in the process (Bozic Yams, 2016: 162).

Dance as an ephemeral, non-verbal practice may lead to a performance but does not leave an artefact and a persistent object of evidence. Art works such as sculptures and paintings in comparison have a longer history in organisations. They often are present as a financial investment in the form of an art collection, decorating walls and spaces in banks and all kinds of companies. They also can be used for art workshops with employees to further their perception capabilities. The can also serve to change the environment, communicating values to those present or potentially affecting the 'creative' ways they interact at work (Schiuma, 2011: 180).

The ephemeral and abstract form of dance can however be considered as promising for interaction. Dance, in its forms and procedures, generates experiences and knowledge that involves all our senses and allows dynamic and changing relations, a constant reorganisation of the abstract and the concrete (Pakes, 2009). In contrast to other arts, dance focuses on the process of abstraction, rather than on the product such as a sculpture, a painting or a theatre play. It thus allows for different understandings of leadership and followership and embodied interaction at work. Artistic interventions generally aim to provide aesthetic experiences that engage people's emotions, stimulating organisational members to reflect on their feelings at work, both positive and negative, and to address them in more open ways than usually possible in a work context (Berthoin Antal and Strauß, 2013: 31).

Given their interactive and open nature, artistic processes cannot be fully controlled. Participants' associations and thoughts can diverge from what was intended in an organisational context. The use of arts in organisations has therefore also been referred to as "arts-based interventions" (e.g. Biehl-Missal, 2014) or "applied art", for example "applied theatre" (Lempa, 2016). The later perspectives originating in the humanities and arts use a more distanced label to point to the fact that the use of arts in organisations often diverges from art 'without purpose' in the cultural realm and is tied to efforts to enhance organisational efficiency. Art as an aesthetic form that addresses the body and embodied knowing can in this context also unfold a manipulative potential trying to enforce organisational values and attitudes, when specific interpretations are suggested rather than encouraging participants to play with their own associations and develop their own meanings. Some forms of theatre for example provided simple answers and solutions rather than encouraging participants' questions (Clark and Mangham, 2004). The fine arts have a long history of political, social and economic involvement and positioning, and art in organisations also can offer multiple views, inspiration and emancipatory impulses. Studies that use the term 'artistic interventions' from organisation and management studies emphasise what is for them the unusual, the use of art in organisations that brings together two so fundamentally different realms. They are also aware of the ambiguous nature and the potential of the arts in organisational context, which depends on how artists, organisations and people work together (Berthoin Antal, 2009).

Working together with movement typically involves multiple performers, as dance is a social art form. It goes back to a tradition of thousands of years when dance and the body serves as a medium for communication, a medium that links the past and the present as a storage of memory and experience, and as a ritual medium of bringing together people and cultures. Also today, through our moving bodies we communicate our needs, wants and feelings, we socialise, interact and negotiate with others. When applied in management and leadership development, dance does not need musical instruments or scores, or a written text as in some theatre performances. Dance neither requires other material such as paint and crafts material, and also does not require much technical knowledge, because dance as bodily movement is a natural part of people's interaction. Anyone can move and dance on an everyday level and with regard to the communicative function of the body, leadership and organisational interaction can benefit from acknowledging a kinaesthetic approach. Researchers have suggested dance-based interventions can help practitioners access emotions stored in the body and expressing them through movement more freely and beyond the constraints of role playing (Bozic Yams, 2016). The abstract form of dance and movement that goes along with open reflection also is a creative counterpoint to every-day work in organisations that often is understood in quite 'rational' terms or at least organised in concrete categories.

Connecting minds and embodied knowing, artistic interventions help people to tap into feelings and hidden understandings that guide their decisions and actions (gut-feeling), a competence that is said to be of particular importance in contemporary situations of uncertainty and ambiguity (Berthoin Antal and Strauß, 2013: 31). Practitioners in the field concur that in dance-based exercises in particular the active involvement of participants and the physical experience leads to "ah-ha!" moments and enables changes in behaviours and mind-sets that cannot be achieved through an intellectual presentation of facts and theories (Powell and Gifford, 2016: 133). Moving bodies in particular create an energetic atmosphere, as discussed in this book with reference to multiple issues such as site-specific dancing and leadership. This factor supports the idea that arts-based interventions are about energising, creating new experiences for participants (Berthoin Antal and Strauß, 2013: 31). The aspect of energy pertains to physical movement and in this view is closely related to the emotional energy employees need to work on organisational issues and possibly to negotiate and change them. Artists can create and release energy that has been pent-up in individuals or groups by restrictive rules, structures, and mind-sets in the organisational culture. The kinaesthetic energy can help embodied knowledge to emerge and to create new experiences.

In contrast to other arts-based interventions that use text and musical instruments, in movement exercises, moving bodies interact without theatrical roles and musical status and hierarchies. Dance is promising to create a space for a group that is beyond traditional hierarchies and allows for a different exchange. Movement exercises foreground the connection to others and an understanding of elements that drive our interactions, including shapes and rhythms, whereby individuals can bring in their personal rhythm and create a confidence that resides on the corporeal level. A consequent engagement with the transitory nature of human interaction, for which dance is the paradigm par excellence, develops critical considerations about the creation and, more importantly in organisations today, the dynamic negotiation and change of the organisational order.

Impact of Dance-Based Interventions

The use of arts in organisations cannot be managed in ways that are similar to other rational and cognitive business processes and they cannot be evaluated by looking at the bottom line or financials. Rather artistic initiatives are assumed to have a wide-reaching impact. When the impact of arts-based interventions across different art forms generally is difficult to measure, dance-based interventions pose an even greater challenge for practitioners and researchers. Dance as an ephemeral, non-verbal practice may leave a performance but no artefact and persistent object of evidence. The fugitive and abstract nature of content and outcome may also be a barrier for dance-based workshops, but it also is reported that clients have shown "an overt acceptance [. . .] that the desired shifts in behaviour and mindset would be difficult or impossible to 'measure' and that desirable outcomes would be seen in the form of subtle behaviour changes that could, nevertheless, have real implications for the effective implementation of the capital projects" (Powell and Gifford, 2016: 135). Providing movement experiences that address forms of embodied, tacit knowing, these exercises do not deliver predicted learning outcomes, rather enable participants to discover and develop new body-based skills that need their time to evolve (Springborg and Sutherland, 2016: 102).

Exploring the impact of dance-based methods in organisations means looking at a smaller number of interventions that have a younger history and practice of employment, accompanied by fewer publications (Bozic Yams, 2016; Zeitner et al., 2016). The use of dance however is documented in dance studies publications and in interdisciplinary fields and in practical areas that use the body as a natural medium to work with people in social contexts. I shall hence draw on findings on artistic interventions in general and enhance them with insights from dance theory and other publications that report on the use of dance, as well as my own field research in this area, building on the categories developed in the sections of the book.

In an extensive review of literature and practitioner experience in this area, evidence for a range of effects of arts-based interventions was found that can be located at the individual, group and organisational level, whereby these levels tend to be interconnected. Organisational impacts are usually spill-over effects from benefits individuals and groups have reaped from an experience with an artistic intervention (Berthoin Antal, 2009: 45). Berthoin Antal and Strauß (2013) present the seven aspects of: relationships, organisational development, personal development, collaborative ways of working, artful ways of working, seeing more and differently, and activation. Personal issues typically referred to include the development of technical skills (communication; self-presentation); better understanding of one-self and colleagues; improved intrinsic motivation and commitment; greater "passion"; more energy; and enhanced creativity (Nissley, 2010). The subsequent discussion will show that dance exercises do not emphasise concrete skill development such as non-verbal communication, rather have their focus on issues of awareness and perceiving things in new ways, kinaesthetic empathy and a subsequent enhanced understanding of leadership and collaboration.

Arts-based initiatives may also have an impact on the public domain and wider society in which the organisation is embedded (Berthoin Antal et al., 2011). The use of the arts within organisations may help to find new sources of funding and to strengthen stakeholder dialogues, for example via exhibitions that are accessible to the public. Dance-based interventions stand in a tradition of community work, although organisations so far rarely have included external stakeholders in projects, neither as participants or spectators. Until now, the young field is more concerned with individual, group and organisational issues that will be the focus here. The use of arts in organisations also is driven by an interest on the side of artists, who are discovering organisations as a site for their own creative and social production, as well as an opportunity to earn a living. Their reports have also driven forward research on dance and organisation.

Arts-based interventions generally may generate an impact on the organisational level that has been described as influence on organisational assets and resources (Schiuma, 2011: 157). Amongst the tangible organisational assets that may be enhanced are office space designs; information and communication technological infrastructure; and other artful products such as an art collection. Intangible assets such as organisational culture, reputation, knowledge, skills and attitudes have been the focus of artistic interventions in organisations as well. In a management studies framework, arts-based initiatives may thus influence operational capabilities, the processes that are used to deploy assets effectively in the market place. As an example, service capability through confidence and improved team co-ordination may be fostered by dance workshops, which in this line of thinking contributes to customers' experience of the service encounter. Arts-based initiatives may also have an impact on dynamic capabilities that create, extend or modify the resource base and help sustain competitive advantage. Important dynamic capabilities are those that support organisational learning, innovation and change. By contributing to capabilities on such a broad level, arts-based initiatives in this view can help to enhance organisational performance and create value.

Given the interdisciplinary scope of the book, some aspects of dance have already been linked to these points, and further references will be built without trying to reproduce such a framework. The difficulty of theorising dance in dance studies has been discussed with regard to the nature of dance as a bodily, transitory practice (Brandstetter and Klein, 2013). When bringing dance and organisation studies together, this challenge gets worse with regard to the positivist and quantitative tradition of the discipline and tendencies to present different kinds of models. Often typical management graphs are challenged in scholarly debates for their reductionist layout and Taylor (2014: 6) has argued with regard to these "silly social science scales", that "there is great power in the particular and in an artful approach to the particular based in staying with your senses and not knowing." The lesson that the arts offer to the social sciences is to embrace subjectivity and contextuality to reach deeper insights than provided by any scale. In this way I can only warmly encourage those interested in the topic to practice these exercises in a self-directed or other-directed context to get a 'feeling for' movement in organisations and what it means for one self personally.

To discuss the impact of dance-based interventions in organisations, the interdisciplinary approach that I am using offers two continua that are combined to create a classic two by two matrix (see Table 6.1). They build on the first four chapters in the book that were used to approach dance and organisation, namely dance as a metaphor, kinaesthetic empathy, kinaesthetic politics and choreography. I found them useful in developing a view on the practical field of movement exercises in organisations that builds on the theoretical foundation that was developed with an interdisciplinary approach. The two continua were labelled as follows: The 'view on dance' includes 'metaphor' and 'kinaesthetic', referring to the understanding of dance as a metaphor and as an actual kinaesthetic practice that builds on kinaesthetic empathy. Of course, when dance is applied in organisations participants are present with their bodies, so the view automatically includes both aspects, but one aspect usually predominates. The argument was that dance can serve as a metaphor to make organisational issues appear in a new light, for example leadership and gender, but provides further insights when actually applied so that it involves the kinaesthetic dimension. On the other continuum, the 'social dimension of the organisation', is 'kinaesthetic politics' as a movement practice produced by the individual, and 'choreography' as a collaborative practice when people interact and coordinate their movements.

Kinaesthetic politics is used as a starting point as it addresses individuals and their movement, also with regard to gender issues and personal attitudes. In the first field in the bottom line (metaphor/kinaesthetic politics) we find dance workshops that work with metaphor when dance presentations illustrate leadership, decision making and gender issues. Choreographies, on the right side of this matrix, include a larger number of bodies that are co-ordinated in the moment, being 'inscribed' through previous experiences and embodied forms of knowing. The collaboration serves to produce a metaphor when bodies give form to their embodied knowing on work and leadership (metaphor/choreography). The practical kinaesthetic experience in the upper line of this table is particularly important for individuals' awareness of the body and the training of connecting to others through body language (kinaesthetic/politics). Exercises for groups in this line on the right (kinaesthetic/choreography) involve the sensing of space, similar to a site-specific performance, or provide a different understanding for the nuances of leading and following, cooperation and team collaboration through shared and co-created choreographies.

Table 6.1 Categorisation of dance-based interventions in organisations

View on the organisation	Kinaesthetic	—awareness of the body —body language and connection	—collaboration and co-ownership —leading and following —site-specific walks
	Metaphor	—illustration of leadership —presentation of gender in leadership	—group sculptures and Gestalten
		Kinaesthetic Politics	Choreography
	Social dimension of the organisation		

The aim is to present the broad range of practices that are reflected in the publications and conference presentations in the young field and the experiences that I have made conducting original research with dance-based methods, and from interviewing practitioners in the field and participating in workshops. The examples given may not be covering all existing approaches but they serve to illustrate where these approaches converge. The table shows what has already been produced and points to trends that are promising for further activity and research in the field, again drawing on the central trajectories developed in the other theory sections.

Metaphor/Kinaesthetic Politics

Illustration of Leadership

Dance as a metaphor for organisations enables new views on organisational issues. As a metaphor, dance performances that are presented and watched by an audience of organisational members can serve to illustrate organisational issues such as leadership and work interaction in ways that go beyond the verbal discourse or a written text as in a management handbook. Dance as an art form performs these issues, addressing the senses of the audience. There are many parallels to artistic dance performances that illustrate kinaesthetic politics, questioning how gender, race and social categories are linked to movement (Chapter 3).

Starting with the notion of kinaesthetic politics, bodily movement in these cases serves as a metaphor and as a starting point to access topics such as leadership and followership. Sharing this approach, other arts-based interventions such as paintings for example may serve as a metaphor when discussed and interpreted by organisational members in workshops to see differently aspects of their work and to enhance their capabilities of abstract sense-making (Biehl-Missal, 2015c). Dance presentations by professional dancers or by amateurs working with a choreographer commonly are used as a metaphor for individual performance, teamwork and leadership processes.

A choreographed piece can for example be observed to gain insights into a managed but creative collaboration between choreographer and dancers. Kerr and Lloyd (2008) report findings from a presentation that included a choreographer giving the group of dancers a set of tasks that were performed drawing on basic dance steps, varying energy, mood and speed, with participants working solo, in pairs of two or in groups, in the beginning reacting to commands, then to more general directions until in the end creating their own choreography. This is followed by a discussion between observers and dancers about the processes and their strategies to deal with constraints and expectations—that can be transferred to other leadership situations.

> For example, one participant felt that the choreographer/manager was too directive and 'inhibited the creativity of the dancers.' That participant felt the dancers would have been better off without a choreographer who inhibited independent construction of the 'work'. Other participants felt the innovation in the dance did require a leader to insure controlled disorder and authentic learning of creative habit.
>
> (Kerr and Lloyd, 2008: 494)

Such a performance shows processes of co-creation that are important for contemporary work and pertain to many artistic interactions, be it theatre groups or jazz bands. Choreographies show that a dancer's role can range from being an instrument to a co-owner (Butterworth, 2004). Other metaphorical insights that were reported include that individual participants understand themselves better as part of a group that moves together and requires motivation to collaborate creatively, taking into account opportunities for transformative critical thinking regarding constraints and leadership (Kerr and Lloyd, 2008: 495).

Watching a performance can also be used to exemplify the constant process of decision making that choreography and management share. Kolo (2016) in this sense refers to Burrows (2010: 40), who wrote in his "Choreographer's Handbook" that "choreography is about making a choice, including the choice to make no choice." When creating a choreography, participants are constantly challenged to make a decision, mostly about questions such as to repeat a movement or leave some degree of improvisation and to what extent. The final performance then gives evidence of the range of decisions that were taken. It can also be read as a result of different leadership dimensions that depend on the cooperative process and the ability of participants to solve issues and to exchange their views in verbal and non-verbal ways.

Presentation of Gender in Leadership

Exploring dance as a metaphor for organisations, Chandler (2012: 876) asked where it would take us if we saw work as dance, suggesting that this view "would give close attention to gendered bodies acting in physical and social space." With regard to the notion of kinaesthetic politics, it was discussed that dance performances including ballet and postmodern dances, historically have dealt with ways of how gender is created through movement onstage and in social life. Dance presentations in organisations in the context of personnel development workshops similarly serve as a metaphor for gender relations in organisations. They can present and question gendered interaction and can help to develop participants' assessments of gendered movement in organisations and leadership situations.

Exercises in leading and following through methods of ballroom dancing build on traditional gender performances that have also been discussed in dance scholarship. In a critical account on heterosexual pair dancing, Polhemus (1988: 177) finds unequal power balance that he links to everyday social practice:

> The male led. The male chose with whom he would dance. The male (if the female consented to dance with him—for she always had, if nothing else, the terrible power of rejection) physically supported the female. The male determined the rhythm and the style of their relationship in time and space. The female—as in 'real life'—followed his lead.

Gender performances in pair dancing have been linked to performances in everyday life, and can be seen, in the context of kinaesthetic politics, as a rehearsal of gendered identity construction. These ideas are echoed in contemporary dance-exercises in organisations, as described by Powell and Gifford (2016: 139):

> While dancing, the woman has to feel exactly where the man's weight is placed in order to receive signals from him as to when and where he wishes her to move. Even though they have a set choreography, the man still has to lead the woman through the transfer of his body weight whenever they are dancing together and connected by one or both hands.

Classical ballroom dance can be seen as a vehicle for the operation of gender politics, which do not seem to fit well to contemporary ideas of diversity and equal opportunities in organisations, when heteronormative behaviour is presented and rehearsed. For example, organisational members can find themselves in a dance workshop, exposed to the following scene: A pair is dancing "a short passage where the woman resists the man's lead and another passage where she does not contribute her own weight and allows herself to be 'pushed around' by the male dancer. The results are aesthetically horrible, and clear for all to see" (Powell and Gifford, 2016: 139). Paralleling the scholarly critique on kinaesthetic politics and gender presentations on dance stages, such a presentation in a workshop would suggest that a woman (in business) would better follow rather than resist a man's lead. Pair dancing also suggests imbalanced issues of trust based on a traditional, contested social model: "When the woman leaps, she must be certain that she will be held [. . .]. If there is even momentary doubt, she will instinctively put her body into a different, defensive position and there will be a disaster" (Powell and Gifford, 2016: 141).

Matzdorf and Sen (2016: 118) admit that ballroom dancing has "undeniably, controversial gender issues that need looking at", but assert that modern competitive ballroom dancing "has moved on and away from stereotypes such as 'the lady's role is just to look decorative' to a concept that takes a partnership approach and sees the contribution of the two roles to the success of a performance as near equal." They see the reason for this trend in the development of dance sport that historically started from elegant movement and turned into an athletic and powerful performance with high risk of injury—a complexity that is not obvious on the metaphorical surface of 'effortless' professional dance performances. They also suggest that the co-operation involves both parties and mutual trust to let the partner take the lead, with the person moving backwards having the initiative, as they must make the physical space for the person going forwards (Matzdorf and Sen, 2016: 123). Going beyond the binary gender divide, Matzdorf and Sen (2016: 124) suggest that only a team with a highly-engaged follower, a 'partner', would succeed in competitive dance as well as in business environments.

Although a still image can hardly capture dynamics and movement, the photo can be used to further illustrate the inter-relationship between leader and follower. Matzdorf and Sen have provided the following explanation: In this situation, the leader offers the space and provides and holds the 'frame' (through the arms, the stance and counterbalance), inviting the follower into a movement that culminates in a big stretch with a kick. It is up to the follower how they accept the invitation and use the space. This move requires practice and trust-building: The partners need to work out and negotiate how energetic their moves can be without losing balance—so they need to know how far they can 'stretch' the limitations of their bodies and their strength.

A detailed verbal discussion in situ of what is presented thus seems useful to address issues that may not be obvious at first sight to generate more insights into leadership interaction. The emphasis on a problematic gendered message can for example be diminished when all participants on a more abstract level discuss the dynamics of the teams in which they are currently working, exemplified by considerations about "whether the parties feel that they are being 'pushed' or are indeed 'pushing', and what would be

Figure 6.1 Fides Matzdorf and Ramen Sen
Photo: Iain Carruthers

needed to achieve the kind of 'allowed leadership' that is demonstrated in dance" (Powell and Gifford, 2016: 140).

Filling the metaphor of the presentation with practical detail makes use of the potential of dance as a practice of critique. When critically reflecting on the need to follow and opportunities to resist, participants can transfer their insights into their role in organisations, as exemplified in the quote by a female follower (Matzdorf and Sen, 2016: 124)

> If I'm being pushed around, lose my balance and fall over my feet, I'm not going anywhere fast . . . So I want to be allowed and enabled to do my best. Similarly, where I'm taking a lead at work, I want co-workers to take ownership and responsibility for what they do, shape their contributions, bring in their own talents and ideas. I'm happy to support and facilitate, to chip in as and when needed, both as leader and follower— I do want to give and receive leadership, feedback and connection.

Early theoretical approaches on dance have used the metaphor to insinuate that a "waltz leader" would prefer a compliant follower, relating it to a hierarchical leadership model and a "well-oiled machine" (Ropo and Sauer, 2008: 564). Upon more detailed life observation and discussion, such an image that does not leave room for dynamic change and interaction in today's business world. The inclusion of further dance theory and insights from practice goes beyond the superficial gender binary into a deeper understanding of interaction and collaboration that is required on the highly competitive dance floor, and in today's businesses as well.

Metaphor/Choreography

Group Sculptures and Gestalten

Co-created and improvised dance can be used as metaphor to approach organisational issues. While dance interventions are transitory, some approaches emphasise the importance of creating an artefact in the sense of a final performance that can give evidence of the creative journey, provide a unifying goal for the group (Zeitner et al., 2016: 715), a greater goal on which all efforts are focused while all egos are subordinated (Powell and Gifford, 2016: 134). In some cases, the final performance can be used for external communication: The intermediary TILLT has matched an energy company with a dance company to work on organisational culture and also to enhance public visibility. The resulting "stapler ballet" as one element of the project can be seen as a video (TILLT, 2009). In most practice cases however the performance itself is not relevant in terms of artistic value, but can—when used as a metaphor—serve as an object of internal discussion and reflection.

Dance shares with other arts-based interventions the possibility of being viewed as representational or symbolic in some sense, when, for example, sculptures have been crafted to express organisational values and processes and personal feelings (Rippin, 2013). Arts-based interventions have been explored, drawing on gestalt theory, as methods that help organisational members "finding a form" and giving a "Gestalt" to experiences in the workplace that relate to teamwork, leadership and organisational culture and that can then be addressed, challenged and developed (Biehl-Missal, 2015a). Consequentially it does not only seem useful to observe and discuss performances, but to encourage organisational members to move in creative ways to show how they feel about their work. Dance-based forms go beyond textual narratives to explore organisations, relating to the use of visual imagery for organisational research, and additionally providing the aspects of movement in space and time. In this vein, choreographies have been developed co-operatively to give form to organisational themes.

Techniques of using dance as a learning metaphor include, for example, "body sculptures"—an approach that has its roots in arts-based research methods and therapeutic interventions in a range of contexts such as health, safety, educational and community development. Participants are invited to "generate meaning in a kinaesthetic way" (Lloyd and Hill, 2013: 68), assuming shapes in a multi-figure sculpture with their bodies, either corresponding to a theme or in an improvised process. One could also say that in the sense that dance is a 'universal language', participants are given the opportunity to speak in a language that is not based on words, letters and verbal utterances but engage in a kinaesthetic exchange. For example, the sculpture of a team interaction may be a metaphor for kinaesthetic politics and choreographies in an organisation with one person adopting a central position and the others the margins, either because they see themselves in such a way or because they are perceived as dominant or reserved by others. This provides a point of reference for participants sharing their perceptions and exchanging their views on how they feel about the topic, negotiating their assumptions and believes. Such a process can help to create innovative responses to organisational issues, when, for example through re-sculpting, alternative positions are imagined and kinaesthetic politics is altered and changed.

Adopting an approach that turns the dancer from a contributor or a creator into a co-owner (Butterworth, 2004: 50), dance exercises can explore further issues that start with kinaesthetic politics. Improvised exercises with movements that cover a spectrum from energetic to comfortable to restrained are a form of bodily theorising about identity and relations. For example, in a project facilitated by Katrin Kolo (2012), participants have considered how physical space is explored and how the body occupies space, and whether the dynamics of 'leading' and 'following' is performed and negotiated in gendered ways. Starting with an empty studio space, participants were encouraged to take the stage in ways that they found suitable. The dance-based intervention has shown that space is used differently depending on the gender: Women interacted and encouraged each other to enter the stage, in other cases men occupied the centre of the stage while women explored the margins. Such an occupation of the margins may not come as a surprise when considering how space is used in meetings or at work in organisations where some are able to generate a larger physical presence than others. Gender performativity has been linked to space and Ann Rippin (2015) has debated in her work that women's bodies are controlled in organisations, excluded from spaces of importance such as the boardroom and the strategy meeting. Women are seen as a distraction, the act of entering a male space is seen as trespassing and an act of aggression: "That is worth thinking about in a post-feminist landscape. Organisations are arenas for men to be men, for male violence, symbolic or otherwise. What shall the women do other than hold the coats and roll the bandages?" (Rippin, 2015: 121).

Dance exercises that use the space may bring to the fore embodied knowing on these issues through co-created movement. Asked about their observations, participants in the project started a discussion about how they felt and how they used space, creating parallels to behaviour at work. Considering the specific organisational space and its impact on people, the exercise bears parallels to artistic work for site-specific performances. This has often has been linked to community work as it involves interviews with stakeholders and research into the history of the site, sensitising people to a place and its problems and also showing a concern for the surroundings. The process of developing and showing a choreography in the place connects the site and the community through the physical and performative process, transforming the relationship of the community and the site, or the relationship of organisational stakeholders and their site.

Using the body as an experiential repository for what we know, which may emerge through movement, the spontaneous choreography has illustrated the dynamics of the group. Through dance, the 'felt experience' of being within an organisation can be explored, to create consciousness of what Ladkin (2013: 330) refers to as the invisible, "bodily based perceptions one feels in leadership relations". Movement brought to light for participants their own assumptions, attitudes and behaviours, taking seriously the bodily basis of doing gender. This movement interaction can be negotiated and changed if bodies adopted a different kinaesthetic politics and moved differently to create new leadership relationships and new organisational orders.

An example for the use of dance as a collaborative choreography is Katrin Kolo's (2012) work on an artistic research project UnternehMENSCHhoreographie ("Organisational Choreography" whereby in German the words "Unternehmen" and "Choreographie" converge into the noun MENSCH (HUMAN) in the middle, pointing to the moving body (lat. corpus) in the centre of the corporation), combining arts-based exploration and presentation of research findings. The project aimed to recreate, through a choreographic process, structures of interaction, leadership and implicit values in an imaginary company (Biehl-Missal, 2015b: 191). Rather than focusing on dance conventions, steps and styles, Kolo's project, like other forms of contemporary choreography, emphasises the kinaesthetic experience that is related to movement in space and time, the bodily and affective co-presence of actors and spectators. People negotiate the empty space and social relations, exerting movements, using a form of bodily theorising about identity and relations. Through dance, the 'felt experience' of being within an organisational interaction is explored. One moment in this transitory performance was termed by Kolo "woman fetches a chair or pulls it away". This moment refers to the ambiguous potential in supporting motions that are commonly demanded from female co-workers.

As I have discussed in the chapter on gender and dance, modern choreography has the potential to explore a multiplicity of juxtaposed movements and breaks, with 'typical' and 'atypical' female and male movements that expose and challenge gendered processes in organisations. Linking to the potential for socio-political resistance of modern dance performances, dance-based forms used for representation of embodied knowing and hidden practices in organisations may also disrupt narrative and preconceptions of gender and movement. Dance in this project is kinaesthetic theorising of

Figure 6.2 "Women fetches a chair or pulls it away"
Courtesy Katrin Kolo; Photo: Lisa Schäubli.

the discursive and performative construction of the female body. Dance as an arts-based form of inquiry and representation can address kinaesthetic politics and, through kinaesthetic empathy convey an understanding of the pressure to bring together body and identity. In this sense, it can potentially affect social choreographies in organisations.

Kinaesthetic/Politics

Awareness of the Body

Going beyond the metaphor of dance, many movement exercises emphasise the potential of the bodily experience for management and leadership development. Cases have been made over and over again for the importance of embodied learning and the connection of mind and body, in dance studies and education (Snowber, 2012) as well as in management education and training: Leaders and managers need to rely upon sensual perception, drawing on the aesthetic properties of their experience in addition to the mentally focused processes of reflection to deal with today's complexity and incongruity (Springborg and Sutherland, 2014: 40). The assumption that cognition and sense-making capacity is grounded in bodily, sensory experience has led to claims to actively include dance as a practice for leadership development: Working with bodily movement patterns, postures, and interactions, leaders can develop their ability to use such sensory knowledge to explore in greater depth many abstract concepts of relevance to practice, for example 'leadership' in terms of physical interaction (Springborg and Sutherland, 2016). This process includes a heightened awareness of the body and its perception.

Movement exercises historically stand for embodied learning more than other arts-based approaches. From workshops in organisations, practitioners report that "clients often realize for the first time that their bodies are more than just 'brain taxis' [. . .], carrying their minds from one cubicle or meeting to another" (Ludevig, 2016: 158). Reports include that organisational members sitting behind their desks for many hours a day often "forget their bodies" and that movement exercises help them to "arrive in the room" and to be attentive and present and ready to connect to others in a co-present situation.

Bozic Yams (2016: 162) in this vein explains that dance methods can help shift the focus from the outside to the inside, forgetting about external expectations, goals and performance indicators, starting with what the body tells people how they feel in the moment. It is about using movement experiences to access tacit knowing in the body that can then be used to act in and with the world around us in skilful ways (Springborg and Sutherland, 2016). Embodied knowing can be assessed through movement—a principle that parallels the use of dance as a tool for self-exploration in other social contexts and that also is the basis for dance-based methods when used for research (Chapter 7). This view is about self-exploration, about making meaning, rather than creating content.

Movement connects dancers to their embodied experiences that are non-verbal and encourages them to develop new understandings. In dance-based exercises efforts are made to work with these experiences of dance as a 'universal language' by verbalising them. Choreographer Katrin Kolo (2016: 44) has observed in her work that "this process of 'moving' words (through the body) and 'translating' these moves back into words can improve communication within groups." In this vein, Kolo suggests movement-based additions to business meetings, similar to the use of poems that are read and interpreted by consultants to open up their views before business meetings. Verbal reflection of what has been experienced on the individual level is valued by many practitioners, who accord lots of time for facilitated verbal debrief, sharing and exploration:

> While for some the "ah-ha" moments take place during the movement exercises themselves, for others it is during the debrief that the connection is made between the felt knowledge that emerges through their bodies and the direct application to their daily work, projects, interactions and goals [. . .]. Often the movement exercises are a gateway to then explore certain topics, like how to establish connection with others or what is the rhythm of a particular organization, in greater depth. Once these topics are felt in the body, the otherwise abstract theoretical conversation regarding how they apply to an organization becomes tangible and lively.
>
> (Ludevig, 2016: 153)

Despite valuing the verbal discussion, it has been advised not to try to intellectualise everything or to jump into trivial conclusions, which may suggest for participants that the learning process is over. When movement exercises are used for developing embodied skills and reflexivity over time, commitment to bodily action and exercise remains essential (Springborg and Sutherland, 2016: 105).

With regard to kinaesthetic politics, dance can become a critical practice when participants develop new ways of interacting in organisations. Valuing individual perception and how it enables interaction also is part of this relationship:

> Understanding this phenomenological relationship between attention and outcome is crucially relevant for organizational and systems change work, as it suggests that our attitudes, interests and habits directly impact the reality we then chose to believe in and experience [. . .] The greater their capacity to pay attention, the deeper, more empathic and

more generative their felt experience. Practicing this first in the body allows them the opportunity to learn how to then maintain an open and curious attention in their daily lives as well.

(Ludevig, 2016: 161)

Body Language and Connection

Dance is about communicating through the moving body, and the relevance of this has been increasingly acknowledged by leadership studies. Different approaches emphasise the importance of body language, for example in charismatic leadership, and leadership education consequently has included the body and its movement. Dance exercises however often go beyond the mastery of body language. In a movement workshop we have done with service staff (Biehl and Volkmann, 2016) a participant described leadership with reference to the use of space and bodily postures: "Like if I saw someone who stands tall, upright, has a goal and knows what they want to accomplish, that, for me, is a leader, so someone to follow, someone to follow in their footsteps." This resonates the idea expressed in the section on kinaesthetic politics (Chapter 3) that to be a leader means to move like one. Participants went beyond the visual to include their kinaesthetic perception when assessing these forms of leadership, emphasising a "natural" feeling, stating they could not be effectively trained to only "pretend" these behaviours on the surface. This quote shows the difficulty of assessing 'natural' leadership but it suggests the relevance of kinaesthetic empathy over visual representation.

A lack of movement in leadership often is noted, also in our workshop. A lecturer, who also took part, had not assumed her role of reference to the students and was "shying away":

> She was in my group, and she was saying to me words to the effect of "don't let me be the leader", blah, blah, blah. [. . .] it kind of goes against the image that she has to create in order to do her job. And also, I mean, as much as it would have been nice to have her as a leader, as a role model, blah, blah, blah, in all fairness to her, it's not exactly in her job description, is it?

Using the body as a medium also resonates Watzlawick's dictum, an idea that is widely expressed in communication studies: you cannot not communicate; you cannot not kinaesthetically react to each other. Body language presents a continuous stream of information in other social and organisational contexts, where meaning is constantly 'in motion'. With regard to this expressivity and the idea of 'e-motion', the innovative modern dancer Martha Graham (1991: 4) once said: "Movement never lies. It is a barometer telling the state of the soul's weather to all who can read it." While in an arts context, the analysis of dance requires an education, connoisseurship and training in decoding movements, the evidence from organisational life presented here shows that organisational members possess some kinaesthetic empathy that enables them to understand and react to others. Generally, this is something to be developed: "Emotions are largely reflected through nonverbal communication. This is hugely important in leadership [and] most people are hopeless at picking up perceptions or emotions" (Ashkanasy, cited in Zeitner et al., 2016: 177). The examples cited also showed that kinaesthetic empathy is not only used to understand and interpret what is experienced, but point to the fact that participants start to work with their experiences.

Different from theatre workshops that also consider bodily communication, dance as a non-verbal method focuses on kinaesthetic perception. Putting less emphasis on the spoken word and the appearance of the outer body, dance exercises target the "lived body" (Snowber, 2012: 55) and provide opportunities to develop new ways of relating to others and interacting. In this regard dance links to transformational leadership (Yukl, 2006) that explores how organisations engage in processes of directed change building on shared practices and understandings that emerge. The concrete experience of dance also relates to theories on embodied leadership, as it supports the process of becoming an embodied leader through developing kinaesthetic empathy. The following discussion will further highlight the importance of not only producing kinaesthetic signs, but reacting to non-verbal feedback from others.

This connection has been referred to as the kinaesthetic feedback loop that goes back and forth between leaders and followers, connecting people through movement and bodily perception (Chapter 4). A shift from outside to the inside is the first step before individuals extend their sensitivity and attention outwards to the social body of the group. As an example I shall cite an exercise that is referred to as "Field Dance" and which—using a different terminology and related approaches—draws on social presencing theatre where sensing capacities are emphasised that connect individual bodies to groups or social bodies, implying greater awareness towards others and situations. The exercise starts from a set-up common to the business world, with one individual standing before a group as if ready to give a presentation. The person standing is encouraged to walk and pause in front of the others, offering a gesture and words, paying increased attention to the connection with those who sit, to the interpersonal field or the atmosphere. The aim is to gain a different felt experience of the possible relationship between both parties:

> This relationship is one in which the stander truly operates on behalf of the community and the sitters learn to let go of expectations and pay attention with equal interest to the stander in front of them as well as their fellow sitters to their left and right. The sense of collective unity

that is achieved through this simple practice is so strong that I've seen more than a few participants moved to tears. It also sets the groundwork for real innovation and fresh idea generation through its utter focus on developing total presence and letting go of any previous agendas.

(Ludevig, 2016: 161)

This idea of achieving a better 'feeling for' situations has also been expressed in theories on social presence (Scharmer and Kaeufer, 2010), where the sensible individual is able to consider with greater consciousness the relationships between themselves, others and their environment, using the self as a medium for sensing, embodying, and, eventually, acting towards future scenarios. The so-called Theory U is also used in this context, whose U-shaped process echoes the idea of inversion ("Umstülpung") as a mechanism of problem solving in complex situations whereby the sudden turn of attention was defined as "learning through insight" (Biehl-Missal and Fitzek, 2014: 258).

The exercise practically links to theory developed in the book, such as considerations on the kinaesthetic feedback loop and the connections between co-present leader and followers: Participants acknowledge and actively sense the space between both parties and the co-creation of the situation. Other approaches as well emphasise the importance of "staying in the moment" and "working in the moment", being acutely aware of what others are doing and reacting appropriately (Powell and Gifford, 2016: 134). Dance as an arts-based learning method can help to develop new ways of expressing and perceiving others, when participants become more sensitive to the signals they send with their own bodies, and to the signals that are being sent from other bodies. Further practical implications are that individuals not only increase self-awareness or their own expression, but organisational members shift their attention from the limited personal experience to perceiving the larger whole of any group and valuing that new ideas can emerge within dynamic and co-created leadership situations.

Kinaesthetic/Choreography

Site-Specific Walks

In a business world where bodies are considered brain taxis and where perception often occurs through a digital filter, movement exercises have been applied to improve managers' embodied perception in the physical world. The kinaesthetic experience in these approaches is related to a site-specific choreography, when bodies react to the surrounding spaces, when a choreographer and performers 'sense' the space and develop ideas how to work with it.

Clive Holtham for example applies the dérive as a method, drawing on Guy Debord and continuing the traditional Situationists' practice of 'drifting' and passing through different environments. The dérive in management education and training is an individual and also group-based slow wandering through typically an urban area, but also through corporate spaces, emphasising close observation and recording of physical detail as well as the dialogue between group members (Holtham et al., 2010). Playfully and constructively paying attention to physical detail and their embodied experience, the creative learners are encouraged to develop their own associations about time, place and space that are used for a form of embodied and critical learning. Participants employ their experiences to tell their own story that deliberately alienates their experiences and puts a new frame to things that normally are overseen and not perceived (for example, in a session that Holtham did with my students in Berlin, construction pipes were imaginatively interpreted as a trace of a civilisation long gone, which opens up new associations about the local business school).

While the small group observation and creative debate is typically emphasised, the role of movement can also be considered as important. This also is reflected in practices of walking in a labyrinth practiced in university teaching. The labyrinth can provide a peaceful, meditative space for deepening reflection contemplating one's life and individual aspirations, as well as for confidence building and creative impulses (Sellers, 2013). Again it is not only about a metaphorical experience or simple existence in the labyrinth, but about moving through the space. Sellers (2013: 221) describes how students are frequently surprised by the inner quietness and depth of reflection, arising form the walk that mirrors a life's journey in unexpected twists and turns, new viewpoints, and travelling alone and alongside others for a while. Despite its strong metaphorical component, the movement is of central importance. Moving through space can be seen as a form of experiencing and sensing the site that is similar to what choreographers do when they develop a project, relating the 'essence' of the space in the social context. Moving and reacting to the space, to one self and the group bears also parallels to the use of movement as a research tool for self-exploration and research (Chapter 7). Many other site-specific choreographies can be done with organisational members, in projects that consider how spaces are used and occupied and work with these issues practically.

Such an approach not only relates to dance theory but to philosophical writings, for example continuing ideas of the flâneur in the works of Siegfried Kracauer. Walking through Berlin and Paris in the early 20th century, through streets and buildings, Kracauer's (1978) flâneur ponders about and analyses the social and political consequences of the modern era that in his view created empty times and empty spaces. Accessing the world through the moving body—similar to site-specific performance or choreographic practice—the flâneur proved that understanding is to posit oneself in relation to the spatial environment, to relate to people in the space, to reach out one's hand, to smell, to hear, to taste. Linking to the accelerated process of dynamics and change that people perceived at the time, passing through the spaces of today's organisations is a practical approach of 'embodied leader-ship' when it is about perceiving and sensing atmospheres, gaining a differ-ent understanding of people and spaces and spaces in-between.

Leading and Following

Dance literally consists of practices of leadership in the sense of 'leading' and 'following'. Going beyond the immediate metaphor of leadership, dance exercises provide a kinaesthetic experience of leading and following, which can be used to frame subsequent discussions of topics relevant to leaders and followers. Taking seriously notions used in leadership studies such as the "embodied practicing of leadership" (Küpers, 2013: 336), movement exercises put the relationships into physical practice, making participants experience the practical meaning of 'leading and following'. Dance exercises make explicit some of the more complex leader–follower dynamics, which are addressed by phenomenological approaches valuing engaged acts and responses informed through bodily perceptions in organisations. Authors in the area report that the use of dance-based sessions, designed to provide a valid physical experience of what dancers do in order to cooperate and to perform successfully, has an impact on participants in terms of changed atti-tudes and behaviours (Matzdorf and Sen, 2016; Powell and Gifford, 2016).

Movement exercises are considered suitable for developing organisational members' embodied understanding of leadership and followership particu-larly when these exercises are not about the mastery of specific steps such as tango or waltz, but integrate creative contribution. For example, in tango exercises that focus on content and technique, the process of learning can take up most of the time leaving little space to reflect on leadership issues (Zeitner et al., 2016: 176). Practical exercises often benefit from simple movement structures and switching of roles, allowing participants to expe-rience both leader and follower parts. The aim is to generate in participants "an embodied sense of the influence that [elements such as rhythm, space and gaze,] have in their team's dynamics and their own personal success in leading" (Ludevig, 2016: 152). Putting the kinaesthetic experience at the centre, many exercises play through different ways of non-verbal leading and following interaction, with participants exploring the impacts on them-selves and others.

An example is a tango exercise in which both participants shift back and forth their weight, realising and reflecting that they did not provide time for the follower to rebalance (Springborg and Sutherland, 2016: 106). This motif was in situ discussed with regard to impatience leaders showed at the workplace, when giving and receiving tasks and feedback, making visible mistrust and fear of judgment in the work relationships. The experience of the ease when the dance movement is cooperatively executed can serve as an embodied experience for leaders to act more cooperatively.

One of many examples is another 'body sculpture' exercise that involves a pair of two moving forward with one participant forming the other's bodily postures through lifting legs and pulling forward limbs, turning the trunk and adjusting the head. I am citing this because when participating in the exercise, I experienced how many metaphorical dimensions of leadership can be felt in the body through kinaesthetic activity—as a complementary exercise to expressing embodied knowing through forming a body sculpture in a group. Examples include the feeling of being 'pushed', 'pulled' or 'dragged', of 'providing' or 'limiting space', 'anticipating directions' and reaching a 'flow'. This helped to gain further insights into my personal leadership style as I realised how uncomfortable I felt when having to direct my dance partner in a hands-on style through the room adjusting every small movement, while others seemed to enjoy just that. Gaining a new embodied understanding about the personal importance of giving space and providing freedom led me to ponder about further questions of communication and trust that would be required in such a process—topics commonly discussed with participants in these workshops. Such exercises are a method of research or 'me-search', and have been used as a research method to explore personal attitudes towards leadership or followership (Chapter 7).

Practitioners and scholars suggest that dance exercises can develop an embodied understanding of many metaphorical concepts. Using the moving

Figure 6.3 Participants of a MOVE Leadership workshop "Dancing with Management"
Courtesy Daniel Ludevig.

body as a tool for making sense of abstract concepts relevant to organisational life, such as leadership or problem solving or relationship building, participants may achieve a better abstract understanding that can be applied to practice:

> Many leaders think about "leading" in terms of the physical interaction of one body dragging another body in a specific direction. [. . .] Through dance exercises, managers may experience leading as a matter of using body postures to open a space for the follower to step into, or as a matter of using the combined structure of two bodies to give a small but clear direction, allowing the follower to be the one supplying energy for his own movement (in opposition to the situation where the leader drags the follower and, hence, uses his own energy to move the follower).
>
> (Springborg and Sutherland, 2016: 97)

Participants make experiences that support an advanced embodied understanding of leading. For example, the experience of indicating direction through small but precise impulses in dance can be transferred onto everyday interaction at work. Managers can also benefit from their experience of pushing and pulling "to find ways of leading in which they draw upon their own energy to overcome perceived inertia or resistance" (Springborg and Sutherland, 2016: 104). Sufficient time needs to be accorded in exercises to allow participants to immerse in these experiences and to work on their embodied understanding before then speaking about it. Again it is about making sense through the body working with individual ideas, which can than can be applied to strengthen the own leadership personality.

To develop personal leadership skills, simple exercises such as contact improvisation for example are used. They help to increase participants' awareness of their often consciously reflected approach to leading and following, including the lack of trust or anticipation of aggression (Springborg and Sutherland, 2014: 43). These topics also are approached in classic trust exercises with participants letting themselves fall backwards to be caught by their colleagues. Establishing a relation and thinking about it is an element that often is used. For example, Powell and Gifford (2016: 139) describe the following exercise:

> Stand facing each other, hold your hands out at just below shoulder height, and rest the palms of your hands against your partners' palms. Take turns to lean forward until your weight is uncomfortable for your partner to support. Now take your weight off your hands until your partner feels that they have lost contact with you. The ideal mid-point between these two states is, in dancing, "the connection".

Upon establishment of this connection, the pair moves by stepping forwards, backwards and sideways. Varying speed and direction, the balance needs to be maintained, otherwise participants lose touch or inhibit the joint movement. Matzdorf and Sen (2016: 115) find that in the fast-paced, highly competitive world of dance-sport, leaders need to be highly aware of their "relatedness" at all times in order to be successful. This "relatedness" links to contemporary models of organisational leadership and can be filled with meaning through dance. After becoming aware of their negative attitudes through metaphor, the next step is to use such exercises in a form of active kinaesthetic politics and choreography to develop new ideas of interaction by alternating and changing behaviour.

Other exercises work in similar ways, providing a new understanding of leading and following through metaphor and kinaesthetic experience. Ballroom exercises (Matzdorf and Sen, 2016: 120–122) show that leaders, among other things, need to have the capacity "to monitor", which includes being "in tune" with the music and the partner; listening to the follower's feedback; and observing the environment for obstacles (static or moving). With regard to organisational life, participants have consequently inferred that a leader needs to "be in tune" with company values, mission statements, goals, stakeholder expectations, market factors, public opinion and regulatory frameworks, but also that leaders literally need to follow the organisational rhythm within the department or team in terms of work cycles and project periods. Other issues such as planning and communicating can also be transferred onto organisational leadership. Relevant insights for followership revolve around 'listening' in terms of 'picking up signals', and 'acting' in terms of being more than a 'sheep' follower, but rather bringing in their own competency, using the space and time and the leeway provided by the leader. Allowing the partner to take initiative for example has provided insights for a manager:

> That helped me to understand . . . that I needed to let my staff do their jobs, and not micro-manage, but to allow them the space to do things their own way, to guide and keep the "grand plan", but not to decide on every last detail myself. I found that allowing followers to be active participants in the equation to be an underrated part of the leadership-followership dynamic, but doing so gave team members the space to develop their own potential, as well as allowing them to develop the best possible solutions to problems that they took more ownership over.
>
> (Matzdorf and Sen, 2016: 123)

A trend to emphasise the follower role can often be found in movement exercises in organisations. For example, in improvised exercises, participants constantly change their roles and are encouraged to explore possibilities of actively leading from their follower position "to understand how they can empower, enhance, support and influence their leaders from this position" (Ludevig, 2016: 153). Developing the follower role links to contemporary co-operative models of work. In ballroom dance exercises as well, facilitators emphasise that skilful following is not about being led, but about taking responsibility for actions and teamwork. Matzdorf and Sen (2016: 119) use the terms "leader" and "co-leader" as they find that the term "follower" implies too passive a role:

> The leader initiates movements and invites the follower to 'follow' this lead by moving and opening up space for the leader to move into, the leader now 'following' the follower into the newly available space. Whilst the leader initiates a movement, the person going backwards (and this switches dynamically between leader and follower depending on the figure being danced) is in control of making the space and controlling the distance travelled.
>
> (Matzdorf and Sen, 2016: 119)

Adding an embodied dimension to theoretical concepts, dance exercises of this kind enable a better understanding of 'shared leadership' or 'relational leadership'. Relational leaders for example are expected to be "aware of the importance of the flow of present moments in making sense of complexity, resolving problems, shaping strategic direction and practical actions" (Cunliffe and Eriksen, 2011: 1446). Replacing a dichotomy of leader and follower with a dynamic approach of co-created and shared leading can contribute to new ways of practicing leadership at work. These new interactions can be created by participants that feel empowered through exercises: "The role of the follower as an active partner in the relationship—as a co-leader—was underlined. We all noticed clearly that 'I myself' am responsible for the nature of the relationship" (Hujala et al., 2016: 28). Dance exercises have an impact as a critical practice when kinaesthetic empathy is applied to generate an experience that affects individuals' kinaesthetic politics, changing and developing interactions or 'choreographies' in organisations.

Collaboration and Co-ownership

Dance and co-operative movement activities go beyond an awareness of body language and individual reflection and can enhance an understanding of collaboration in organisations and in leadership situations. Bearing many parallels to organisational leadership, choreography can be seen as a process of setting human agents, movements and ideas into a relationship, as the coordination of humans in space and time. Choreography includes different forms of control that are negotiated not only in artistic, but also in social processes that occur between choreographer and dancer(s) in different dance-making approaches.

Exploring opportunities of cooperation in choreographic practice, Butterworth (2004: 46) has drafted a continuum of choreography ranging from a 'didactic' approach (artistic apprenticeship and 'teaching by showing') to a 'democratic' approach at the other end of the spectrum (rejection of traditional hierarchies and preference for cooperation and collective working). This model has been used by students and tutors of choreography in the dance world, and can be applied to dance-based approaches in organisations as well. Butterworth's (2004: 55) model of choreographic processes identifies five forms of leadership and followership on a didactic/democratic continuum:

1) Choreographer as expert—dancer as instrument: The choreographer is generating the material, while the dancers imitate and replicate. Social interaction is passive and can be impersonal. The learning process is about receiving and processing information.

2) Choreographer as author—dancer as interpreter: Control of concept, style and content is with the choreographer, the dancer imitates, replicates and interprets. Both parties exert separate, but still receptive activities, whereby dancers learn to receive and process instructions, utilising their experience as performer.

3) Choreographer as pilot—dancer as contributor: The choreographer initiates the concept, directs and sets tasks, the dancers can replicate, but also improvise and create content. This requires active participation. Learning is about responding to tasks and contributing to guided discovery.

4) Choreographer as facilitator—dancer as creator: The choreographer in a more nurturing and mentorial approach provides leadership and stimulus, the process and concept is created and negotiated with dancers in active participation.

5) Choreographer as collaborator—dancer as co-owner: Research, negotiation and decision-making about concept, intention and style are shared and developed by choreographer and dancers, content is co-created in shared authorship. The learning approach is experiential as dancers can contribute fully to concept, content, form and process.

These different styles of co-operation can be used to work with organisational members. A straight-forward way is model 3 when participants at a large organisational event learn a short choreography in which they can replicate, but also improvise content. Such an event with large businesses Daimler and Deutsche Bank for example, creates an energetic atmosphere and a 'joint spirit', and can be read as a corporate statement for fitness (Walz, 2016). Models 4 or 5 for example can help to change the behaviour and mind-set of project managers, encouraging a more flexible, reactive approach to highly complex scenarios and a more collaborative, 'ensemble' approach to working with outside partners (Powell and Gifford, 2016). Zeitner et al. (2016: 171) find that these models can be transferred to non-dance contexts of collective activity: For example, successful co-ownership in a non-hierarchical setting "might provide learners with insights into cooperative action and teamwork, which can then be transferred into other organizational contexts, such as organizational change management". Through the kinaesthetic experience, these exercises can develop an embodied understanding of leadership practice.

In the world of arts, there is a trend among communities, groups and subjects that directors, performers and participants increasingly collaborate (Husemann, 2009). Self-directed agency articulated in choreographic practices parallels developments in organisations where leadership is shared and negotiated. Dance-based trainings in organisations also tend to emphasise democratic models of choreography and use movement in non-hierarchical leadership situations, making model 5 particularly suited for dance-based interventions. Model 5 when used outside the art world typically is applied in the area of social and community work and in organisations. These areas emphasise the shared, collaborative process and experience over issues of artistic representation. Groups develop a common understanding of things, share the research process (if there is one), and have individual opportunities to bring in their knowledge, views and insights. As the choreography is a democratic endeavour, members can contribute to a different extent, negotiating, embodying expression and applying personal experience, and also may assume the role of the observer (Butterworth, 2004: 62). Choreographers who work with organisational members also have expressed that they prefer co-created works, seeing their "role very much in the spirit of a curator who considers every person a masterpiece of art and helps each one to get the right space to unfold its full potential and offers opportunities to relate to each other thus unfolding their collective potential" (Kolo, 2016: 44). As dance-based interventions in organisations do generally not work towards an artistically valuable product, it is easier than in artistic choreographies to balance out varying levels of experience within the group and to experiment with ideas.

The choreography continuum can be applied to experiential learning and dance-based interventions and can also be used for theory building by organisational scholars who explore forms of leadership. Looking into leadership issues in dance practice and in the work of choreographers is believed worth studying for organisational scholars (Bozic and Olsson, 2013) to gain inspiration for creative practices and to see from a different perspective leadership practices. Dance scholars for example have discussed that shifting between "a choreographer's puppet", passively following movement instructions and being partners in creation requires the ability to coordinate levels of engagement with the choreographic process (Rowe and Zeitner-Smith, 2011: 41). Following up such insights in interdisciplinary scholarship can provide new views on organisational followership. The five models could also be compared to different leadership approaches to raise awareness of details and to develop new insights into practice. Researchers could for example look at highly scripted service interactions to see which opportunities beneath replication (model 2) are used when participants improvise (model 4) and maybe co-create new processes (model 5)—as discussed earlier with regard to choreographies (Chapter 5).

Further research is required as dance scholars find that issues such as colonisation, racism and gender discrimination are constantly neglected in the critical discourse: For example the gendered relation between a dancer and a choreographer, the reproduction of an economy of subjection and authorship, of obedience and command, of vocalising orders and following orders, micro-fascims performed in commanding speech acts, and racial and racist formations (think of what kind of bodies dance displays, what kind of bodies is perceived as dancing the 'contemporary') (Lepecki, 2013: 157). These issues echo concerns of many critical organisational scholars.

Dance exercises may increase a connection among the group through kinaesthetic empathy and on a broader level, these exercises work towards a choreography as an invisible network which members create. To illustrate this, I shall refer to a workshop that we have done with service staff in the hotel sector (Biehl and Volkmann, 2016). In an exercise the choreographer asked participants to express through their movement and posture "confidence" (type A) and "self-consciousness" (type B) and to match with another participant expressing the opposing feeling while walking through the space. The exercise was a challenge, as explained by a participant:

> I think [. . .] there had to be a distinct difference between somebody who's miserable and somebody who is really confident. I think some people, the way they portrayed confidence didn't seem like it, so they could have seemed miserable. So I think I definitely found it quite hard to find someone to match with. So yes, I actually had to ask, which was kind of cheating—I was like "are you a B?" or whatever—because I wasn't sure, because they didn't portray it in such an extravagant way for me to know that they were A or they were B.

Subsequent verbal discussions have dealt with the issue that junior service staff did not yet feel comfortable when moving through the space, hesitant to being "confident", which they linked to "owning the space", sending out signals that they did not intend to send. Participants had difficulties in making sense of others' non-verbal signals and reading their emotions—a widespread deficiency that I pointed out earlier in this chapter. In the words of Springborg and Sutherland (2016: 97), they were lacking the "ability to perceive and distinguish between sensory states" as a prerequisite for engaging in 'aesthetic reflexivity': Without the ability to perceive differences in non-verbal forms of expression such as postures of colleagues or customers, managers "could not use experiences of subtle differences in interactions between two bodies in motion to achieve skilful knowing and doing". Skilful doing in this sense would be a form of "aesthetic agency", using specific aesthetic experiences as tacit knowledge to act in and with the world around us (Springborg and Sutherland, 2016: 95).

Going beyond this form of individual understanding and agency, our study however found that a form of kinaesthetic coordination on the group level started to emerge. In this situation, we discovered a kinaesthetic dynamic: Participants attempted to eliminate differences between confident and self-secure postures. They explained how a choreography emerged:

> Yes, so it's a bit awkward. I don't know what it's like for everyone else, but when you're working in the hotel and someone is a bit nervous, you try and help them; you don't just . . . You try to build it so they're as confident as you are, in a way. So it's a bit of a strange situation to be in, almost, because you don't just have the shy person and the confident person, in a way; you try to get everyone to be as confident as each other and at the same level of manage . . . Do you know what I mean? [. . .] you do all kind of try—you want to be similar because obviously you're all working towards the same standards and the same level at the same time.

Participants from this group of team-oriented service employees worked towards an equal level of kinaesthetic activity, trying to remove hierarchy and leadership that they associated with specific kinaesthetic activity. With reference to the concept of the kinaesthetic feedback loop introduced earlier, the kinaesthetic experience sets 'in motion' subsequent efforts to work with the situation, in this case efforts were undertaken to eliminate differences in kinaesthetic energy and to coordinate participants towards a joint performance.

The choreography and kinaesthetic coordination that brought participants on an equal level also showed in the analysis of a workshop exercise: The group moved through the space as a huddle, with leadership changing to the person in front when the huddle switched direction. The video made visible some use of the space in terms of horizontal and sagittal (front to back) movement although the use of effort, along with a consideration of how body parts move (dynamics, energy) was rather low. This indicated that participants felt reluctant to take the leader role and uncomfortable, which also was verbalised in response to our subsequent interviews questions:

> One thing that I noticed is that people weren't overly prepared to take the leadership role because of the fact that they kind of felt embarrassed or they weren't entirely sure what to do in that kind of situation, and they didn't like being put on the spot. But people, for me personally, I was more comfortable just to take the back seat, as it were, and let someone else kind of . . .

These exercises show how a choreography or joint collaboration is gaining momentum, based on kinaesthetic empathy and heightened awareness towards the group. This connection may for example be referred to as "pressure" both on the movement level and the metaphorical social level.

> But then again, if you did it individually then you don't have the pressure of the people behind you and that sort of peer pressure—especially

having your friends behind you as well, following every action that you do. But if you were doing it individually then it's just you, and then it's a sort of different pressure.

Extending individual embodied perception to include the group as a basis for further coordination is a feature commonly observed in dance exercises. Ludevig (2016: 163) for example cites participants who refer to "learning about the importance of 'seeing' with all senses of their body, and not over prioritizing only that which comes, for example, through their visual senses". In her work with organisational members, Kolo (2016: 43–44) also observed that they developed a sense for what is happening behind their backs, integrating the space behind their bodies into their radius of attention and action:

> We were caring much more for the whole group and people started to trust each other even more. In the discussion following our movement sequence we found that this sight of the space behind one's back is a very special sort of 'seeing the space behind you'—what we before called 'respect'. After this, every time, when we used the word 'respect' again, we had this common experience and therefore also in mind this new meaning. Having 'respect' meant more than before and at the same time it felt much clearer to all of us, what we meant by it.

This understanding of 're-spect' as a form of kinaesthetic empathy is exemplified in dance education when dancers train with a mirror, not solely to watch themselves but to see what is next and behind them: "As a dancer you are trained to 'see' this space in order to be able to perform on stage without a mirror. One of my teachers called this ability the 'compound eye' of the dancer" (Kolo, 2016: 44).

Groups coordinate each other using their kinaesthetic empathy and 're-spect', and then make efforts towards an assimilation on a kinaesthetic level that eliminates hierarchical differences in an effort of co-created leadership. Dance exercises can raise individuals' embodied awareness of how their movements follow social choreographies when they bring themselves in position and exert specific gestures and movements, potentially performing hidden political strategies without knowing it, embodying and "re-member-ing" these practices in their body parts (members). Employing verbal discussions of the experience, dance exercises can help to criticise and not unconsciously accept these moving orders and social structures. Theatre exercises have a tradition to consciously reflect on attitudes and to potentially change them. Bertolt Brecht (1961) plays through different forms of gestures and attitudes and via the Verfremdung (alienation) illustrates how these are socially constructed, affec the inner attitude and can be negotiated. For example, in Brecht's plays "He Said Yes" (Der Jasager) and "He Said No" (Der Neinsager), actors rehearse two alternative plots, causing them to 'play through' developments and reflect on their personal attitudes, in order to become aware of opportunities 'to act' their lives differently.

Working on a more abstract and embodied dimension, dance exercises contain an emancipatory element when framed as "an invitation to think with our entire beings" (Snowber, 2012: 56–57), which opens up opportunities "of grappling more deeply with the complexity of ways [participants] can critically think, sift, perceive, and eventually come to fresh understanding of whatever subject they are studying." When conceiving of the moving body as the element that links us to the world, a different relationship with our bodies enables a deeper understanding of the world that surrounds us and also may open up considerations of changing these relations.

Applying a dance perspective has shown that organisational members do much more than imitating and re-presenting. Rather they perform their own choreography as a kinaesthetic network that is created through training and constantly negotiated and in flux. By going beyond the dance metaphor and in detail considering kinaesthetic processes and empathy, the dance perspective explores how social routines and structures are not only reproduced but also how improvisation, co-ownership and alteration of bodily movements potentially changes social interaction.

Literature

Alkemeyer, T. and Schmidt, R. (2003) Habitus und Selbst: Zur Irritation der körperlichen Hexis in der populären Kultur, in Alkemeyer, T., Boschert, B., Schmidt, R. and Gebauer, G. (eds.) *Aufs Spiel gesetzte Körper: Aufführungen des Sozialen in Sport und populärer Kultur*. Konstanz: UVK Verlag, 77–102.

Barry, D. and Meisiek, S. (2010) Seeing more and seeing differently: Sensemaking, mindfulness, and the workarts, *Organization Studies* 31(11): 1505–1153.

Berthoin Antal, A. (2009) *Research report: Transforming organizations with the arts*. Gothenburg: TILLT. http://www.wzb.eu/sites/default/files/u30/researchre port.pdf (Accessed 1 Feb 2016).

Berthoin Antal, A. (2012) Artistic intervention residencies and their intermediaries: A comparative analysis, *Organizational Aesthetics* 1(1): 44–67.

Berthoin Antal, A., Gómez de la Iglesia, R. and Vives Almandoz, M. (2011) *Managing Artistic Interventions in Organizations: A Comparative Study of Programmes in Europe*, 2nd ed. Gothenburg: TILLT Europe.

Berthoin Antal, A. and Strauß, A. (2013) *Artistic Interventions in Organisations: Finding Evidence of Values Added. Creative Clash Report*. Berlin: WZB.

Biehl, B. and Volkmann, C. (2016) *Research Paper 'Choreography and Organisation'.* unpublished, The University of Essex.

Biehl-Missal, B. (2014) Die Kunst des Management: Wie Unternehmen kunstbasierte Methoden zur Personal—und Organisationsentwicklung einsetzen, in Henze, R. (ed.) *Kultur und Management: Eine Annäherung*, 2nd ed. Wiesbaden: Springer, 239–251.

Biehl-Missal, B. (2015a) Finding form: Gestalt theory as a development of aesthetic approaches to organisation and management, *Dialogue & Universalism* 4: 163–172.

Biehl-Missal, B. (2015b) 'I write like a painter': Feminine creation with arts-based methods in organizational research', *Gender, Work & Organization* 22(2): 179–196.

Biehl-Missal, B. (2015c) Kunstsammlung und Wert: Neue Einsatzmöglichkeiten der Corporate Collection im Kontext der Personal-und Organisationsentwicklung und internen Kommunikation. *Kommunikationsmanagement* 3.114, 1–22 (Losebl. Neuwied 2001 ff., edited by Bentele, G./ Piwinger, M./ Schönborn, G.).

Biehl-Missal, B. and Fitzek, H. (2014) Hidden heritage: A Gestalt psychology approach to the aesthetics of management and organisation, *Gestalt Theory: Official Journal of the Society for Gestalt Theory and Its Applications (GTA)*, 36(3): 251–266.

Bozic Yams, N. (2016) Choreographing creative processes for innovation, in Johansson Sköldberg, U., Woodilla, J. and Berthoin Antal, A. (eds.) *Artistic Interventions in Organizations. Research, Theory and Practice.* New York: Routledge, 149–164.

Bozic Yams, N. and Olsson, B. (2013) Culture for radical innovation: What can business learn from creative processes of contemporary dancers? *Organizational Aesthetics* 2(1): 59–83.

Brandstetter, G. and Klein, G. (eds.) (2013) *Dance [and] Theory.* Bielefeld: transcript.

Brecht, B. (1961) On the experimental theatre, trans. by Carl Richard Mueller, *The Tulane Drama Review* 6(1): 2–17.

Burrows, J. (2010) *A Choreographer's Handbook.* New York: Routledge.

Butterworth, J. (2004) Teaching choreography in higher education: A process continuum model, *Research in Dance Education* 5(1): 45–67.

Butterworth, J. and Wildschut, L. (eds.) (2009) *Contemporary Choreography: A Critical Reader.* London and New York: Routledge.

Chandler, J. (2012) Work as dance, *Organization* 19(6): 865–878.

Clark, T. and Mangham, I. (2004) Stripping to the undercoat: A review and reflections on a piece of organization theatre, *Organization Studies* 25(5): 841–851.

Cunliffe, A. L. and Eriksen, M. (2011) Relational leadership, *Human Relations* 64(11): 1425–1449.

Graham, M. (1991) *Blood Memory: An Autobiography.* London: Palgrave Macmillan.

Holtham, C., Ward, V. and Owens, A. (2010) Slow knowledge work—designing space and learning. Paper presented at the 26th EGOS (European Group for Organizational Studies) Colloquium, 1–3. July, Lisbon.

Hujala, A., Laulainen, S., Kinni, R., Kokkonen, K., Puttonen, K. and Aunola, A. (2016) Dancing with the bosses: Creative movement as a method, *Organizational Aesthetics* 5(1): 11–36.

Hujala, A., Laulainen, S. and Kokkonen, K. (2014) Manager's dance: Reflecting management interaction through creative movement, *International Journal of Work Organisation and Emotion* 6(1): 40–58.

Husemann, P. (2009) *Choreographie als kritische Praxis: Arbeitsweisen bei Xavier Le Roy und Thomas Lehmen.* Bielefeld: transcript.

Johansson Sköldberg, U., Woodilla, J. and Berthoin Antal, A. (eds.) (2016) *Artistic Interventions in Organizations: Research, Theory and Practice.* New York: Routledge.

Kerr, C. and Lloyd, C. (2008) Pedagogical learnings for management education: Developing creativity and innovation, *Journal of Management and Organization* 14(5): 486–503.

Klein, G. (2011) Dancing politics: Worldmaking in dance and choreography, in Klein, G. and Noeth, S. (eds.) *Emerging Bodies: The Performance of Worldmaking in Dance and Choreography.* Bielefeld: transcript, 17–28.

Klein, G., Barthel, G. and Wager, E. (2011) *Choreografischer Baukasten*. Bielefeld: transcript.

Kolo, K. (2012) (How) can you choreograph a company? https://unternehmenscho reographie.wordpress.com/english/ (Accessed 1 Feb 2016).

Kolo, K. (2016) Ode to choreography, *Organizational Aesthetics* 5(1): 37–46.

Kracauer, S. (1978) *Straßen in Berlin und anderswo*. Berlin: Das Arsenal.

Küpers, W. (2013) Embodied inter-practices of leadership—phenomenological perspectives on relational and responsive leading and following, *Leadership* 9(3): 335–357.

Laban, R. von (2011) Modern educational dance (1948), introd. Ann Carlisle, in McCaw, D. (ed.) *The Laban Sourcebook*. London: Routledge, 237–256.

Ladkin, D. (2013) From perception to flesh: A phenomenological account of the felt experience of leadership. *Leadership* 9(3): 320–334.

Lempa, F. (2016) The aesthetics of applied theatre: An interview, *Organizational Aesthetics* 5(2): 25–33.

Lepecki, A. (2013) Dance and politics, in Brandstetter, G. and Klein, G. (eds.) *Dance [and] Theory*. Bielefeld: transcript, 153–158.

Lloyd, C. and Hill, G. (2013) Human sculpture, a creative and reflective learning tool for groups and organisations, *International Journal of Professional Management* 8(5): 67–75.

Ludevig, D. (2016) Using embodied knowledge to unlock innovation, creativity, and intelligence in businesses, *Organizational Aesthetics* 5(1): 147–161.

Matzdorf, F. and Sen, R. (2016) Demanding followers, empowered leaders: Dance as an 'embodied metaphor' for leader-followership, *Organizational Aesthetics* 5(1): 114–130.

Nissley, N. (2010) Arts-based learning at work: Economic downturns, innovation upturns, and the eminent practicality of arts in business, *Journal of Business Strategy* 31(4): 8–20.

Pakes, A. (2009) Knowing through dance making: Choreography, practical knowledge and practice-as-research, in Butterworth, J. and Wildschut, L. (eds.) *Contemporary Choreography: A Critical Reader*. London and New York: Routledge, 10–22.

Polhemus, T. (1988) Dance, gender and culture, in Carter, A. (ed.) *The Routledge Dance Studies Reader*. London and New York: Routledge, 171–179.

Powell, M. and Gifford, J. (2016) Dancing lessons for leaders: Experiencing the artistic mindset, *Organizational Aesthetics* 5(1): 131–149.

Rippin, A. (2013) Putting the Body Shop in its place: A studio-based investigation into the new sites and sights of organization as experience, *Organization Studies* 34(10): 1551–1562.

Rippin, A. (2015) Feminine writing: Text as dolls, drag and ventriloquism, *Gender, Work & Organisation* 22(2): 112–128.

Ropo, A. and Sauer, E. (2008) Dances of leadership: Bridging theory and practice through an aesthetic approach, *Journal of Management and Organization* 14(5): 560–572.

Rowe, N. and Zeitner-Smith, D. (2011) Teaching creative dexterity to dancers: Critical reflections on conservatory dance education in the UK, Denmark and New Zealand, *Research in Dance Education* 12(1): 41–52.

Scharmer, C. and Kaeufer, K. (2010) In front of the blank canvas: Sensing emerging futures, *Journal of Business Strategy* 31(4): 21–29.Schiuma, G. (2011) *The Value of Arts for Business*. Cambridge: Cambridge University Press.

Sellers, J. (2013) The Labyrinth: A journey of discovery, in McIntosh, P. and Warren, D. (eds.) *Creativity in the Classroom: Case Studies in Using the Arts in Teaching and Learning in Higher Education.* Bristol: Intellect, 209–224.

Snowber, C. (2012) Dance as a way of knowing, *New Directions for Adult and Continuing Education* 134(1): 53–60.

Springborg, C. and Sutherland, I. (2014) Flying blind? Teaching aesthetic agency in an Executive MBA course, in Taylor, S. and Ladkin, D. (eds.) *The Physicality of Leadership: Gesture, Entanglement, Taboo, Possibilities.* Bingley: Emerald Books, 37–58.

Springborg, C. and Sutherland, I. (2016) Teaching MBAs aesthetic agency through dance, *Organizational Aesthetics* 5(1): 94–113.

Svendler Nielsen, C. and Burridge, S. (eds.) (2015) *Dance Education Around the World: Perspectives on Dance, Young People and Change.* New York: Routledge.

Taylor, S. (2014) Silly social science scales: Embracing the particular, *Organizational Aesthetics* 3(1): 4–6.

TILLT (2009) Truckbaletten Veera Suvalo Grimberg Landvetter Airport 090512. https://www.youtube.com/watch?v=Eo7aGybvL7s (Accessed 1 Sep 2016).

Walz, P. (2016) Austausch & Vernetzung. https://blog.daimler.de/2016/05/13/austausch-vernetzung-pathfinder-kongress-in-berlin/ (Accessed 20 Sep 2016).

Yukl, G. (2006) *Leadership in Organizations*, 6th ed. Upper Saddle Creek, NJ: Prentice Hall.

Zeitner, D., Rowe, N. and Jackson, B. (2016) Embodied and embodiary leadership: Experiential learning in dance and leadership education, *Organizational Aesthetics* 5(1): 167–187.

7   Dance as a Method (Research)

Dance-based methods have been used with other arts-based research methods by organisational scholars to access and analyse organisational life. Arts-based and aesthetically sensitive approaches (Warren, 2008) emphasise the sensual experience, which often is difficult to access and to verbalise due to its embodied and tacit nature. Rippin (2013: 1554) suggests that "organizations are located in our experience of them, and that art is an appropriate and useful way for organization scholars to explore and represent that experience".

Dance is a new approach in organisation studies, inspired by research in the area of performance studies and social studies, which look back on a longer tradition of using dance as a method. Following the suggestion of early studies on dance and organisation to attempt a "close observation of who moves, how they move, and with what consequences", including the "rhythms" (Chandler, 2012: 876), such a method goes beyond using 'dance' as a metaphor. Applying dance for research links to embodiment research and phenomenological approaches that promote the body as a central source of data and that have lead to a general increase in dance as a methodological tool in other disciplines results (Leavy, 2009: 182). Working from the premise that the body is a repository for what people know, dance and movement as a method can help to access this embodied experience. This approach suggests that there are kinds of data that our bodies experience before our minds though the physical interaction with the world, making movement a means to access bodily knowing (Snowber, 2012: 54).

Dance is a very particular addition to arts-based research approaches in organisation studies as it is in many ways the most abstract art form, combining elements from other arts such as the performative, the visual and the poetic. Dance has been referred to as a 'universal language', despite and probably because of its abstract from, with the potential to express experiences through the body. In comparison with other arts-based research approaches, dance has a particular strength to deal with aesthetic and tacit knowing in organisations:

> The use of artistic forms to look at aesthetic issues offers a medium that can capture and communicate the felt experience, the affect, and

something of the tacit knowledge of the day-to-day, moment-to-moment reality of organizations. Not just the cleaned-up, instrumental concerns of 'the business', but the messy, unordered side as well. In short it provides a holistic way to get at the whole of the experience, something that the intellectualization and abstraction of traditional organizational research often seems to miss.

(Taylor and Hansen, 2005: 1224)

Dance as a research method communicates without words and directly starts with the body as a tool and its motion. Using the body as a starting point and a medium, dance-based methods fit very well to aesthetic approaches in organisations and related perspectives, for example in gender research and feminist, postmodern, psychoanalytic perspectives that put the body at the centre of attention. Positing that social experience and organisational experience is embodied, it is only logical to start exploring by using the body. In addition to considering the body as an instrument that through kinaesthetic politics and choreographies, through voice, gesture and movement performs social practices and communicates cultural messages, the body can be viewed as a locus of discovery (Halprin, 2000), being "inscribed" as a site where social meanings are created and resisted, and being the "lived body" that experiences the world.

Dance studies go beyond a Cartesian dualism positing the body and the mind as two distinct and mutually exclusive regions of human experience. Following phenomenological approaches, dance studies see the body as a source of data and knowledge, and as an experiential memory repository for what we know, which may, consequentially, emerge through dance and movement. This perspective posits that people's bodies are in immediate physical touch with the world and gather experiences that are stored in the body and exist there in ways that differ from rational understandings. The body is inscribed by many social, cultural and political discourses and is a legitimate site to explore how and who we are and perceive others. This makes movement workshops, exercises and performances a means to access bodily knowing and to communicate this knowledge. Dance as a body-based research tool uses a 'universal language' and non-verbal way to access and express experiences individuals made while being in an organisation.

These embodied, tacit forms of knowing can not only be represented through artistic forms—different from explicit knowledge that can be represented through text and discursive forms—but can also be accessed through these forms. Langer (1942) argues that the different media we use to map reality (e.g. painting, music, dance and language) have different properties and, therefore, distort reality in different ways. Different art forms make it possible to capture and express aspects of reality, which cannot be captured or expressed when using the medium of language. For example, because the medium of language consists of words, which appear one at a time like beads on a string, this medium distorts reality so it appears more as if it consists of discrete objects appearing in sequences. In contrast, using painting or picture to map reality opens the possibility of capturing and expressing simultaneously occurring, contradictory aspects of reality. However, static paintings and pictures leave little room for capturing developments in time. Dance, by contrast, as a 'universal language' can capture and express both simultaneously occurring, contradictory aspects *and* their development in time. It can be argued that in this sense dance-based media are superior to language in their ability to capture and express complex and aesthetic organisational phenomena.

Artistic research is a major topic in contemporary dance research (Brandstetter and Klein, 2013) and the use of movement to explore inter-personal issues in organisations seems a natural continuation of and complementary addition to an historic tradition of dance as a medium in social and political life. The idea of using arts-based forms is fairly new to management scholars and extant arts-based methods include poetry, visual narratives and imagery, fabrics and materials.

To outline the value of dance as an organisational research method, the rationale behind arts-based organisational research methods is presented in a next step. This is followed by a description of dance as a means to generate data and an explanation of approaches to dance analysis to access the data. Dance and movement workshops are often followed by a viewing of video recordings, and the analysis of video recordings, and can be complemented with qualitative interviews. Methods from dance studies that draw on choreographic notation of dance are introduced, for example Laban Movement Analysis. Then discussed is the use of dance as a representational form, i.e. a way to give form to research findings that is different from written and verbal presentation. Further links between dance and research in the humanities and critical and feminist approaches to organisational research will be explored to develop the argument that a dance-based method has a particular potential to present, challenge and negotiate many aspects relating to kinaesthetic politics and choreographies in organisations.

Arts-Based Methods

The idea of using arts-based forms is rather unconventional for many scholars in management, but they have been used in different contexts following the performative turn in social sciences and qualitative paradigm that emerged during the 20th century. Arts-based research methods are employed by qualitative researchers in organisation studies, looking back on a longer tradition of application across the humanities and social sciences. These methods are useful during all phases of research, including data collection, analysis, interpretation and representation. Arts-based methodologies draw on different forms such as visual art, music, theatre performance, literary and poetic writing. Representational forms include a variety of ways of expression such as theatre plays, poems, collages, songs, paintings, drawings, and dance and movement performances.

Theoretical developments and interdisciplinary scholarship have led to methodological advances, and epistemological changes have brought about a redefinition of the qualitative paradigm in the social sciences and a growing body of literature on art as a method of inquiry (Knowles and Cole, 2008). Arts-based research methods in management studies still remain a somewhat marginal practice (Buchanan and Bryman, 2009). Positivist science, also referred to as empiricism, became the model for scientific research across disciplines and is the dominant approach in management and organisation studies. Despite the incorporation of many different methodological positions within organisation studies, the long-term trend, also fuelled by increasing pressures to publish in peer-reviewed journals that have a bias towards quantitative data, is still in favour of positivist empirical analyses. Management studies is seen to be dominated by seemingly rational approaches such as the 'rigorous method', and Phillips and colleagues (2014: 315) critically quote unrealistic ideals of the researcher as a person being able to approach 'perfect rationality', preferably in quantitative (hard) ways as 'real men don't collect soft data'. These ideal models in positivist approaches favour masculine (white) ideals and forms of expression (Höpfl, 2000), and are complicit in the oppression of minority und less privileged groups of all genders. They exclude diverse forms of thinking and representations and the main concern levied against these methods centres around basic issues of validity and trustworthiness (Leavy, 2009: 6). The debate about including arts-based methods is hence linked to larger discourses on scientific standards and ways to build knowledge.

The arts-based approach has been received sceptically by traditional management studies dominated by positivism, because it adopts subjective views hardly capable of claiming to reveal generalisable knowledge. Ann Rippin (2006) has described how her arts-based explorations with fabrics were referred to derogatively and as self-indulgent by particular members of the academic management community. With a little imagination one can guess how the use of dance may be received, as dance often has been labelled a 'female' art form and that has seen much rejection in the academic community when it evolved into an academic discipline. With regard to kinaesthetic politics and the oppression and rejection of many bodies in organisations, inclusive the female body, it might be a difficulty that dance and movement exercises put the gendered body, its properties and capacities into the centre.

Dance and arts-based research methods can be situated in a context that challenged positivist approaches over the past decades. Qualitative and aesthetic approaches to management often follow a constructivist perspective, questioning a knowable reality and 'truth' that exists independently of the research process and can be discovered, measured and controlled via objective means, in a deductive process, through an objective researcher (Hesse-Biber and Leavy, 2007). For example, ethnography with its 'thick descriptions' came to challenge positivist assumptions about social reality and the researcher and from the 1960s a growing diversity with female researchers and people of colour came to reframe research questions and approaches because of power dynamics and related questions such as voice, authority and representation that make 'objectivity' appear as a practice of exclusion and oppression. Other influences such as globalisation, economic and media change and emerging schools of thought such as postmodernism and critical approaches lead to a development of the qualitative paradigm to deconstruct, challenge and question extant research.

When researchers work with data generated through moving bodies, they draw on their own bodily perceptions and kinaesthetic empathy. This challenges ideas of traditional concepts of academic research based on neutrality and rigorous standards. In this regard "dance knowledge" has been considered as sensual-dynamic knowledge bearing a critical potential towards traditional science: Dance knowing confronts traditional studies that try to capture dynamic processes in static concepts (Klein, 2007: 33). Dance is critical as it makes obvious the shortcomings of intellectual inquiry, distorting and disrupting frontiers between knowing and science.

Dance as an abstract art form situates itself in attempts to push borders in a research tradition that is strongly influenced by positivist approaches. Arts-based approaches have gained more ground and in other disciplines, for example in performance studies, concepts of 'practice as research' have seen a strong development. Its rise was influenced not only by the epistemological arguments that were outlined, but also by political and economic considerations. As the contribution of the arts and cultural industries to national health and prosperity has mounted in the political agenda, a growing number of performing arts and related university departments have developed degrees that place practice at their centre (PARIP, 2006), in many ways preceding contemporary management education. This has led to new practical research approaches in the performing arts (drama, theatre, dance, music) and related disciplines (film, video, television, radio). Most notably, the use of performance as research has massively expanded over the last three decades and includes a variety of methods for data generation, analysis and representation, ranging from ethnodrama to theatre scripts and performances often strongly related to the social context and people's lives (Leavy, 2009) and which also serve as an inspiration for dance-based approaches to organisation studies. The surge in performance-based research methods has also been traced back to early qualitative and metaphorical theorising on organisations 'as theatre' for example. When conceiving of social interaction as a performance with front stage and back stage and rituals of impression management, it is only a small step to use actual theatre-based methods for inquiry (Leavy, 2009: 7). The growing body of research that theorises 'dance and organisation' will likewise drive forward the applied use of dance for organisational inquiry.

Arts-based research approaches and related arts-based interventions have received positive feedback when stakeholders are involved. Their practical use-value and the demand to make an impact has furthered the fast and smooth adaption of arts-based methods in the humanities and arts departments in UK Higher Education and determines funding success for researchers. Critics find that practice as research is often instrumentalised as social work, for example when theatre projects are made with stakeholder groups. The same opportunity and risk can apply to dance-based projects when they are used primarily to work with organisational members according to organisational aims, rather than providing the freedom to get to the bottom of organisational issues. As with dance-based training workshops, researchers need to be aware of the history of bodies in organisations that were used in many destructive ways to not further pressure organisational participants. Cancienne and Snowber (2009: 211) in this regard suggest that we need to be interested "in using the body to release the tension, understand relationships of self and other, and ultimately heal bodies that are silenced, stressed, and restricted in ways that are unhealthy". This idea also links to the tradition of using dance as a therapeutic tool in a self-directed way that can help build an enhanced bodily awareness and understanding of social relationships.

Analysing Movement

To make use of dance to generate new insights into organisational life, researchers and practitioners have resorted to actual dance and movement exercises for data generation. Movement data can stem from different situations and can have different forms. Studies on social spaces for example have used video recordings from people moving, which can be measured with regard to time and spatial dimensions, also applying quantitative methods. The focus of this chapter however is on dance-based research that bears many parallels to the use of dance as an arts-based intervention in organisation. The dance-based approach requires somebody to 'move' the participants: This can be the researchers if they can choreograph in the sense of linking movements to concepts and the research question; or data generation can be facilitated through a choreographer.

While dance-based interventions often use language to reflect on the experiences and to bring to a higher level the insights, many of the experiences remain in the individual's bodies. The use of dance as a research method at this point makes an effort to access the body as a repository for what we know and to bring to lights these insights. When using dance as a part of data collection, dance can serve as a source of information on cultural, social and organisational practices. Dance can be useful to gain insights into, for example, social choreographies in organisations and kinaesthetic politics including gender and individual perception. When culture and social inscription is expressed in movement, dance analysis goes from the outer form to describe what is expressed through movement. Researchers need to find ways to evaluate data from, for example, movement workshops that are video-recorded or observed live, in which groups of participants or individuals use movement as a tool. This approach, as other qualitative approaches as well, take all steps in the ethical approval process and fully disclose their methodology to participants and readers of subsequent publications.

To analyse movement, organisational researchers can draw on their experience and theoretical knowledge as the activities of analysing movement and locating it within its context are inextricably linked (Carter, 1998: 237). Many cultural analyses of dance have shown that not only analytical skill is important to capture the meaning and implications of movement, but a knowledge of the prevailing political context, and also often an analysis of the circumstances of the production process. This resonates with the extended discussion of the social embeddedness of movement and choreographies. Some of the extant examples in organisational research using dance-based approaches that I will refer to in this section also have addressed both the aesthetic and organisational and cultural dimensions of the movement performance and have included the voices of producers and performers.

The use of dance as a research method confronts traditional research approaches and also brings up the question of competence and prerequisites for academic research on body movements. Berger and Schmidt (2009) have asserted that some bodily competence and sensory-motoric, embodied knowledge is necessary for the perception of movement. This does not automatically mean that researchers need a profound knowledge on representational forms of dance and codes useful for classical ballet for example, but that they use their own kinaesthetic empathy and bodily reception, their kinaesthetic experience and observations that often cannot be put into objective words. The processes of dancing and dance-making can be felt, but not to a full extent represented verbally (Foster, 2013: 26). Kinaesthetic empathy resides in our bodies already but can be developed: Referring to the "responsive body", the choreographer William Forsythe emphasised the value of training bodily intelligence that complements the understanding in the mind (Berger and Schmidt, 2009: 75).

Dance analysis does not remain at the level of a detailed description of movement and is more than examining elements such as effort, shape and the use of the body that are suggested as categories in Laban Movement Analysis for example. The choreographer William Forsythe has created a research project for the documentation and notation of choreography that is called "Motion Bank" (www.motionbank.org) and encouraged the development of a video annotation software called "piecemaker". Breaking dance into smaller units leads to some questions that pertain to the difficulties of notating movements that are multi-dimensional, highly dynamic and transitory:

> But questions emerged of what to notate, in which ways and in which media? Is it the steps, the movement in space, the quality of movement, in words, drafts or videos? Who is notating, from which perspective: is it what the choreographer designs, the performance of dancers or what

the spectator remembers? Who is reading the final notation? Is the purpose of notation a prescript before a dance is performed or a description after it has been performed? The answers to these questions vary. Standards therefore are difficult to develop and establish.

(Kolo, 2016: 38)

Digital technologies are appreciated by dance educators (Kipling Brown, 2015), for example cameras to record, stream and view performances, and programs such as DanceForms and Labanwriter that offered a means to both choreograph and notate movement and dance, as does the iPad app KineScribe, which displays and edits scores in Laban movement notation. Many computer-based applications for dance including motion capture, Internet-based performance, and interactive technology show that even if the body in dance interacts with a chosen spatial environment, there is strong interest in not only enhancing people's learning in the digital age, but with working with digital technology—a practical bridge between dance and digitization, in addition to the conceptual discussion in this book on the value of dance with regard to embodied knowing, kinaesthetic empathy and collaboration.

Further pursing the idea of making sense of movement in research data, the notion of interpretation of dance requires that "the character of the dance, its subject matter, the treatment of that subject matter and the qualities that might be ascribed are also understood" (Adshead, 1988: 167). In order to appreciate dance, the individual needs certain skills of noting and observing movement components and their relationship. A dance analysis is based on the ability to construct a big picture of the components and participants and the ways in which they coexist, interact and create something special. Appreciating dance is linked to ascribing certain qualities and attributing meanings, achieving an interpretation, based on a description of the movement and supported by additional knowledge of the context of the dance (Adshead, 1998: 167). This also applies to some extent to the analysis of movement in an organisational context, and means that an understanding of the historical and social context or the organisational culture is of relevance, as well as site-specific aspects, particular social choreographies and kinaesthetic politics.

An example from earlier studies on dance and organisation is from Kavanagh et al. (2008), who have presented an analysis of Irish dance, finding that the genre of Riverdance stands for a transformation of working relations and can serve as a lens through which globalised work and management can be discussed. The authors frame their discussion around the historical development of Irish dance that is immersed in larger organising discourses, historical narratives about national identity and attempts to control the body. Riverdance illustrates a shift towards a more liberated approach to the body, with body-hugging materials, short skirts and tight shirts designed to subtly sexualise dancers' bodies. In this sense Riverdance liberated locked-up elements of Irish tradition and became a parable of the modernisation of Irish culture (Kavanagh et al., 2008: 738). The merit of this paper is that it presents an under-researched approach in organisation studies to kinaesthetic politics, interpreting movement as an expression of culture. Such an approach would benefit from an aesthetic analysis of dance movements or a detailed description of the dance presentations that would have been valuable to illustrate some of the power, drive and energetic sexuality that is brought to life in these presentations and tie them back to organisational life. More generally, when dance is used for research with organisational members, movement is not used as a metaphor but as a bodily expression of tacit and embodied knowing.

In dance studies, Freedman (1991: 335) for example has made the point that to understand the meaning inherent in dance as a form of communicative, it is necessary to analyse both the movement text (the dance itself) and the cultural context of the dance event. She has done an interpretative ethnography of dance in the courtship and marriage rituals of a Romanian village, focusing on the dance performance and gender differences in movement (kinaesthetic politics). She approached dance movement as a system of meaningful, coded signs that are performed through different movements and dynamics by women and men. The analysis of videos, informed by data about the cultural specifics in the area, showed how gender-specific dance movements are performed on the level of movement and position and are learned from childhood. Differences can be perceived in bodily postures and in the ways energy is mobilised and in the way the bodies move through space. The detailed description used categories such as "body", "effort" and "space" is as follows:

> Body: While the cultural level stance is neutral erect, with an erect torso, (. . .) women show a slight curve in the upper body (. . .) The women also show more twist in the waist than the men. (. . .)
>
> Effort: While strength is the predominant effort fall all dancers, the women show more lightness than the men. The greater use of lightness shows in more body parts, for a longer duration of time and in more combinations with more effort factors. [. . .]
>
> Space: The women use large, arc-like movements to change direction in turns. Men's direction changes are much more angular. Both groups stop the turn with a diagonal use of space, thrusting one foot diagonally forward in a narrow fourth position. Women distribute their weight evenly in this position, whereas the men prefer an uneven distribution, with the weight on one foot. [. . .] During the upbeat of the stamping motif, women stress the sagittal dimension of the sagittal plane, which is composed of the two dimensions of sagittal and vertical. The men, however, stress the vertical dimension of this plane. [. . .] While both sexes lean away from each other, the lean differs by sex. Women lean from the knees or ankles while the men lean angularly from the hip.
>
> (Freedman, 199: 341–343)

Reading this detailed description in categories conveys some idea of the kinaesthetic experience and aesthetic richness of the dance and develops a better understanding of the argument that the movements and their combination make part of a subtle system of communication of intended messages. The framework that is used to categorise movements in such a way is presented in the next section.

Laban Movement Analysis

An established framework used to analyse dance performances is Laban Movement Analysis (LMA). One part of what also is referred to as Laban-analysis is Labannotation, a system for the notation of movement structure, and the other part is a system for the description of dynamic movement qualities, or energy use, called Effort/Shape. The three elements that are commonly considered are: 1) use of body (height; weight; depth); 2) use of space (the horizontal axis, vertical and sagittal (front to back); 3) use of effort. In the context of these categories, the researcher can specify which body parts move in which ways through space and time, and what sort of energy can be perceived. The use of body also includes issues such as: transference, trunk articulation, the relationship between body parts, and the organisation of body parts within phrases such as simultaneous or sequential phrasing. It also includes the point of initiation of the movement, which can be central, from the trunk, or peripheral, from the limbs (Freedman, 1991: 226). The use of effort includes when the weight of the body is used to exert force or is used in light ways. The issue of flow concerns the tension in the body, which allows to immediately stop the continuity of movements, or makes it hard to stop. The perception of time also is relevant, varying from hectic movements to the relaxed use of available time.

These categories of analysis have been applied in gender research on movement as well, for example in early observations on young women making less use of horizontal, vertical and sagittal space when "throwing like a girl" (Young, 1980: 137). Later studies have developed fine-grained observations. In the analysis of Romanian dancers (Freedman, 1991: 341), categories that were used contain the body (stance; waist twist; forward lean; sequencing of turns), effort (weight; space; time; flow) and space (spatial; space use; lean), to develop a gender movement profile by noting the differences. For example, in a corresponding diagram, the line on the analysis of "weight" says: "mostly strong; more lightness in more body parts combined" (women)—"mostly strong; little lightness—in only one body part at a time" (men).

Such profiles delineate the strong difference between qualitative movement styles of women and men. The research also gave evidence that participants understood and reacted to these movements and subtle movement elements—without using technical terms, but through their kinaesthetic empathy and embodied knowing of lived cultural practice. Labanalysis in this study helps to explain subtle but meaningful movement messages that are part of the definition of the local gender role to a wider audience so that they can be used to reflect on the definition of non-local gender identities as well.

In organisation studies, Labananalysis has only recently been used by Ralf Wetzel and Natalie Van Renterghem (2016), who asked participants to engage in creative movement. Different from standardised management teaching with a strongly cognitive language, movement improvisation provided MBA students with a different experience of topics such as formal and informal coordination, which was then used for further reflection in a learning context. Wetzel and Van Renterghem (2016: 48) included "the body as both a variable to be addressed in the teaching and as a focus of experience of the students". Video recordings from two forms of group coordination, formal and informal coordination, were analysed with Laban Movement Analysis. The analysis showed how the bodies responded differently in terms of the use of body, space, and effort, depending on the management style. The video showed that in an emergent, informal way of coordination, participants' bodily expression pointed to much more calmness, openness and self-assuredness in the coordination, while the formal, hierarchic way was related to anxiety, insecurity and the fear of failing:

> In the formally directed way of coordinating, there was almost no connection between the different players but a strong connection between each of them and their respective manager/choreographer. We experienced a lower responsibility of individual performers for the whole picture the group was drawing, it appeared more as if individuals were following instructions. In the second part of the exercise, the overall groups appeared to be more connected and aware of each other, they seemed to be more observing of what is happening (eye contact, flexibility of bodies towards new things occurring).
> (Wetzel and Van Renterghem, 2016: 57)

This exercise again expresses the concept of kinaesthetic empathy that is used to achieve a social choreography as a collaborative interaction. While in improvisational theatre language tends to keep cognition awake, Wetzel and Van Renterghem (2016: 51) use movement improvisation that emphasises the kinaesthetic empathy of multiple players in a room, the experience of the instantaneousness of individual decisions, of an "embodied deciding" outside the routines of everyday work. With regard to the transformative potential in dance, improvisation leads to new movement patterns and promotes discovery. Acknowledging the embodied nature of organisational interaction, the exercise helps to develop ideas on the adaptability of groups and organisations.

Such an example for dance-based teaching goes some way towards what Celeste Snowber (2014: 254) refers to as "body pedagogy". This approach emphasises teaching embodied human beings and reclaiming the body as a place of knowledge and understanding. Linking learning to creative understanding, teachers need to be attentive to students' movements: "A big part of creativity is about listening, and as a dancer, writer, and educator, my task is to listen to the language and nuances of movement, words, and the subtleties of the gestural and tonal language of my students" (Snowber, 2014: 258). Students are challenged to connect to their embodied ways of being and knowing to reflect on their visceral activity. Attending to our own embodied knowledge is important in organisations and can be trained in the classroom as well.

Movement Analysis and Interviews

Dance-based methods can be combined with qualitative interviews, and also with focus group interviews that often are used in addition to dance-based methods (Leavy, 2009: 181) when film sequences are presented for the purpose of discussion to participants. In a multi-method approach, videos from movements to be analysed with Laban Movement Analysis for example are often combined with interviews as a verbal reflection. For a research project we have worked with a choreographer who has led movement workshops with participants. Looking into social choreographies, the project (Biehl and Volkmann, 2016) examined movements from hotel school students who were trained on the job. The method of dance was deemed suitable when considering movement as a performative element of social interchange. We found that participants use their kinaesthetic empathy to coordinate their movements, also collaborating towards a new choreography beyond predefined patterns and a professional habitus.

To develop suitable exercises, we worked through the literature on social choreographies to identify issues that could be approached through movement exercises. The ideas were then discussed with the choreographer, also with regard to his repertoire that one of the researchers has experienced in an earlier workshop. Improvisational movements were included that typically break patterned movements and promote discovery outside the routines of everyday work (Leavy, 2009: 180). Similar to a research process, the choreographic process is one of organising, sorting, examining, editing, doing and re-doing—a process of discovery. For example, an exercise that required joint clapping in pairs was devised that aimed to gather data on kinaesthetic coordination. It showed how hesitations were negotiated and how bodies were coordinated non-verbally. Another exercise involving confident and timid postures aimed to get insights into kinaesthetic empathy and the non-verbal transfer of emotions through movement. Participants in another exercise were asked to move through the space in a huddle whereby leadership and directions were constantly shifting and improvised.

The workshops were videotaped and analysed with Laban Movement Analysis considering the three perspectives: 1) use of body; 2) use of the space (horizontal, vertical, sagittal [front to back]; and 3) use of effort, along with a consideration of how body parts move (dynamics, energy). We used the categories to identify issues that related to the research questions and to other phenomena to be followed up in the interviews, for example when group movements suddenly expanded in space or diminished their extent. For example, we have observed restricted body movements in certain situations that transported feelings of uneasiness, whereas in other moments the used space expanded or decreased, prompting further questions.

The video analysis of the leadership exercise for example shows some use of the space in terms of horizontal and sagittal (front to back) movement whereas the use of effort, along with a consideration of how body parts move (dynamics, energy, rhythm) was rather low. This indicated that participants felt uncomfortable and reluctant to take the leader role, as expressed in the subsequent verbal interviews. Videos showed how participants react to influences that are perceived kinaesthetically, not through seeing, also referred to as "pressure of people behind you" by one participant. Feelings of insecurity were shared by the collective body of a group, which became clear for individuals and for observers as well.

> Yes, I think it was quite ironic, the fact that we're watching a group of hotel managers and they're all trying to get to the back. We're meant to be doing a course in leadership, and people are scuttling round, hiding away. [. . .] You know, in the hotel—I've witnessed it myself—a lot of people in that room can be leaders and they can do those roles properly, but obviously different situations bring up different parts of people. Some of the same people, like I said, are hiding behind their team members, which would be the last thing you'd see in the hotel.

The identification of issues in the videos not only is a result of rational coding but also emerges as a bodily understanding of the researchers when watching movement and reacting with kinaesthetic empathy when these movements resonate in the own body (Berger and Schmidt, 2009). This understanding was enhanced by the participation of two researchers in a separate workshop. This form of kinaesthetic empathy when watching also was helpful for the subsequent focus group interviews in which film sequences were presented to participants.

The example again shows that dance as a research-method has a two-fold effect, linking to forms of kinaesthetic training: Movement does not only help researchers to access embodied social structures, but can also enhance participants' understanding of their everyday choreographies.

Catalogue for Performance and Dance Analysis

Researchers analysing dance performance often draw on a framework for performance analysis going back to Patrice Pavis (2003). This framework can be used both for dance and performance and has already been applied in organisation studies to study the aesthetic dimension of interaction (Biehl-Missal, 2011). While dance shares with the performance of theatre many transitory aspects, theatre researchers in many cases and in classical plays have a text to look at. The practice of movement however is transitory and difficult to capture, unlike visual or textual artefacts, and poses additional methodological challenges. A catalogue for performance analysis accounts for perception occurring in a non-hierarchical way, not primarily through the visual sense or the understanding of what has been said. It extends beyond earlier, more semiotic, models for theatre analysis that have a strong focus on a dramatic text or a story-line in dance and neglect many relevant elements that are hardly materialised, often invisible, are energy and atmosphere (Pavis, 2003: 36).

Dance and performance researchers use Pavis's (2003) framework considering in detail distinct elements such as space, movement, light, sound and people's bodily interaction. This procedure is a "mise en pièces" (Pavis, 2003: 8), a complementary process to the structured planning process of the mise en scène, requiring the researcher to deconstruct and reconstruct the performance to identify its motifs and aesthetic impact. Analysis of organisational phenomena would require a remodelled version of the catalogue (Biehl-Missal, 2011), which is initially designed to be adapted. I shall refer to Pavis's original framework to provide an overview of a range elements, whose inclusion can be considered.

Its first category is the 'general discussion of the performance' (1), which identifies intellectual themes that emerge from the analysis. Movement performance can thus be tied to places as a site-specific performance, to issues of kinaesthetic politics, choreographies and leadership. The scenography (2) and stage properties (4) relate to the material framing and describe the impact of the space. The sensual category of smell (Pavis, 2003: 195) that pertains to a room can be added here. Lighting (3) considers the intensity, colour and distribution of light, and can often be linked to the category 'music and sound effects' (7). The functions of theatrical costume (5) largely coincide with clothing in social life, as an important element expressing general values and a person's role in organisational contexts.

The actors' performances (6) are described with regard to the interplay of gestures, postures and voice. This part would be elaborated on in greater detail when a dance and movement performance is analysed. This would also be the place to integrate further insights of Laban Movement Analysis, which categorises human movement according to the body, the effort and the space.

Pavis's category of the '(dramatic) text in performance' (10) is irrelevant for non-dramatic performances, whereas story-lines (9) can be addressed in an organisational context, for example in terms of topic (e.g. leadership). The 'pace' (8) refers to the perceived time or duration that is an interesting element particularly in movement performances that can be energetic, extremely slow, hesitant or in flow, generating a corresponding kinaesthetic experience. The separate category on the audience and their actions (11) stems from a traditional theatre/dance setting, and can be referred to throughout the analysis, emphasising that the situation is co-created by all participants, as expressed by, for example the kinaesthetic feedback loop. The database and modes of analysis are addressed by Pavis's section on the notation (12), along with incoherencies and remarks (13 + 14), and would typically be listed in a methodology section.

Applying Pavis's questionnaire as a structuring frame for their data, researchers typically draw on further theory that assesses the impact of individual elements, which is not fully subjective but depends on culture and context. When considering movement in organised space in terms of

Table 7.1 Questionnaire for performance analysis, adapted from Pavis (2003)

1 *General discussion of performance* what holds elements of performance together; what do you find disturbing about the production; strong moments or weak moments?	7 *Function of music and sound effects* 8 *Pace of performance* overall pace, steady or broken, dynamics
2 *Scenography* relationship between audience space and acting space; principles of organisation of space; colours and their connotations; relationship between off-stage and on-stage	9 *Interpretation of story-line in performance* story; dramaturgical choices; plot structure 10 *Text in performance* 11 *Audience* Audience actions, co-production of meaning
3 *Lighting system* 4 *Stage properties* type, function, relationship to space and actors' bodies	12 *How to notate (photograph and film) this production* 13 *What cannot be put into signs* 14 *Final assessment* any comments, further suggestions, additions to the questionnaire
5 *Costumes* style; function; relationship to actors' bodies	
6 *Actors' performances* style of acting; relation between actor-group/ text-body/ actor-role; quality of gestures, mime and voice	

'site-specific performance' (Chapter 5) for example, one may consult books on architecture and also popular books that may have been published on the specific space, if available. Further textual or visual material pertaining to the phenomenon, from media publications and blogging and social network sites, can be included as these online contributions have become vehicles through which experiences are being logged and exchanged among participants. Dance analysis often is part of a multi-method research project that does not simply 'add' methods, but rather lets them inform each other: A questionnaire and personal experience of dance and discussions with participants would operate synergistically with traditional qualitative interviews as all these approaches seek to yield insights on the same aspects.

Researchers on dance situations have for example included data from background talks with participants in situ, interviews with DJs and dancers (Biehl-Missal, 2016; Pfadenhauer, 2009). When movement is related to sound, it is useful to not only dance but simultaneously immerse yourself in the sound, via recordings for example. Referring to these experiences is particularly important in performances linked to electronic sound as they are disconnected from the textual meaning found in many theatre performances (Pavis, 2003: 47). The latter aspects point to the use of the body to collect data that also part of the approach.

When in arts-based research, the researcher is an instrument that interprets and makes sense of things, in dance-based practice, the researcher's moving body is an instrument. The body is used as a tool to access embodied knowing (see next section), but also to complement the application of the Pavis catalogue and for ethnographic approaches. As the dance experience cannot be fully articulated in a written text, Foster (2013) argues for dance as a form of research, which includes that researchers dance themselves and reflect on their movement. This requires personal visits to and participation in the dance performances that commonly are practiced by dance researchers. Such a form of movement participation becomes increasingly important when considering realist forms of movement and not highly codified artistic forms such as ballet or socially coded dance. Studies on dance and on raves as non-codified practices for example include in their analysis participatory observations and accounts of personal experiences (Gerard, 2004). Joint movement in other contexts as well is not primarily a representational practice that can be analysed with an external perspective, but revolves around bodily presence and experience, calling for an internal perspective (Klein, 2004: 250). As in ethnographic dance research, dance scholars include their personal experiences from dancing and refer to their kinaesthetic responses (Pavis, 2003: 101) to the situation.

The Pavis questionnaire as a research tool is particularly useful when organisational life is not considered metaphorically 'as dance', but when the kinaesthetic experience is in the focus. Working with the questionnaire requires researchers to experience the situation and to involve themselves and their moving bodies. For example, in a study that analyses the experience of a techno club (Biehl-Missal, 2016) I undertook personal visits during the club nights and one visit during daytime, being physically receptive and responsive to the place in a way that choreographers are when they develop a site-specific dance performance. It is about 'tuning into the site' on a sensual level, observing architectural shapes and people's movement or the absence of it, balancing considerations of what impact possible changes to objects and movement pattern have, contemplating how and why our movements are controlled in various places, and question factors of influence.

Huopalainen (2015) in her work on bodily movements in a fashion show followed the suggestion of mobility researchers to "move towards the subject or topic of research" (D'Andrea et al., 2011: 153), generating empirical material from many hours of participant modes of fieldwork that includes observations in a "what-goes-on-here" style, informal conversations with participants and a reflection of how the researcher herself feels in the space among the moving people. Exploring how bodily movements construct organising, means "being mobile and reflexive in the field myself" (Huopalainen, 2015: 832). In this endeavour, the researcher based her analysis on a close reading of her raw field notes from which fuller and more comprehensive narrative descriptions have been constructed, being aware of the difficulties of generating in a selective manner ethnographic material and presenting it.

Body Narratives

Bodily movement is used as a dance-based method to access and enhance embodied knowing, based on the idea that: "We do not have bodies; we are bodies" (Snowber, 2012: 55). Bodies experience realities before and in other ways than the mind, which makes dance and movement a valuable method to explore and represent our bodies and bodily knowledge. Celeste Snowber uses improvisational dance as a method to collect knowledge. Exploring the connection between autobiographical narrative and dance she finds that improvisational movement can give a better understanding of the performers and their lives. The dance-based method called "body narratives" brings together movement and word, dance and autobiographical narratives. Similar to arts-based interventions in organisations, which however take place in a more controlled space, the purpose of this method is discovery: "I would suggest that the process of improvisation and creation in all the arts in an embodied ritual which leads us into not-knowing, and ultimately into knowing" (Snowber, cited in Leavy, 2009: 189).

Dance is a way to more deeply understand and question the world around us and movement exercises can be thus be employed by organisational scholars in various ways for purposes of embodied discovery. Snowber (2012: 56–57) explains how movement helps to make sense of all kinds of phenomena:

> Movement and dance are not just ways to illustrate ideas but a way of grappling more deeply with the complexity of ways [people] can critically think, sift, perceive, and eventually come to fresh understanding of whatever subject they are studying. Dance is an invitation to think with our entire beings. It ushers in a way to connect biology and body, economics and intuitive thinking, human geography and physicality, and psychology and visceral awareness.

Movement and dance has been used by scholars as a research tool in an auto-ethnographic approach 'to think with their entire beings' about complex organisational issues such as leadership. For example, Anneli Hujala and colleagues (Hujala et al., 2014, 2016) used dance as "a living and embodied interview" to create an understanding of the leader–follower relationship in an organisation. They drew on their own physical experience that was accessed through dance exercises under the guidance of a dance pedagogue. Using dance and creative movement as a method, the team, following a phenomenological approach, wanted to access knowledge that is beyond the discursive and rational level.

Each participant presented an individual performance to a chosen piece of music with the aim to express her personal experiences of a leader–follower relationship. The task was to 'invite' one's boss to dance with the boss(es) being present either in an imaginary way or represented by other participants (Hujala et al., 2016: 19). Following the "embodied interview", a reflective discussion among all participants was led by the dance pedagogue who also gave a feedback. A video recording was used in the subsequent interpretation process that involved questions such as: What kinds of feelings were aroused by my own performance? What did the creative movement reveal about my own leader–follower relationship (a current relationship or in general)? How did I feel about this experiment with dance/creative movement as a method? (Hujala et al., 2016: 20).

Different from other approaches that were presented in this chapter, researchers in this case did not use a framework for interpretation such as Laban Movement Analysis or Pavis's catalogue, because they felt that they did not have enough expertise in interpreting movements. Using dance was used to access emotions and knowledge and reveal new insights into the leader–follower relationship. In the auto-ethnographic approach it was an individual matter and the responsibility of the participants themselves, whilst the others were able to give impulses through their feedback and kinaesthetic empathy that does not require formal training in dance. In the focus of the phenomenological study, individuals turned dance as a "universal language" into "a mirror of the soul" (Leavy, 2009: 179).

Drawing on kinaesthetic relations between dance and organisational leadership of 'leading' and 'following', participants chose different forms of dance and music that expressed their follower-style, ranging from tango ('search for a common tune'), to a performance to Edith Piaf's "Je ne regrette rien" ('independent agency and survival') to the Paso doble ('challenging and fighting'). The Paso doble dancer says that she performed her follower role as a challenger, not being subordinate but taking control.

> [The Paso doble dancer] went near each of "the bosses" quite soon and made physical contact with them by pulling them by the hand onto the dance floor. However, if you feel that there is an imaginary threshold to be crossed between you and your boss, this kind of active attack may serve as a defensive tool to overcome this feeling. In the Paso doble the invitation to dance was not a kind one but presented as a challenge to the bosses.
>
> (Hujala et al., 2016: 23)

Figure 7.1 "Challenging and fighting II (Paso doble dancer)"

Courtesy Emma Vilina Fält (Drawing out loud, www.emmafalt.net, 2014) (art work) and Anneli Hujala.

The setting in which the interaction with the bosses was danced provided a new, albeit transitory, and embodied form to this relationship whereby the individual and her body was posed as the central actor, which also encouraged critical self-reflection. This role of the follower as an active and responsible agent in the relationship, or a co-leader, was reflected in a central finding expressed by a dancer: "I myself am responsible for how I feel [in the relationship] and I suppose I am the one who should do something about it" (Hujala et al., 2016: 29). In a research context, such an outcome acknowledges the increased interest in follower-research in leadership studies and more generally emphasises the perspective of co-creation that the discussion of dance in this book has elaborated on.

While the researchers found that the setting with the dance floor distinct from everyday work encouraged participants to express their emotions through movement, the research design however pointed to barriers such as courage or cultural stereotypes that may have discouraged potential participants. The presence of a professional dance pedagogue was considered positive, also in case emotions surfaced in unexpected ways in the unusual exercise. The interpretation of embodied experience and the transfer into a discursive mode is challenging and the findings are not fully transferable, rather constitute individual and contextual examples of the leader–follower relationship. The researchers however found that the embodied form revealed to them knowledge and meanings beyond their rational understanding to be further developed conceptually.

Dance as a research method revealed knowledge and meanings beyond people's rational and discursive-level understanding, and, like arts-based interventions, may also unfold an impact on participants. Berthoin Antal and Strauß (2013: 3) suggest that "the power of artistic interventions in organizations resides in the opening of spaces of possibility," which enable participants to "experience new ways of seeing, thinking, and doing things that add value for them personally". In this sense, participants can benefit from an extended awareness. Movement can have a healing effect (Halprin, 2000) and also can function as action research: Dance-based methods that empower the follower to take the lead can remodel those social choreographies in which leaders and followers are embedded.

Writing on Movement

The interplay between dance and writing needs to be addressed, when wanting to articulate the meaning of movements after having used dance-based methods. While dance itself may serve as an artistic form to represent research findings—to be discussed in the next section—academic research typically is written down to be published. When researchers on the aesthetic aspects of organisations find that a written text is not able to fully capture and transmit the experience, researchers on kinaesthetic elements face similar issues. Dance scholars face the challenge to put into words and text the perception of transitory movement. They need to find words to transmit an experience of movement, which is difficult. When the processes of dancing and dance-making can be felt, but not represented verbally, creating a theoretical bridge between live performance and written text is difficult. Sometimes dancers have a talent to write about dance because they can adopt a distant perspective but also bring their embodied knowing and their kinaesthetic experience of dance to it. Trying to present findings of actual bodies moving in relation to other bodies points to many abstract issues but still requires some lived experience that cannot be found in a standard text. In her work on fashion shows for example, Huopalainen (2015: 842) reports that she has attempted to capture embodied elements and experiences of organizing and tried to do so by "creating a mobile text": "Somewhat ironically, the end result turned out to be more linear than I would have preferred, at times positively immobile, demonstrating the difficulty and challenge of writing bodily movements in practice."

Looking for ways to add more experience to writing, Celeste Snowber and Mary Beth Cancienne (2009: 210) point to the fact that "writing begins not only when we put pen to paper or fingers to the keyboard, but also (begins) in the way we are consciously embodied—the way we breathe, think, and feel in our bodies." Writing is not only recording, but a process that needs attention to details of experience. This process can benefit from dance as a research method that is a process that leads to new insights: "Dance allows us to taste the grammar of the gut, the alphabet of the bones, the etymology of the pelvis" (Cancienne and Snowber, 2009: 210). This links to approaches used in aesthetic studies on organisations, namely participant construction as opposed to participant observation (Taylor and Hansen, 2005: 1225). Involvement through the moving body is achieved, for example when researchers aim to 'experience' a site, moving or dancing among the people present. Generally, a heightened awareness of the body can be furthered through dance-exercises that can in this regard positively contribute to the process of academic writing.

The writing process might obviously benefit from a subjective, first-person perspective that is accepted in arts-based research and also has been applied in organisational research. Taylor (2004: 72) asserts that first-person research is advanced in modern management theory, particularly in the organisational change and development literature, which suggests that transformational organisational change must include changing yourself: "The underlying logic is that if we do not first look at our own behavior when we try to change others, then those others will see us as hypocrites as we ask/push/direct them to change but remain unwilling to change ourselves." So when it is about the body and embodied perceptions in movement, researchers would need to explore a more personal and adventurous style to approach their research object and present their research findings in traditional journals and outside them.

Using Movement as a Representational Form

The application of arts-based, sensual methodologies has led to new forms for the representation of research findings. Arts-based methods go beyond rationalist forms of academic writing to include poetic forms, visual narratives and imagery, fabrics and materials, and actual bodily movement in choreographies (Knowles and Cole, 2008). Arts-based methods have been used in many ways to communicate findings on the felt experience and hidden, tacit forms of influences in organisational life and they are suitable to evoke experiences in the viewer (Rippin, 2013: 1559). These approaches can capture issues that intellectual forms of inquiry represented by traditional journal articles cannot address fully. Whilst explicit knowledge can be represented through discursive forms of writing in journal articles and books, aesthetic and embodied forms of knowing requires a more intricate, emotional and multi-layered form (Taylor and Hansen, 2005: 1214). Arts-based methods are presentational forms, which, due to their multi-layered aesthetic nature, are able to convey a more holistic understanding of organisational life. Artistic forms, through their immediacy, may be very powerful to address emotions and aesthetic perceptions.

Dance in particular, through its bodily-based form and the kinaesthetic experience it evokes, may even be 'moving' in a more immediate sense. Dance as a performance-based method can bring research findings to life, adding dimensionality, and exposing emotional and interpersonal issues that are otherwise hidden (Leavy, 2009: 135).

While written forms of research can be read anywhere, it can be assumed that the communication of arts-based forms to a recipient works best as an aesthetic experience in a co-present situation, shared by participants and the art work or performance. Particularly in dance performance, the kinaesthetic experience is stronger in the moment. Dance, more than most other arts-based forms such as painting, is a method that creates data or representations that are fugitive, that cannot be hold onto. Other methods as well such as theatre and music can cannot be put into words without losing the very essence they intend to capture and transmit. The co-present situation is deemed central to presentational forms of arts-based research as it may involve a complex negotiation of meanings and articulate multiple research purposes that include consciousness-raising, empowerment, emancipation and political agendas (Leavy, 2009: 135).

However, new technologies and social media are particularly important in this regard and open ways for researchers to transmit their data, for example as a dance video that can be searched for and be viewed online. A source widely referred to is Cancienne and Bagley's (2002) book *Dancing the Data* that comes with a CD-Rom *Dancing the Data, Too*. These objects show the ways in which educational research and the visual and performing arts can embrace each other to engender a culture of feeling and meaning and in so doing evoke new ways of knowing, learning and teaching.

Dance can be used as a representational form to illustrate research findings. One quite well-known example is the yearly competition called "Dance Your Ph.D.", where scientists from physics, chemistry, biology and the social sciences create dance videos to communicate their research. Many of these presentations seem to use dance as a metaphor to illustrate figuratively processes that are related to movement, when, for example, chemical elements 'approach' or 'disconnect'. Other submissions from social science scholars and the humanities make more use of the potential of dance to illustrate not only what movement literally represents, but to give an aesthetic form to ideas, concepts and processes that are felt and embodied. The particular potential of dance can unfold when the lived experience of people is addressed through a movement performance.

At the AoMO Art of Management and Organization Conference, Sam Warren (2016) has performed an academic DJ set intended as an embodied, corporeal encounter to present findings of her study on the work of a DJ that takes place in hedonistic and ecstatic leisure places. She played a mix of progressive tech-house and techno, in order "to move you to feel the data". Interview data and central theses on the embodied work situation of DJs were presented in a mix with further visual cues on PowerPoint ("embodied music is not disembodied"). Participants were dancing or listening to the tunes, actually experiencing a situation that was co-created and in which "the body of the DJ subsumes the bodies of the dancers into the music as (s)he plays or produces tracks". Such an approach is particularly appropriate to report findings that can hardly be intellectualised, but still are so strong that they energise work careers and an entire industry of clubbing and music.

To transmit an experience of research findings, in a similar vein dance-based methods have been used with academics at conferences. Fides Matzdorf and Ramen Sen (2016) as well as Anneli Hujala and colleagues have done ballroom dancing exercises with researchers at Art of Management and Organization Conferences as well as at the EGOS conference to make participants experience practices of leadership, collaboration and co-creation. These presentations harness the potential of arts-based approaches to promote dialogue and to facilitate conversations. By connecting participants on a kinaesthetic level, they also help to build a shared 'feeling' for the research and can promote acceptance of dance-based approaches in the academic community. A valuable approach in this endeavour is the postperformance dialogue with the audience, when the researchers distributed questionnaires and asked for feedback on the impact and insights and personal responses. This may also increase the validity of the data and build an extended dialogue.

When movement is a performative practice of knowledge (Huschka, 2009), it transmits knowledge in an organisation and different understandings of the dynamic nature of leadership and followership for example. On

a broader level, such representational forms that involve different participants may bring scholarship to a wider audience. As indicated earlier and
throughout this chapter, the typical academic form of management studies
writing is not only restrictive in terms of aesthetics and the body but also
does little service to the public when hidden behind a pay wall in commercial journals. Dance-based forms in particular that do not need a musical
instrument or crafting tools but use bodies that move and could seize this
possibility for wider dissemination.

The use of dance as a representational form in organisation studies brings
up the question of what counts as acceptable research output. It is worth
considering the standards of what is acceptable as academic research and
the positivist tradition of focusing on written research outputs, as the latter
inhibits the acceptance of presentational forms of non-text research output.
Across the disciplines there is a trend to accept performative and artistic
research outputs, but dance may again face more difficulties in this context
given its transitory nature, its existence in the moment.

Looking beyond business schools into the wider academic context,
arts-based methods have grown. The University of Bristol's Practice as
Research Project (PARIP, 2006) has explored creative-academic issues and
developed "frameworks for the encouragement of the highest standards in
representing practical-creative research within academic contexts", which
are necessary to legitimise research towards structural frameworks and
funding bodies. In management and organisation studies, journal rankings
are criticised as particularly 'managerial' and oppressive (Mingers and Willmott, 2013), providing fewer opportunities of qualitative expression than
other fields. Performances as research output may constitute an alternative to the publishing treadmill for those who question the sense of journal
rankings and commercial publishing with its restricted access. Arts-based
approaches would be somewhat outside this realm and their style an immanent rejection of all the publishing pressure. Arts-based forms of expression even operate beyond this discourse, using many non-verbal, corporeal
and emotional forms hospitable to different gendered and political forms
of thinking and expression. Arts-based forms are also an advantage for an
international faculty that is affected by a publishing and ranking system
dominated by white males of Anglo-American origin (Özbilgin, 2009).
The arts are a truly international form of communication and may fit well
in today's diverse management research community. Dance as a "universal language" in particular uses the body and does not put an emphasis
on an exclusive form of scholarly British English or American English that
poses challenges not only to non-native speakers but also to scholars from
India and other countries who report that they experience discrimination in
review processes. A form of scholarly expression that combines bodily language and verbal language would thus be more inclusive and open up other
opportunities for a plurality of scholars.

An institutionalisation of the arts-based research approach and output would constitute another transformative development of "Taylorized" business school research (Mingers and Willmott, 2013), but depends on its attributed legitimacy. The establishment of arts-based research output in management studies would need some strategic or grass-root lobbying. This leads to a range of questions which already have been debated in other fields and which include how original contributions to knowledge might be conceptualised and assessed, evaluated, and judged (e.g. Rowe and Buck, 2013). Of relevance also is who decides. Furthermore, specific kinds of resourcing and infrastructures needed to be defined and developed for performance-based research.

In the humanities, academics create artistic projects that may include the direction of a performance or the organisation of an exhibition, and which count towards institutional research audits. The Research Excellence Framework in the UK for example, REF (2011: 22) states that, in addition to printed academic work, "research outputs may include, but are not limited to: new materials, devices, images, artefacts, products and buildings; confidential or technical reports; intellectual property, whether in patents or other forms; performances, exhibits or events; work published in non-print media", emphasising that no particular form will be regarded as higher than another in the assessment. Non-text or practice-based outputs (performances, artefacts and so on) should normally be accompanied by a description of the research process with a maximum of 300 words (REF, 2011: 22). Emphasising the importance of a theoretical framing, PARIP (2006) suggests that in order to comply with university norms and to make manifest a research contribution for the community (which typically is demonstrable by bibliography, abstract, literature review and citations) researchers doing performances have to "have a set of separable, demonstrable, research findings that are abstractable, not simply locked into the experience of performing it".

Given the abstract nature of dance and the tradition of dance studies it can be suggested that this approach may be particularly tantalising for academic researchers, wanting to bring together the abstract and the theoretically concrete. However, for artists who also contribute to management studies, this issue is contested as it poses the question of "divided competences" (Schrat, 2011: 34) and requires a double effort to excel both artistically and intellectually. Scholars in the organisational field using hybrid artistic methods for representation also have to face judgements that do not primarily revolve around objectivity, rigorous method and theoretical contribution, but are likely to include aesthetic categories such as beautiful, or judgements of the innovative or artistically original. Doing art and 'moving' people is a qualified craft and typically involves extensive training that scholars do not have. However, the postdramatic trend in contemporary dance and theatre in particular may be lowering barriers for academics to contribute. These forms are more realist and do not derive their artistic value primarily from a holistic representation and a complex artistic form, such as classical ballet for example that requires techniques and careful staging. Movement as a direct bodily expression for a contemporary dance performance does not only need to be based on technical finesse and extensive training. Kinaesthetic perception has moved into the focus of many contemporary techniques of dance in the heterogeneous field of dance, along with different body concepts, in contrast to classical ballet, for example, which values a specific physique and the outer representational form.

While modern dance is a highly specialised art form, dance performances can also derive creative and aesthetic value of its concept and organisation, when all kinds of bodies move and make something move in the audience. This may be interesting for organisational scholars as there already is an affinity between performance and qualitative research that involves enhanced aesthetic awareness and visual understanding of people, space and artefacts; working with qualitative texts, interview transcripts and field notes; and symbolic and metaphorical thinking and storytelling.

The substantial contextualisation of the arts-based research is important for organisational scholars. Taylor and Hansen (2005: 1222) argue that if an intellectual framing is not included for artistic methods or illustrations, the authors "would simply (not to suggest that it is ever simple) be creating art around instrumental issues". The process of creating dance 'around' organisational issues can however be seen as part of the data gathering process. It is often difficult to distinguish between process and outcome as artistic means infuse and accompany the entire process, including an aesthetically mediated dialogue in so-called studio-based work (Rippin, 2013: 1554). This approach also raises questions about trends and developments in academic research. Using poetry as a representational form, Darmer (2006) once posited: "Imagine what kind of world this would be, if science were turned into poetry." Arts-based research embraces subjectivity rather than hiding behind a dubious neutrality, taking a position towards the recipient that differs from traditional management scholarship. Art at its best typically provides some opportunities to play with own associations rather than transmitting a logical, holistic argument in textual form. Pursuing the aim to explore multiple viewpoints and the intricate, aesthetic nature of organisational life that are made imperceptible by traditional research inquiry, researchers using arts-based forms of representation open up a space for co-construction and individual understanding. Recipients can in different ways relate to what they see, hear and feel, linking these impressions to their own embodied understandings they have about social interaction, emotions and work.

Arts-based methods question what organisational researchers are allowed to produce and what their "readers" are allowed to experience, thereby producing a different form of knowledge. Dance with its rhythm, vision and corporeal perception, generates forms of knowing that involve all our senses and allow dynamic and changing relations, a constant reorganisation of the abstract and the concrete. Exposing researchers and organisational members to arts-based methods sensitises them to their own embodied responses, attending to the intangible aspects of the research field. Arts-based forms of dance, via their production of aesthetic and embodied knowing, could oppose what Fotaki (2011: 50) called the "fantasy of the knowledge creation process as a pure product of the (masculine) academic mind without the 'contaminating' influence of the body".

Feminist Critique

Traditional forms of organisation studies writing limit what organisational researchers are allowed to produce and restrict what 'readers' are allowed to understand. Arts-based research methods allow for research findings to be experienced aesthetically, including gender issues, creating a form of presentational knowledge that differs from propositional knowing that is created by standard academic writing and its rational theories and methods (Taylor and Hansen, 2005: 1213). By doing this, they can contribute to efforts to "destabilize, undermine and confuse the implicit yet powerful dominance of masculine theorizing in organization studies" (Phillips et al., 2014: 5). Feminist perspectives in management studies have pointed out that we need to open up language and allow for ambiguity in order to imagine and understand alternatives and the use of arts-based and dance-based methods can be a way to do this.

The use of arts-based forms, including dance, to represent research findings can be seen as a critique towards the widely accepted standard of academic writing with 'rational' scientific language that stands in the positivist and also masculinist tradition of management studies. The only seemingly neutral form of academic writing has been criticised from an aesthetic perspective and also from a gender and feminist perspective. Feminine issues are strongly related to the aesthetic, involving the body, its experience and appearance and cannot adequately represented in text. Organisation studies writing is shaped by masculine stereotypes of scientific rationality, objectivity and rigorous method. Phillips et al. (2014: 3) argue that "the legacy of science, as a privileged mode of inquiry and knowledge production, both formally and in terms of a culture of scientificity, is central to the pervasion of masculinity as the mode par excellence of organizational theorizing." This leads to a state where the only gender that can be done legitimately in research by all genders is masculinity, conforming to a phallogocentric order (Höpfl, 2000).

Feminist perspectives in organisation studies have suggested, as alternatives, styles of writing that diverge from the standard, and I have suggested that arts-based forms can be seen as another alternative to masculine academic writing as 'feminine creation' with an emphasis on female corporeality and experience in organisations (Biehl-Missal, 2015). I have made this argument with reference to Kristeva (1977): Arts-based methods such as dance as a form of kinaesthetic politics can be seen as political by being in opposition to the political, in the sense of Kristeva who finds that the political is subject to the law of the law, it cannot help but posit an order, a rule, a power that is applicable to all, a common measure. Arts-based forms can deconstruct the traditional form of academic writing by not writing directly against it but by illustrating its limits through the aesthetic form. Arts-based methods do not need to be seen as the anti-rule or the anti-power to positivist forms of research and representation, but as the exception. Höpfl (2000: 104) wrote that for Kristeva, "the attempt to use language against itself is to create an untenable position," so it may be suggested that arts-based forms can be a way to act against written language as representative of academic publishing by not writing. From a feminist perspective, dance as an arts-based method can unfold their potential to deconstruct established practice by remaining multiple and diffuse, going some way to break the traditional dialectic binary towards a bisexual form of expression (Phillips et al., 2014: 15).

It is difficult to imagine new understandings without having the language, but dance as an embodied language can through kinaesthetic empathy convey other forms of understanding, opening up meanings, imagining change, complementing empiricist research methods that aim 'to set the record straight' on many feminist topics for example. Dance as a universal language has a potential to give voice to suppressed experiences of women and all genders (Hesse-Biber and Leavy, 2007), responding to an on-going concern of feminist research to include a diverse range of women's experiences and to give voice to other marginalised groups.

Critical Practice

Dance-based forms of representation along with, for example theatre-based, approaches can also be considered as critical, given the relation of art and management. Performance art in particular makes a commitment to pretence, raises questions rather than providing solutions, and can confront many researchers' and practitioners' "morals" like, for example, Steven Taylor's (2000) play "Capitalist Pigs" at the Academy of Management that clearly voiced practices of oppression and discrimination. Much of the critical potential resides on the discursive dimension, on the level of the spoken word. Dance performances did not create controversy to such an extent as all kinds of theatre scandals, as the non-verbal abstract nature of dance and moving bodies leave much room to overlook, to understand or to misunderstand content. While people with an aesthetic training such as dance scholars, dancers and people that feel affiliated to other artistic areas and abstract forms of representation, have the capability to decode and understand dance performances in many ways, many viewers trained in a more positivist science and work tradition may find it hard to work with these forms of representation.

Controversy in dance performances can of course be caused without any verbal framing through movement and on the visual level, and culturally often happened when bodies were shown that in their existence, relation or movement were perceived as offensive or inappropriate, for example when audiences understood them as 'too sexualised', or sexualised in ways that do not fit with their morals. From an artistic perspective, it would be a way to challenge audiences when a performance is created that deals with the many forms of oppression of bodies of whichever gender in an organisation. Dance performances as a representational form may thus be particularly apt for topics and themes that revolve around the body, its relation to bodies and things, and its movement. At this point, a theatre performance at the AoMO Art of Management and Organization Conference in 2014 by Jean-Luc Moriceau and Isabela Paes comes to my mind: The female performer was heavily pregnant and boasted her expanded belly half naked, while also pouring cold water over herself. While I felt uncomfortable through empathising kinaesthetically, I could sense that audience members were irritated and sometimes repelled by this rather unusual setting in a male dominated area of scholarship. One colleague left the performance rumbling something about it being "too French". This suggests it would be worth further exploring topics that revolve around the body and embodied identity through dance in particular. This would be an attempt to continue a tradition of arts-based research that aims at not only giving voice to marginalised subjects, but providing them with a bodily presence in an organisational context that often suppresses bodies that are not heterosexual white male.

In this sense, when arts-based methods are used as a presentational form, they can be seen as critical art performances as well. From a critical management studies perspective, they could be considered an initiative of 'anti-management', undermining it through critique, being provocative and offensive. Contemporary artists came to practice actual artistic resistance against capitalism, using paintings, plays and performances with powerful imagery and emotional experiences that are different from and absent in intellectual, written approaches. It can be assumed that these approaches will remain difficult to absorb by mainstream management research and practice not only because of their qualitative, but because of their open, interpretive and potentially subversive nature and their artistic intent that rejects efforts to control reality. Dance as a transitory, fugitive bodily practice can be seen as an initiative par excellence in this context.

Literature

Adshead, J. (1988) An introduction to dance analysis, in Carter, A (ed.) *The Routledge Dance Studies Reader*. London and New York Routledge, 163–170.
Bagley, C. and Cancienne, M. B. (2002) *Dancing the Data*. New York: Peter Lang.
Berger, C. and Schmidt, S. (2009) Körperwissen und Bewegungslogik: Zu Status und Spezifik körperlicher Kompetenzen, in Alkemeyer, T., Brümmer, K., Kodalle, R.

and Pille, T. (eds.) *Ordnung in Bewegung: Choreographien des Sozialen. Körper in Sport, Tanz, Arbeit und Bildung.* Bielefeld: transcript, 65–90.

Berthoin Antal, A. and Strauß, A. (2013) *Artistic Interventions in Organisations: Finding Evidence of Values Added. Creative Clash Report.* Berlin: WZB.

Biehl, B. and Volkmann, C. (2016) *Research Paper 'Choreography and Organisation'.* unpublished, The University of Essex.

Biehl-Missal, B. (2011) Business is show business: Management presentations as performance, *Journal of Management Studies* 48(3): 619–645.

Biehl-Missal, B. (2015) 'I write like a painter': Feminine creation with arts-based methods in organizational research, *Gender, Work & Organization* 22(2): 179–196.

Biehl-Missal, B. (2016) Filling the 'empty space': Site-specific dance in a techno club, *Culture and Organization.* DOI: 10.1080/14759551.2016.1206547.

Brandstetter, G. and Klein, G. (eds.) (2013) *Dance [and] Theory.* Bielefeld: transcript, 35–80.

Buchanan, D. and Bryman, A. (eds.) (2009) *The Sage Handbook of Organization Research Methods.* London: Sage.

Cancienne, M. B. and Snowber, C. (2009) Writing rhythm: Movement as method, in Leavy, P. (ed.) *Method Meets Art: Arts-based Research Practice.* New York and London: The Guildford Press, 198–214.

Carter, A. (1998) Analysing dance: Introduction, in Carter, A. and O'Shea, J. (eds.) *The Routledge Dance Studies Reader.* London and New York: Routledge, 237–240.

Chandler, J. (2012) Work as dance, *Organization* 19(6): 865–878.

D'Andrea, A., Ciolfi, L. and Gray, B. (2011) Methodological challenges and innovations in mobilities research, *Mobilities* 6(2): 149–160.

Darmer, P. (2006) Poetry as a way to inspire (the management of) the research process, *Management Decision* 44(4): 551–560.

Foster, S. L. (2013) Dancing and theorizing and theorizing dancing, in Brandstetter, G. and Klein, G. (eds.) *Dance [and] Theory.* Bielefeld: transcript, 19–32.

Fotaki, M. (2011) The sublime object of desire (for knowledge): Sexuality at work in business and management schools in England, *British Journal of Management* 22(1): 42–53.

Freedman, D. C. (1991) Gender signs: An effort/shape analysis of Romanian couple dance, *Studiea Musicologia Academiae Scientarum Hungaricae* 33(1): 335–345.

Gerard, M. (2004) Selecting ritual: DJs, dancers and liminality in underground dance music, in St John, G. (ed.) *Rave Culture and Religion.* London: Routledge, 167–184.

Halprin, A. (2000) *Dance as a Healing Art: Returning to Health With Movement and Imagery.* Mendocino, CA. LifeRhythm.

Hesse-Biber, S. and Leavy, P. (2007) An invitiation to feminist research, in Hesse-Biber, S. and Leavy, P. (eds.) *Feminist Research Practice: A Primer.* London: Sage, 1–26.

Höpfl, H. (2000) The suffering mother and the miserable son: Organizing women and organizing women's writing, *Gender, Work & Organization* 7(2): 98–105.

Hujala, A., Laulainen, S., Kinni, R., Kokkonen, K., Puttonen, K. and Aunola, A. (2016) Dancing with the bosses: Creative movement as a method, *Organizational Aesthetics* 5(1): 11–36.

Hujala, A., Laulainen, S. and Kokkonen, K. (2014) Manager's dance: Reflecting management interaction through creative movement, *International Journal of Work Organisation and Emotion* 6(1): 40–57.

Huopalainen, A. (2015) Who moves? Analyzing fashion show organizing through micro-interactions of bodily movement, *Ephemera: Theory and Politics in Organizations* 15(4): 825–846.

Huschka, S. (ed.) (2009) *Wissenskultur Tanz: Historische und zeitgenössische Vermittlungsakte zwischen Praktiken und Diskursen.* Bielefeld: transcript.

Kavanagh, D., Kuhling, C. and Keohane, K. (2008) Dance-work: Images of organization in Irish dance, *Organization* 15(5): 725–742.

Kipling Brown, A. (2015) Dance education: Embodied knowing in the digitalized world, in Svendler Nielsen, C. and Burridge, S. (eds.) *Dance Education Around the World: Perspectives on Dance, Young People and Change.* New York: Routledge, 141–148.

Klein, G. (2004) *Electronic Vibration: Pop Kultur Theorie.* Wiesbaden: VS Verlag.

Klein, G. (2007) Tanz in der Wissensgesellschaft, in Gehm, S., Husemann, P. and von Wilcke, K. (eds.) *Wissen in Bewegung: Perspektiven der künstlerischen und wissenschaftlichen Forschung im Tanz.* Bielefeld: transcript, 25–36.

Knowles, J. and Cole, A. (eds.) (2008) *Handbook of the Arts in Qualitative Research.* Thousand Oaks, CA: Sage.

Kolo, K. (2016) Ode to choreography, *Organizational Aesthetics* 5(1): 37–46.

Kristeva, J. (1977) *Polylogue.* Paris: Seuil.Langer, S. (1942) *Philosophy in a New Key.* Cambridge, MA: Harvard University Press.

Leavy, P. (2009) Dance and movement, in Leavy, P. (ed.) *Method Meets Art: Arts-Based Research Practice.* New York: Guilford Press, 179–214.

Matzdorf, F. and Sen, R. (2016) Demanding followers, empowered leaders: Dance as an 'embodied metaphor' for leader-followership, *Organizational Aesthetics* 5(1): 114–130.

Mingers, J. and Willmott, H. (2013) Taylorizing business school research: On the 'one best way' performative effects of journal ranking lists, *Human Relations* 66(8): 1051–1073.

Özbilgin, M. (2009) From journal rankings to making sense of the world, *Academy of Management Learning and Education* 8(1): 1–9.

Pavis, P. (2003) *Analyzing Performance, Theatre, Dance, and Film.* Ann Arbor: University of Michigan Press.

Pfadenhauer, M. (2009) The lord of the loops: Observations at the club culture DJ-desk, *Forum Qualitative Social Research* 10(3), Art. 17.

Phillips, M., Pullen, A. and Rhodes, C. (2014) Writing organization as gendered practice: Interrupting the libidinal economy, *Organization Studies* 35(3): 313–333.

Practice as Research in Performance. (2006) Department of drama: Theatre, film, television, University of Bristol. http://www.bristol.ac.uk/parip/ (Accessed 1 Aug 2016).

REF Research Excellence Framework (2011) *Assessment Framework and Guidance on Submissions* online at http://www.ref.ac.uk/media/ref/content/pub/assessmentframeworkandguidanceonsubmissions/GOS%20including%20addendum.pdf (Accessed 1 Oct 2016).

Rippin, A. (2006) Refusing the therapeutic: Marion Milner and Me', *Culture and Organization* 12(1): 25–36.

Rippin, A. (2013) Putting the Body Shop in its place: A studio-based investigation into the new sites and sights of organization as experience, *Organization Studies* 34(10): 1551–1562.

Rowe, N. and Buck, R. (2013) Moths, candles and fires: Examining dance as creative practice research in a Master's degree, *Higher Education Research & Development* 32(6): 1022–1036.

Schrat, H. (2011) *Meanwhile . . . Wham! Comic and its communication value in organizational context.* PhD thesis, Essex Business School, University of Essex, UK. http://www.henrikschrat.de/2011/PhD/PhD.htm (Accessed 1 Jun 2016).

Snowber, C. (2012) Dance as a way of knowing, *New Directions for Adult and Continuing Education* 134(1): 53–60.

Snowber, C. (2014) Visceral creativity: Organic creativity in teaching arts/dance education, in Piirto, J. (ed.) *Organic Creativity in the Classroom: Teaching to Intuition in Academics and the Arts.* Waco, TX: Prufrock Press, 253–266.

Taylor, S. (2000) Aesthetic knowledge in academia: Capitalist pigs at the academy of management, *Journal of Management Inquiry* 9(3): 304–328.

Taylor, S. (2004) Presentational form in first person research, *Action Research* 2(1): 71–88.

Taylor, S. and Hansen, H. (2005) Finding form: Looking at the field of organizational aesthetics, *Journal of Management Studies* 42(6): 1211–1231.

Warren, S. (2008) Empirical challenges in organizational aesthetics research: Towards a sensual methodology, *Organization Studies* 29(4): 559–580.

Warren, S. (2016) Fire and warmth: Bodies, music and space in the craft of underground DJing, paper and DJ performance presented at the Art of Management and Organisation Conference, Bled, Slovenia, 1–4 Sep.

Wetzel, R. and Van Renterghem, N. (2016) How to access organizational informality: Using movement improvisation to address embodied organizational knowledge, *Organizational Aesthetics* 5(1): 47–63.

Young, I. M. (1980) Throwing like a girl: A phenomenology of feminine body comportment motility and Spatiality, *Human Studies* 3: 137–156.

Concluding Thoughts

In every academic discipline and in everyday life, our conceptions of the world influence what we see and how we act. The purpose of this book was to bring the disciplines of dance and organisation together to open up some new ways of seeing organisations. By approaching movement and dynamic aspects of human interaction on a micro-level—usually overlooked or taken for granted—this approach shows a different understanding of agency and organising, valuing co-created, embodied practices that are performed and negotiated, delimited and broken up, in an ongoing manner, and matter to us more broadly.

I believe that it does matter how we think about organisations. It makes a difference if we think of organisations as a 'machine', or as a 'theatre' or as 'dance' with human bodies in motion, co-operating, co-ordinating actions in ever changing constellations. It is different when we conceive of leadership as something that is done by one strong leader, or as something that is a relational, mutual, co-created and dynamic activity. It also has different implications if we do not conceive of space as a stable form of influence, but see it as a ground on which people create something new. Considering movement as something that is natural and does not deserve attention, we miss out on issues of gender and kinaesthetic politics and many other things that happen in-between people and spaces. This also included an addition to qualitative research methods, when movement is used to access transitory actions and embodied forms of knowing.

In previous conference discussions on the topic we have figured out challenges of interdisciplinary research bridging two different fields. One challenge is to do justice to the professional and advanced work scholars, dancers and choreographers do when receiving and discussing it from a different perspective that also is unusual for those involved in dance. Keeping in mind the difficulties, I would assert that knowledge is not on object that is diminished when 'taken away' from those who 'possessed' it first, rather it can grow and flourish when it is shared. To achieve this, an open, respectful and curious attitude from organisational scholars is required and many have already gone far beyond an instrumentalist and positivist mainstream view and have literally moved their 'embodied minds' into other fields. Dance scholars and practitioners on the other hand can also conceptually or in their practical work benefit from links and bridges that are built to the world of organisations.

One of the advantages of thinking about organisations as dance is that issues have been emphasised that commonly were overlooked by traditional management thinking and theorising. Organisation studies is in need of a development and other scholars have already pointed out the relevance of the body in organisation, the influence of aesthetic, sensual perception and also have presented criticism towards authoritative forms of leadership or the suppression of women's bodies and non-masculine identities in organisations. Many scholars in the broad organisation and management field have expressed that contemporary ways of organising and managing are reaching their limits and fail to secure progress for so many of us. While not having intended or being able to sketch a new form of economic organisation, the dance approach is an interdisciplinary and critical perspective as it discusses many forms of power and resistance that take place on the embodied, kinaesthetic and intangible dimension in organisations and also points to forms of non-hierarchical interaction and change.

Paying attention to the body in motion, the book has addressed a very salient issue today. Despite and because all digitisation, the body is a target of economic and social power. This includes all forms of surveillance and biological data, aggressive marketing of body-related goods and services, health management, and the management of spaces in which bodies reside. Contemporary dance practice shows the body as something that is influenced and formed socially, the aim and result of social power, gender hierarchies, political issues and also shows how people negotiate and try to resist these influences. In the book, the focus on embodied practice is not to be interpreted as a romantic return to the body, rather is a critique of views that try to influence the body or neglect it, promoting in merely instrumental ways forms of leadership and co-operation as completely disembodied, impersonal and uncreative. The dance perspective keeps in mind the complexities of current organisation and leadership practices and emphasises the embodied sensorium of practice and its dynamic and relational nature. Such a view may help to foster a more cooperative and potentially sustainable culture of organisational interaction and leadership.

Another hope in approaching organisations from the perspective of dance is an emphasis not on only transience and the decline of structures, which is exemplified by dance practice, but also on issues of dynamics and change. Theory on choreography proved to be promising in this respect. When contemporary dance and choreography does not merely present the body, like ballet does, as an expression of a defined and stable individual, rather as a site and result of social power, the aestheticisation of everyday movements became a central element to reflect on the inner movements, shared influences and the outer constitution of an individual. When choreography now has entered the world of organisations, it has continued its development to work with bodies as a site of social influence and also as a site of opportunity. The examples that were to date discussed in organisation scholarship have shown how participants in workshops co-create their choreographies, negotiating their own forms of leadership and followership and their relation to social spaces. Different from manipulating or controlling, these dance workshops put the subjectivity of the dancers in the centre, opening up a space to negotiate and potentially challenge and resist everyday practices in organisations. Researchers on dance and organisation have suggested that kinaesthetic experiences of the body are used as tacit knowledge to achieve skilful knowing and doing across a broad range of contexts. Playing with embodied choreographies and testing out new ways of movement interaction in kinaesthetic forms of training can be read as a reaction to new organisational challenges, including gender in management and new forms of leadership, and can also be seen as a way to provide people with some new insights and choreographic agency and control.

Contemporary choreography on a more general level has changed and is not to be considered as a macro-structure that brings under control, orders and delimits micro-movements, as a Foucauldian instrument of power and repression, rather is an aesthetic practice, a performative and conceptual tool to discuss and reflect on order, its forms, strategies and dynamics (Klein, 2015: 47). In this sense, further studies on dance and organisation could explore what can be learned from contemporary choreography that does not only deal with a presentation of the moving body, but with the absent or present body in time and space, with questions of construction of subjectivity, identity and representations, and includes processes of studying and research. These choreographic practices are promising in terms of collaboration innovation in organisations.

When seeing contemporary choreography not as an ordering structure, but as a space of opportunities, created by collective actions and participatory processes that are performed, further studies would need to identify and explore these movement performances in organisations that previously were under-researched, because invisible from an immobile management studies perspective. The book has presented some early insights on how organisational members negotiate their network of bodies rather than following pre-defined roles or a professional habitus, or how gendered performances can be addressed and changed. Before providing some more comments on the topic, I shall embed these thoughts in a critical and political perspective.

Dance as a theoretical perspective and practice that puts the moving body into the centre has many political aspects that are of relevance to organisation studies. Movement and dance is a transitory practice that produces something 'more' that is non-discursive, cannot be easily captured or represented. In this sense, it may be seen as a critical perspective and practice that operates against normative structures and dominant perspectives. Peggy Phelan (1993) has suggested that the resistant potential in dance resides in the fact that it is transient and not to be reproduced, thus offering something more that cannot easily be accessed discursively in text and writing, but resides in movement. Developing this idea, Klein (2009: 206) does not only see dance as 'the ephemeral' but as 'the dynamic', as permanent movement that erects an order, then deconstructs and transforms this order. In this sense dance can be a negative metaphor and representation for neoliberal liquidation of 'attitudes' and individual 'stability', of work structures and securities. It can also open up a positive perspective when it raises our awareness to the permanent construction and decline of these orders and points to change and its possibilities.

With regard to contemporary organisations and their demands for artistic forms of working, flexibility and creativity, dance theory tries to locate a space where dance as an artistic practice can still be political. Considering new requirements for leadership for example, dance can be affirmative when insights only are absorbed with the aim of increasing organisational efficiency. Movement in organisation may also be affirmative when it merely follows new office designs with staircases and open spaces that aim to enhance circulation and knowledge exchange. Dance and choreographic practice can however be political when is resists, challenges and undermines orders, norms and conventions—and eventually changes them (Klein, 2015: 48).

In this sense, the notion of kinaesthetic politics was used to discuss that the gendered and social body, whose motion has been neglected in organisation studies, is an unstable, constantly evolving and transient phenomenon. Dance is political in the sense that it shows the dominant order and its weaknesses, through falling and raising, deconstructing and foregoing classical ideals of movement. It transforms norms that include some and exclude others. Not only media changes society (for example when new forms of dance change our view of gender), but changes in society also change media (when feminist movements in the 1960s were reflected in a new movement vocabulary presented on dance stages). The body in dance takes a position towards contemporary challenges such as virtuality, audio-visual stress and everyday mechanisation of the human body. In many modern dance forms, performers subvert the audience's gaze by changing patterns of characteristic movement. When art operates from the margins, we can also understand how women as constituents of the margins in an organisational world might be in a position to transgress boundaries, using not only static appearance but the moving body to create a space of change.

When organisational culture is a bodily, performative practice, critique and transformation can happen through the medium of the body, in the performances in everyday life, in interactions, movements and attitudes. Doing leadership for example is not seen as a matter of having a body and taking it into an organisation. Rather, leadership "is about creating and experiencing our bodies, our careers, our lives, through embodied participation with others" (Mavin and Grandy, 2016: 270). When there is ambiguity around the 'one right way' for a female elite leader to 'look' or to 'move', and increasing pressures to manage appearances, the body can become a source of agency, changing practices and understandings of leadership. When embodied and practical techniques are modified, actors modify their relationship to themselves and to each other. When in trainings, experiences are produced that challenge participants' identity and previous experiences and ways of doing, opportunities emerge for new forms of interaction and a new kinetic form of the self and the relationship to others. Moving together is a dialogical, relational, co-created experience that creates knowledge that is the basis not for static, but for dynamic structures.

With the evolving practice of contemporary choreography, also the places of dance have changed. Dance is not only created in studios, but in the social world and in business organisations. Dance performances outside concert halls can affect today's organisations, for example when artistic forms of resistance appear as site-specific performances. When dance exercises are now used in organisations as arts-based interventions, there is a possibility to change movement, gender roles, leadership and collaboration through the medium of dance. So dance for organisation studies can be more than a critical metaphor or a theoretical lens. With regard to applied methods of dance for leadership development, it needs to be gauged whether the practice of dance can be political by letting participants engage with performative aspects of existing orders and movements to engender reflection and possible change of its constitutive elements. Dance, after all, is political when it does not aim to set up functional networks, but creates a community as a precondition for practice. Scholars have put many hopes in arts-based methods in general to further community and human-centred thinking and mutual understanding.

On a more general level, also academic life is 'in motion'. Movement in social life, play and sports has always been tied back to economic life. For example, skating and roller blading and the 'flow' that people perform has been interpreted as an embodied anticipation of new social impositions of 'flexible' and 'effortless' conditions of work (Alkemeyer and Schmidt, 2003: 99). Dance has become a model for today's dynamic and ever changing organisations and the dancer a role model for the flexible worker, the nomad, the artist. On the positive side however, recently management scholars at a conference act as DJs and others rave to the tunes, and scholars and practitioners perform dance exercises to explore their ways of 'leading' and 'following' and to access and work with their embodied knowing on their life in organisations. We can see this as a bodily anticipation of new developments in the scholarly world and maybe a further rejection of 'rigorous' method and 'established' ways of doing things that have privileged a few people, perspectives and topics, and excluded many others. After all, different from the positivist view, performative acts like performative utterances show that things are not 'true' of 'false', they themselves not only describing a given reality, but also changing the social reality they are describing. To be successful, they rely on the receiving side and the meaning that is given to actions. I have used the analogy of a leader and a DJ, who is undeniably noticing when the crowd does not dance and when people are not 'moved' or simply leave the dance floor. In this way the perspective of dance expresses the hope that followers become co-owners of their dance—and their organisation.

Literature

Alkemeyer, T. and Schmidt, R. (2003) Habitus und Selbst. Zur Irritation der körperlichen Hexis in der populären Kultur, in Alkemeyer, T., Boschert, B., Schmidt, R. and Gebauer, G. (eds.) (2003) *Aufs Spiel gesetzte Körper. Aufführungen des Sozialen in Sport und populärer Kultur*. Konstanz: UVK Verlag, 77–102.
Klein, G. (2009) Das Flüchtige. Politische Aspekte einer tanztheoretischen Figur, in Huschka, S. (ed.) Wissenskultur Tanz. Historische und zeitgenössische Vermittlungsakte zwischen Praktiken und Diskursen. Bielefeld: transcript, 199–208.
Klein, G. (2015) Zeitgenössische Choreographie, in *Choreographischer Baukasten. Das Buch*. Bielefeld: transcript, 17–49.
Mavin, S. and Grandy, G. (2016) A theory of abject appearance: Women elite leaders' intra-gender 'management' of bodies and appearance, *Human Relations* 69(5): 1095–1120.
Phelan, P. (1993) *Unmarked: The Politics of Performance*. London: Routledge.

Index

Printed in the United States
by Baker & Taylor Publisher Services